Perpetrators and Accessories in International Criminal Law

Individual Modes of Responsibility for Collective Crimes

Neha Jain

·HART·
PUBLISHING
OXFORD AND PORTLAND, OREGON
2014

Published in the United Kingdom by Hart Publishing Ltd
16C Worcester Place, Oxford, OX1 2JW
Telephone: +44 (0)1865 517530
Fax: +44 (0)1865 510710
E-mail: mail@hartpub.co.uk
Website: http://www.hartpub.co.uk

Published in North America (US and Canada) by
Hart Publishing
c/o International Specialized Book Services
920 NE 58th Avenue, Suite 300
Portland, OR 97213-3786
USA
Tel: +1 503 287 3093 or toll-free: (1) 800 944 6190
Fax: +1 503 280 8832
E-mail: orders@isbs.com
Website: http://www.isbs.com

Hart Publishing is an imprint of Bloomsbury Publishing plc.

British Library Cataloguing in Publication Data
Data Available

ISBN: 978-1-84946-455-0

Typeset by Hope Services, Abingdon
Printed and bound in Great Britain by
CPI Group (UK) Ltd, Croydon CR0 4YY

Acknowledgements

This book began its life as my DPhil thesis at Balliol College in Oxford. My deepest gratitude goes to my DPhil supervisor, Andrew Ashworth, who showed infinite patience with the various twists and turns that this research entailed, and who was unfailingly generous and supportive of the project. I am also grateful to my DPhil examiners, Claus Kress and Rebecca Williams, whose thorough examination and detailed comments greatly assisted in the revision of important parts of the book.

The book would not have been possible without the help of my colleagues at the Max Planck Institute for Foreign and International Criminal Law, who provided support, encouragement and assistance throughout the arduous and occasionally frustrating process of learning the German language and understanding German criminal law. Special thanks to Ulrich Sieber, Emily Silverman, Marianne Wade and Andras Csuri.

The extremely fast-paced nature of international criminal law resulted in significant revisions to the original thesis, especially in light of new forms of commission being developed at the *ad hoc* tribunals and at the International Criminal Court. For rich and productive conversations, which contributed significantly to the development of my thoughts on the nature of international criminal responsibility, I am grateful to my colleagues at Georgetown University Law Center and the University of Minnesota Law School, including David Luban, Robin West, Larry Solum, Julie O'Sullivan, John Mikhail and Antony Duff.

Several scholars, who acted as informal mentors and guides at various points in time during the development of the book, helped shape my thoughts on the comparative nature of the enterprise, especially Maximo Langer, Jacqueline Ross, Mathias Reimann, Larry Alexander and Don Dripps. Others, who have thought deeply about these issues before me, were the inspiration for many of the ideas in the book, including Elies van Sliedregt, Judge Christine van den Wyngaert and Jens David Ohlin.

Lastly, I am grateful to Kevin Schawinski for his unstinting support and general good cheer throughout the course of this project.

Contents

Table of Cases

United Kingdom

Germany

International Criminal Tribunal for the former Yugoslavia

International Criminal Tribunal for the Rwanda

International Criminal Court

Extraordinary Chambers in the Courts of Cambodia

Post World World II Military Trials

Miscellaneous

Table of Statutes and International Instruments

1

Introduction

MASS ATROCITY HAS been an unfortunately persistent occurrence throughout human history; the phenomenon of holding individuals criminally responsible for its commission is, in contrast, a relatively recent development.[1] 'Crimes against international law are committed by men, not by abstract entities and only by punishing individuals who commit such crimes can the provisions of international law be enforced'[2] – this ringing pronouncement by the International Military Tribunal at Nuremberg has become a talisman for international criminal lawyers ever since the historic trials conducted after World War II.[3] Banishment of the spectre of collective guilt has been sought with repeated incantations of the principle of individual responsibility in constitutive documents of international tribunals, judgments and scholarly writing.[4] The puzzle of the collective nevertheless endures: like an unloved

---

[1] On the development of collective and individual criminal responsibility in international law see, eg, A Levy, 'Criminal Responsibility of Individuals and International Law' (1945) 12 *University of Chicago Law Review* 313; TLH MacCormack, 'Selective Approach to Atrocity: War Crimes and the Development of International Criminal Law' (1996–1997) 60 *Albany Law Review* 681; E van Sliedregt, *The Criminal Responsibility of Individuals for Violations of International Humanitarian Law* (The Hague, TMC Asser Press, 2003) 15–39; A Eser, 'Individual Criminal Responsibility' in A Cassese et al (eds), *The Rome Statute of the International Criminal Court: A Commentary Vol I* (Oxford, Oxford University Press, 2002) 767, 774–78.

[2] *France v Goering* (1946) 22 *International Military Tribunal* 411, 466.

[3] See, eg, AM Danner and JS Martinez, 'Guilty Associations: Joint Criminal Enterprise, Command Responsibility, and the Development of International Criminal Law' (2005) 93 *California Law Review* 75, 82, 85; G Simpson, 'Men and Abstract Entities: Individual Responsibility and Collective Guilt in International Criminal Law' in A Nollkaemper and H van der Wilt (eds), *System Criminality in International Law* (Cambridge, Cambridge University Press, 2009) 69, 73 (noting the pervasiveness of this notion in international criminal law). It should be noted, though, that this affirmation coincides both with an argument that the responsibility may not lie exclusively with the individual but also with the State and, of late, with increasing demands for organisational responsibility for international crimes. See, eg, PM Dupuy, 'International Criminal Responsibility of the Individual and International Responsibility of the State' in A Cassese, P Gaeta and JRWD Jones (eds), *The Rome Statute of the International Criminal Court: A Commentary* (Oxford, Oxford University Press, 2002) 1085; A Clapham, 'Extending International Criminal Law beyond the Individual to Corporations and Armed Opposition Groups' (2008) 6 *Journal of International Criminal Justice* 899; M Kremnitzer, 'A Possible Case for Imposing Criminal Liability on Corporations in International Criminal Law' (2010) 8 *Journal of International Criminal Justice* 909.

[4] See, eg, Rome Statute of the International Criminal Court, 17 July 1998, UN Doc A/Conf 183/9*, 2187 UNTS 90 (*entered into force* 1 July 2002), Art 25(2); Statute of the International Tribunal for the Prosecution of Persons Responsible for Serious Violations of International

catchy tune it lingers, lodging in the crevices of modes of responsibility fashioned by international criminal tribunals. How can individual responsibility adequately reflect the manner in which such a crime comes to pass, including the multifarious ways in which various persons contribute to it, ranging from the lowly soldier to the head of a government? Who should be considered the perpetrator of a crime such as genocide – an offence that necessarily involves participation by several hundreds of individuals? And what of our usual notions of responsibility that are manifested in the case of an everyday criminal act – if X stabs Y intending to kill Y then X is the murderer. If X was a jealous spouse who was told by Z that his wife Y was being unfaithful to him, and X murdered Y in a fit of passion, he would be the murderer and Z only the instigator. Is this also true of the ordinary civilian who harms, kills or tortures in a climate of conflict and chaos orchestrated by a few high-level policy makers? In other words, should the intellectual authors of a genocidal policy be held to account as the perpetrators of the crime, or should they be labelled instigators and aiders, and punished accordingly?

I. DISTINCTIVE FEATURES OF INTERNATIONAL CRIMES

The difficulty in identifying principles that can distinguish adequately between the various participants in mass atrocity and label their responsibility accurately stems from the peculiar nature of international crimes. The most telling of the characteristics is that an international crime, when contrasted with its domestic counterpart, is inherently collective in nature, for the perpetrator as well as the victim.[5] While the perpetrator of a crime

Humanitarian Law Committed in the Territory of the Former Yugoslavia since 1991, UN Doc S/25704/Add 1 (3 May 1993), adopted by Security Council on 25 May 1993, UN Doc S/RES/827, Art 7(1); Statute of the International Criminal Tribunal for Rwanda, SC Res 955 (8 November 1994), UN Doc S/RES/955, Art 6(1); Secretary-General, *Report of the Secretary-General Pursuant to Paragraph 2 of Security Council Resolution 808*, delivered to the Security Council, UN Doc S/25704 (3 May 1993), para 53; *Prosecutor v Tadić*, No IT-94-1-A, Appeals Chamber Judgment (15 July 1999), para 186; A Cassese, 'Reflections on International Criminal Justice' (1998) 61 *MLR* 1, 6; M Sassoli and LM Olson, 'The Judgment of the ICTY Appeals Chamber on the Merits in the Tadic Case' (2000) 82 *International Review of the Red Cross* 733, 755. Some scholars have taken a more nuanced view of the relationship between guilt and responsibility, holding that collective guilt can be an appropriate response to collective wrongdoing and that its recognition does not necessarily justify collective responsibility: GP Fletcher, 'Collective Guilt and Collective Punishment' (2004) 5 *Theoretical Inquiries in Law* 163, 168–78. Others would not go so far as to advocate collective guilt, but instead favour collective sanctions as more suited to dealing with accountability for mass atrocity: M Drumbl, 'Collective Violence and Individual Punishment: The Criminality of Mass Atrocity' (2005) 99 *Northwestern University Law Review* 539, 576–77; M Drumbl, 'Pluralizing International Criminal Justice' (2005) 103 *Michigan Law Review* 1315.

[5] P Akhavan, 'Justice in the Hague, Peace in the Former Yugoslavia? A Commentary on the United Nations War Crimes Tribunal' (1998) 20 *Human Rights Quarterly* 737, 781; GP Fletcher, 'The Storrs Lectures: Liberals and Romantics at War: The Problem of Collective

such as ethnic cleansing or waging aggressive war is individually culpable, he invariably commits this crime on behalf of, or in furtherance of, a collective criminal project, whether of a state or some other authority.[6] The hypothetical figure of the lone *génocidaire* rarely exists in practice: the perpetrator is part of, and acts within, a social structure that influences his conduct, in conjunction with other people.[7] Similarly, the victims of international crimes are mostly chosen not based on their individual characteristics, but because of their actual or perceived membership of a collective.[8] This is reflected in the provisions of the law as well as in practice. Genocide, for instance, is defined as performing certain acts such as killing or causing serious harm, 'with the intent to destroy, in whole or in part, a national, ethnical, racial or religious group, as such'.[9] International crimes are also collective in the sense that they are committed with the consciousness on the part of the individual perpetrator that he is part of a common project. While it would be far-fetched to say that there is a 'corporate mens rea'[10] at work in all international crimes, what can hardly be disputed is that crimes such as crimes against humanity that are committed as a systematic and widespread attack against a civilian population cannot be understood solely in terms of the mental state of each perpetrator. Rather, one must address the social structures and group solidarity that renders them possible – whether that is based on fear of violence, ethnic hatred or religious intolerance.[11]

The second distinctive aspect of international crimes is that the individual crimes do not deviate from, but conform to, the prevailing social norm.[12] In this sense, they are indeed 'crimes of obedience', as coined by Kelman: they are acts carried out under explicit instructions from makers of official policy, or at least in an environment in which they are sponsored, expected or tolerated by them, and which are considered illegal or immoral by the larger community.[13] Drumbl uses the terminology of *jus*

Guilt' (2002) 111 *Yale Law Journal* 1499, 1531; LE Fletcher and HM Weinstein, 'Violence and Social Repair: Rethinking the Contribution of Justice to Reconciliation' (2002) 24 *Human Rights Quarterly* 573, 605.

[6] RD Sloane, 'The Expressive Capacity of International Punishment: The Limits of the National Law Analogy and the Potential of International Criminal Law' (2007) 43 *Stanford Journal of International Law* 39, 56.

[7] Ibid.

[8] Drumbl, 'Collective Violence', above n 4, 571.

[9] Convention on the Prevention and Punishment of the Crime of Genocide 1948, 78 UNTS 277, Art 2.

[10] Sloane, above n 6, 58.

[11] MJ Osiel, *Making Sense of Mass Atrocity* (Cambridge, Cambridge University Press, 2009) 187–88.

[12] A Nollkaemper, 'Introduction' in Nollkaemper and van der Wilt (eds), above n 3, 1, 6; Fletcher, above n 5, 1541; I Tallgren, 'The Sensibility and Sense of International Criminal Law' (2002) 13 *European Journal of International Law* 561, 575.

[13] HC Kelman, 'The Policy Context of International Crimes' in Nollkaemper and van der Wilt (eds), above n 3, 26, 27.

cogens norms and basic conceptions of human decency when speaking of this larger community.[14] This is regardless of whether the crimes are also committed for personal motives or with zeal.[15] The perpetrator of an international crime acts within a moral and cultural universe where his actions correspond to the values of the group to which he belongs. He may conceive of himself as being in the right and working to prevent injustice, or even in self-defence.[16] The victims are transformed into the guilty parties, and the group dynamic is reinforced by a myth of ethnic, religious, racial or national superiority that is under threat from the victims.[17] Scholars and journalists who analyse genocide and ethnic cleansing have documented such experiences in cases such as Rwanda and Yugoslavia.[18] It is even claimed that in such a climate, it is paradoxically those who refuse to commit the crimes who deviate from the social norm. Criminal law, in these circumstances, appears to be something that can be adhered to only by exceptional individuals.[19]

George Fletcher offers a slightly different account of this dimension of international crimes in terms of the denial of the perpetrator's opportunity for self-correction. The moral climate of hate does not cause the crime to be committed; rather, it deprives people of their second order capacity for self-restraint (from criminal conduct). The perpetrator is subject to the world of the senses, but always has the capacity to choose the world of reason and let his conduct be governed by the moral law. However, the circumstances in which he operates can make this exercise of choosing the moral order far more demanding.[20] It is for this reason that the dramatically different background, which Carlos Nino terms 'radical evil',[21] in which international crimes are committed, as compared to isolated acts of murder or rape, must be paid serious attention to in any theory of responsibility for international crimes.

Lastly, a theory of modes of participation in international crimes has to be sensitive to the number and motivations of the participants in the crime. It must be able to accommodate the fact that these participants will be spatially and temporally dispersed, and that for this reason, unlike in domestic crimes, a theory of responsibility cannot afford to focus solely on the time and place where each individual offence (such as rape) con-

---

[14]   Drumbl, 'Collective Violence', above n 4, 567.

[15]   Kelman, above n 13, 27.

[16]   See JE Alvarez, 'Crimes of State/Crimes of Hate: Lessons from Rwanda' (1999) 24 *Yale Journal of International Law* 365, 396–97; MA Drumbl, 'Punishment, Postgenocide: From Guilt to Shame to *Civis* in Rwanda' (2000) 75 *New York University Law Review* 1221, 1243, 1245.

[17]   Alvarez, above n 16, 396–97; Tallgren, above n 12, 574; Drumbl, 'Collective Violence', above n 4, 567–68.

[18]   See, eg, on Rwanda, A Des Forges, *'Leave None to Tell the Story': Genocide in Rwanda* (New York, Human Rights Watch, 1999).

[19]   Drumbl, 'Collective Violence', above n 4, 568; Tallgren, above n 12, 573.

[20]   Fletcher, above n 5, 1541–43.

[21]   C Santiago Nino, *Radical Evil on Trial* (New Haven, CT, Yale University Press, 1996) vii.

stituting the overall crime (war crime) occurred. It should also be cautious of simplifying the social, cultural and structural forces that make mass atrocity possible, and should resist the temptation to make all cases of mass violence fit into a preconceived mould. International crimes can take place in diverse organisational settings – they may be highly organised and rigidly hierarchical ones, or deliberately encourage arbitrariness and spontaneity.[22] The crimes may rely on anonymity and functional speciali- sation to facilitate their commission.[23] Conversely, they may thrive on proximity between the perpetrators and the victims, where neighbours, friends and family are motivated to kill and rape people with whom they previously had close ties, in a ritual cleansing affirming the division of religion, race or ethnicity.[24]

It is also important to keep in mind that the image of the participant as a soulless bureaucrat, who is merely 'doing his job' as part of the enter- prise of mass atrocity,[25] presents only part of the truth about the reality of mass atrocity. This image is of significance, and has proved quite influen- tial in the development of a theory of perpetration. As we shall discuss in chapter seven, Roxin's picture of the fungible intermediary as a human automaton clearly relies on this conception of the physical perpetrator in order to shift control onto the *Hintermann*. However, as academics have noted in their studies of the phenomenon of mass atrocity, more often than not, there is a 'communal engagement with violence'.[26] Atrocity can- not be perpetrated on such a widespread basis unless it is accompanied by the vigorous participation of a very large number of ordinary people.[27] Some studies even question whether crimes on such an epidemic scale can be committed by people simply acting under the instructions of authority figures, unless they have internalised the ideology behind the instructions and actually wish to assist in its operationalisation.[28] People can be motivated to commit such acts only when the ideology resonates with their own psychological dispositions.[29]

While the calculating bureaucrat and the crazed ideological killer per- haps represent two extremes of the kinds of actors in international crimes, most perpetrators will display some or a combination of various kinds of

---

[22] MJ Osiel, 'Constructing Subversion in Argentina's Dirty War' (2001) 75 *Representations* 119, 127.

[23] See Sloane, above n 6, 64. Against Osiel, above n 11, 99.

[24] AJ Vetlesen, *Evil and Human Agency: Understanding Collective Evildoing* (Cambridge, Cambridge University Press, 2005) 32; Drumbl, 'Collective Violence', above n 4, 569–70.

[25] See Sloane, above n 6, 64.

[26] Fletcher and Weinstein, above n 5, 605.

[27] Drumbl, 'Collective Violence', above n 4, 569; LE Fletcher, 'From Indifference to Engagement: Bystanders and International Criminal Justice' (2005) 26 *Michigan Journal of International Law* 1013, 1026.

[28] Vetlesen, above n 24, 25–26.

[29] Ibid, 50.

motives.[30] Mann even classifies perpetrators according to their motives: ideological killers, bigoted killers, fearful killers, careerist killers, materialist killers, disciplined killers, comradely killers and bureaucratic killers.[31] In fact, no case of mass atrocity will involve only one type of perpetrator. This is true even in the case of atrocities committed by the Nazi regime, where it is now acknowledged that while the personnel in concentration camps were part of an oppressive organisational matrix, they still had considerable freedom to act and perpetrate violence as they wished without fear of retribution.[32] Commentators on mass conflict note that in quite a number of these scenarios, subordinates enjoy considerable autonomy in the interpretation and execution of the policy directives of leaders, and sometimes this control over the fate of their victims is appropriated rather than granted voluntarily.[33] For example, during Argentina's Dirty War (1976–1983), junior officers who acted at the lower levels exercised considerable discretion as to how to treat their victims after interrogation.[34]

These distinctive features of international crimes – their collective nature, conformity to the prevailing social norms and widespread participation in their commission by different levels of participants acting on different motives – must be kept in mind while attempting to construct a theory of responsibility for international crimes.

II. THE NEED FOR AN ACCOUNT OF MODES OF PARTICIPATION

One might argue that the categorisation of the various participants in mass atrocity into principals and accessories is not particularly necessary, or even useful. As long as we respect the concept of individual accountability and adhere to fundamental criminal law principles, the exact label we attach to the accused is irrelevant. After all, the offender is held accountable in either case and, in the absence of any mandatory mitigation of sentences for accessories, punished equally. Indeed, quite a few domestic criminal law systems consider the distinction between principals and accessories to be largely redundant.[35] I argue that a sophisticated

---

[30] On Rwanda, see Drumbl, above n 16, 1246–51.

[31] M Mann, *The Dark Side of Democracy: Explaining Ethnic Clensing* (Cambridge, Cambridge University Press, 2006) 27–29.

[32] Vetlesen, above n 24, 36 (quoting Sofsky).

[33] Osiel, above n 11, 22–23, 26.

[34] Ibid, 102.

[35] For instance, 'formal unitary systems', such as those in Denmark and Italy, do not recognise the distinction between principal and secondary responsibility, whereas 'functional unitary systems', like those of Austria and Poland, formally distinguish between the two but do not consider secondary responsibility to be derivative in nature: H Olásolo, *The Criminal Responsibility of Senior Political and Military Leaders as Principals to International Crimes* (Oxford, Hart Publishing, 2010) 18–19, fnn 35–37. In the United States, the Model Penal Code and the majority of states have abandoned the traditional common law distinctions between principals and accessories: WR LaFave, *Criminal Law* (St Paul, MN, West Academic Publishing,

understanding of the status of the accused in relation to the offence committed is crucial for the ascription of responsibility. Statements of responsibility perform an expressive function: the censure of the conduct of the accused. However, this expression is not confined simply to evaluating whether the accused is innocent or guilty; it also assesses exactly what he is guilty of.[36] The rules of criminal responsibility would fulfil this essential communicative function only if they accurately expressed[37] the nature of the censure, its appropriate target and the conditions under which it is deserved.[38] A theory of attribution of responsibility for international crimes must therefore be capable of representing, as accurately as possible, both the nature of the crime in question and exactly how the accused is connected to its commission.[39]

This communicative function of criminal responsibility is perhaps even more important in international criminal trials than in domestic ones. Apart from the more standard aims of criminal justice[40] – retribution, deterrence, incapacitation and rehabilitation – proponents of trials for international crimes have come to view these as embracing increasingly more ambitious goals. The international criminal trial is touted as a venue for giving voice to victims of mass violence, expected to create a historical record of wrongdoing and even to contribute to the prevention of conflict.[41] There is also emphasis on the potential didactic function of the

---

2010) 706–08. English criminal law treats the principal and the accomplice identically for the purposes of punishment in that they are both guilty of the full offence, but the distinction between the two still has some limited significance. Most importantly, the status of an accomplice is in part contingent upon the existence of a principal who commits an offence, and there are some practical differences: strict liability offences require *mens rea* on the part of the accessory, there is also no vicarious liability for the act of an accomplice and the definitions of certain offences allow for the possibility of their commission (as a principal) only by a defined class of persons. See AP Simester and GR Sullivan, *Simester and Sullivan's Criminal Law: Theory and Doctrine* (Oxford, Hart Publishing, 2010) 206.

[36] V Tadros, *Criminal Responsibility* (Oxford, Oxford University Press, 2005) 80.

[37] Gardner holds that rules of responsibility, in the relevant sense, are ascriptive rather than normative. They are therefore directed towards making our judgements on whether and how we should count what people have done more accurate, rather than more desirable or valuable. See J Gardner, 'Criminal Law and the Uses of Theory: A Reply to Laing' (1994) 14 *OJLS* 217, 220.

[38] Tadros, above n 36, 3.

[39] For recent powerful counterarguments to this position, see JG Stewart, 'The End of "Modes of Liability" for International Crimes' (2012) 25 *Leiden Journal of International Law* 165, 211–13.

[40] See, eg, JN Shklar, *Legalism: Law, Morals, and Political Trials* (Cambridge, Mass, Harvard University Press, 1964) 158; LN Sadat, *The International Criminal Court and the Transformation of International Law* (Ardsley, NY, Transnational, 2002) 73–75; RJ Goldstone, 'Justice as a Tool for Peace-making: Truth Commissions and International Criminal Tribunals' (1996) 28 *NYU Journal of International Law & Politics* 485, 491; D Wippman, 'Atrocities, Deterrence and the Limits of International Justice' (1999) 23 *Fordham International Law Journal* 473.

[41] 'Developments in International Law – International Criminal Law' (2001) 114 *Harvard Law Review* 1943, 1961; M Schrag, 'Lessons Learnt from ICTY Experience' (2004) 2 *Journal of International Criminal Justice* 427, 428; M Damaska, 'What is the Point of International Criminal Justice?' (2008) 83 *Chicago-Kent Law Review* 329, 331.

process – creating a public sense of accountability for severe violations of human rights through exposure, stigmatisation, and internalisation of norms and values that respect human rights.[42] Champions of these trials assert that it is only through justice – establishing accountability for abuses, creating an accurate historical record and providing some relief for victims – that a conflict society can transition to a peaceful and stable one based on the rule of law.[43] Commentators disagree on whether these are all legitimate aims of the international criminal trial, whether they are capable of being operationalised and how they should be prioritised. However, if the truth- and history-telling and didactic functions of international criminal trials are to be realised, it is essential not only that they reflect, quite precisely, the position of the accused in the context of mass atrocity, but also that they situate him within the political and cultural climate that made this violence possible.

Indeed, it is precisely this motivation for accurately reflecting the accused's role in the commission of mass atrocity[44] that has led international criminal tribunals to develop two competing doctrines – Joint Criminal Enterprise (JCE) on the one hand and indirect perpetration and co-perpetration on the other – as modes of responsibility.[45] Joint Criminal Enterprise is largely a common law-influenced doctrine, with close analogues in the doctrine of joint enterprise in English law[46] and the *Pinkerton* conspiracy doctrine in US law.[47] It has been in vogue for much of the existence of the *ad hoc* criminal tribunals, especially the International Criminal Tribunal for the Former Yugoslavia (ICTY) and the International Criminal

---

[42] Akhavan, above n 5, 741–42, 746–51; Damaska, above n 41, 345–47.

[43] JE Méndez, 'In Defense of Transitional Justice' in AJ McAdams (ed), *Transitional Justice and the Rule of Law in New Democracies* (Notre Dame, IN, University of Notre Dame Press, 1997) 1, 7; RG Teitel, *Transitional Justice* (Oxford, Oxford University Press, 2001) 28; JE Alvarez, 'Rush to Closure: Lessons of the Tadić Judgement' (1998) 96 *Michigan Law Review* 2031, 2031–32; AKA Greenawalt, 'Justice without Politics?: Prosecutorial Discretion and the International Criminal Court' (2007) 39 *NYU Journal of International Law & Politics* 583, 602.

[44] See, eg, C Kress, 'Claus Roxins Lehre von der Organisationsherrschaft und das Völkerstrafrecht' (2006) *Goltdammer's Archiv für Strafrecht* 304, 308; F Zorzi Giustiniani, 'The Responsibility of Accomplices in the Case Law of the *Ad Hoc* Tribunals' (2009) 20 *Criminal Law Forum* 417, 419; E van Sliedregt, 'The Curious Case of International Criminal Liability' (2012) 10 *Journal of International Criminal Justice* 1171, 1182, 1185.

[45] On the international tribunals' embrace of the differentiated model of participation, see, eg, S Wirth, 'Committing Liability in International Criminal Law' in C Stahn and G Sluiter (eds), *The Emerging Practice of the International Criminal Court* (Leiden, Martinus Nijhoff Publishers, 2009) 329; G Werle and B Burghardt, 'Indirect Perpetration: A Perfect Fit for International Prosecution of Armchair Killers?' (2011) 9 *Journal of International Criminal Justice* 85, 88; D Guifoyle, 'Responsibility for Collective Atrocities: Fair Labelling and Approaches to Commission in International Criminal Law (2011) 64 *Current Legal Problems* 255, 285.

[46] For a succinct account of the doctrine of joint enterprise in English law, see A Ashworth, *Principles of Criminal Law* (Oxford, Oxford University Press, 2009) 420–27; AP Simester, 'The Mental Element in Complicity' (2006) 122 *LQR* 578; Simester and Sullivan, above n 35, 233–44.

[47] See *Pinkerton v United States*, 328 US 640 (1946).

Tribunal for Rwanda (ICTR).[48] Co-perpetration and indirect perpetration are based on established forms of participation in German criminal law and are currently the favoured doctrines at the International Criminal Court (ICC).[49] Both doctrines have come under considerable criticism from academics and courts, for reasons ranging from the methodological to the substantive, including the uncomfortable truth that they lack a secure foundation in customary international law or even in general principles of law recognised by civilised nations.[50] The most recent jurisprudence of the ICC also demonstrates some ambivalence towards the acceptance of indirect perpetration and co-perpetration at the court.[51] Having never been on a firm footing to begin with, a coherent account of the basis for attribution of responsibility for international crimes seems more precarious than ever. If international criminal tribunals are to fulfil their goals of ending impunity for international crimes and establishing individual accountability, this is a task that they simply cannot afford to postpone any further.

III. STRUCTURE AND METHODOLOGY

In this study, I take up the challenge of constructing a theoretical framework for distinguishing between parties to an international crime, which yields modes of perpetration and accessorial responsibility that account

[48] For an excellent analysis of the prominence of JCE at the *ad hoc* tribunals, see generally G Boas, JL Bischoff and NL Reid, *International Criminal Law Practitioner Library Vol I: Forms of Responsibility in International Criminal Law* (Cambridge, Cambridge University Press, 2007) 8–141; WA Schabas, 'The ICTY at Ten: A Critical Assessment of the Major Rulings of the International Criminal Tribunal Over the Past Decade: Mens Rea and the International Criminal Tribunal for the Former Yugoslavia' (2003) 37 *New England Law Review* 1015, 1030–33; N Piacente, 'Importance of the Joint Criminal Enterprise Doctrine for the ICTY Prosecutorial Policy' (2004) 2 *Journal of International Criminal Justice* 446.

[49] On the recent ascendance of the doctrines at the ICC and their background in German criminal law, see F Jessberger and J Geneuss, 'On the Application of a Theory of Indirect Perpetration in *Al Bashir*: German Doctrine at the Hague?' (2008) 6 *Journal of International Criminal Justice* 853, 857; HG van der Wilt, 'The Continuous Quest for Proper Modes of Criminal Responsibility' (2009) 7 *Journal of International Criminal Justice* 307.

[50] On JCE, see, eg, Danner and Martinez, above n 3; JD Ohlin, 'Three Conceptual Problems with the Doctrine of Joint Criminal Enterprise' (2007) 5 *Journal of International Criminal Justice* 69; ME Badar, '"Just Convict Everyone!" – Joint Perpetration: From *Tadić* to *Stakić* and Back Again' (2006) 6 *International Criminal Law Review* 293. On indirect perpetration and co-perpetration, see Jessberger and Geneuss, above n 49, 868; *cf* G Werle, 'Individual Criminal Responsibility in Article 25 ICC Statute' (2007) 5 *Journal of International Criminal Justice* 953, 963–64 (stating that while perpetration by means is recognised in major legal systems, it had not been regulated by international criminal law instruments or courts prior to the Rome Statute).

[51] See *Prosecutor v Lubanga*, No ICC-01/04-01/06-2482, Judgment Pursuant to Art 74 of the Statute, Separate Opinion of Judge Adrian Fulford, Trial Chamber I (14 March, 2012); *Prosecutor v Mathieu Ngudjolo Chui*, No ICC-01/04-02/12, Judgment Pursuant to Art 74 of the Statute, Concurring Opinion of Judge Christine Van den Wyngaert, Trial Chamber II (18 December 2012).

for the collective nature of these crimes. This new conception of responsibility reflects the doctrinal concerns at the core of debates on responsibility in highly theorised domestic criminal law systems, and is simultaneously attuned to the unique features of international crimes. I consider the theoretical foundations of the distinction between perpetrators and accessories in English and German criminal law, as prominent representatives of the common law and civil law traditions respectively. I assess the points of convergence and difference between these systems, and apply this analysis to the unique features of international crimes in order to develop an account of principal and secondary responsibility for international crimes. In this process, I develop a theoretical account of JCE liability which engages with domestic criminal law principles to assess whether it can be justified as a mode of principal or accomplice liability. I also take on the task of considering the doctrines of co-perpetration and indirect perpetration that have been put forward as alternatives to JCE, and examine whether these are true to the doctrinal bases of responsibility in domestic legal systems and to the nature of international crimes.

The argument developed in this study has the following structure. Part One of the book comprehensively reviews the development of forms of perpetration or principal responsibility in international criminal law. It analyses the development of the JCE doctrine at international tribunals, including its historical underpinnings, its initial formulation by the ICTY, and its subsequent explication by tribunals and academics. It then conducts a similar examination of the concepts of indirect and co-perpetration, beginning with their incorporation in the jurisprudence of the ICTY and their later adoption by the ICC. It identifies the main loopholes and contradictions in the construction of these theories, and presents factual scenarios for which these theories have either no answers or only problematic ones.

Part Two develops a concept of perpetration for international criminal law, drawing on domestic criminal law theory. It looks at the concept of a perpetrator in English and German criminal law, and uses the doctrinal insights gleaned from this analysis to assess whether JCE, indirect perpetration and co-perpetration are appropriate modes of perpetration responsibility for international crimes. It also proposes a new, modified version of the doctrine of *Organisationsherrschaft* as a more accurate characterisation of the role and function of high-level participants in mass atrocity.

Part Three of the book focuses on the concept of accomplice liability in German and English criminal law and doctrine. Based on this assessment, it addresses whether JCE II and JCE III can be justified as forms of secondary criminal responsibility, and whether there is any merit to retaining them as distinct modes of liability that capture the collective dimension of international crimes. It concludes that a more tightly circumscribed version of JCE II may be retained in international criminal law. The status of JCE III is more precarious, given that domestic criminal law theory yields inconsistent results on its advisability. While JCE III may be justified independently using expressive and risk justifications rationales, it may be more prudent for international criminal law to abandon it as a mode of secondary responsibility.

A word on methodology is in order here: I choose to focus on English and German criminal law for my examination of responsibility for several reasons. First, in the field of domestic criminal laws, these legal systems constitute two of the most sophisticated and influential systems representing the common law and civil law worlds respectively. Secondly, existing modes of responsibility in international criminal law have borrowed heavily from these legal systems in their jurisprudence on modes of responsibility. Thirdly, my task is not to advocate the wholesale adoption of any doctrine that may be found in any particular legal system, but rather to restructure and combine divergent theoretical perspectives on perpetration responsibility in order to develop a suitable account of the criminal responsibility of senior and mid-level participants in mass atrocity. The attempt, therefore, is to engage fully with domestic criminal law principles and theory while simultaneously capturing the unique features of international crimes. In this sense, the legal systems serve as sources of ideas and concepts, and not as true sources of 'law'.

It is entirely possible that there are other legal systems and traditions that would also have something useful to teach us about the rationale for distinguishing between parties to a crime and how best to attribute criminal responsibility. I am wary, however, that any attempt to address all these systems, while being more inclusive, would also be more superficial, and less well suited to the aim of developing a normative structure for international crimes. The more judicious course of action is to begin by focusing on jurisdictions one can represent, fairly, and welcome a broadening of the debate as scholars from other traditions in turn contribute their insights to the task. A different approach would risk losing both depth and accuracy.

Part One

Modes of Participation in International Criminal Law

2

The Origins of Individual Responsibility in International Criminal Law

I. INTRODUCTION

A S FIRST ARTICULATED by the Appeals Chamber of the International Criminal Tribunal for the Former Yugoslavia (ICTY) in *Prosecutor v Tadić*, Joint Criminal Enterprise (JCE) liability comprises three categories of cases.[1] The *actus reus* elements common to all three categories, JCE I, JCE II and JCE III, are:[2]

(a) a plurality of persons;
(b) the existence of a common plan, design or purpose which amounts to or involves the commission of a crime provided for in the Statute; and
(c) participation of the accused in the common design.

The *mens rea* element differs for each category of JCE. For JCE I, the accused must share the intent to commit a certain crime. For JCE II, the accused must know of the system of ill-treatment and intend to further it. For JCE III, the accused must intend to participate in and further the criminal purpose of the group. In addition, he will be liable for a crime other than the one envisaged in the common plan if the crime was a foreseeable consequence of the common plan and the accused willingly took that risk.[3]

Initially developed by the ICTY based upon a controversial interpretation of 'commission' liability in Article 7(1) of the ICTY Statute,[4] JCE has

---

[1] *Prosecutor v Tadić*, No IT-94-1-A, Appeals Chamber Judgment (15 July 1999) ('*Tadić Appeals Judgment*'), para 195.

[2] Ibid, para 227.

[3] Ibid, para 228.

[4] The Statute of the International Tribunal for the Prosecution of Persons Responsible for Serious Violations of International Humanitarian Law Committed in the Territory of the Former Yugoslavia since 1991, UN Doc S/25704/Add 1 (3 May 1993), adopted by Security Council on 25 May 1993, UN Doc S/RES/827 ('ICTY Statute'), Art 7(1) stipulates: 'A person who planned, instigated, ordered, committed or otherwise aided and abetted in the planning, preparation or execution of a crime referred to in Articles 2 to 5 of the present Statute, shall be individually responsible for the crime.' The ICTY Appeals Chamber held that the term 'commission' in Art 7(1) of the ICTY Statute encompassed an individual's liability for participation in the realisation of a common design or purpose: *Tadić Appeals Judgment*, above n 1, paras 188–89.

come to occupy pride of place in prosecutions before international and hybrid tribunals around the world.[5] It has been resorted to increasingly by prosecution teams in a plethora of cases before the ICTY,[6] the International Criminal Tribunal for Rwanda (ICTR),[7] the Special Court for Sierra Leone (SCSL)[8] and the Dili Special Panels for Serious Crimes (SPSC).[9] It finds place in the first few applications before the International Criminal Court (ICC)[10] and is key to the prosecution case before the Extraordinary Chambers in the Courts of Cambodia (ECCC).[11] It is also included in the Statute of the Special Tribunal for Lebanon (STL), despite the fact that the substantive crimes in the Statute are domestic rather than international

[5] For an account of the increasing importance and use of JCE, see WA Schabas, 'The ICTY at Ten: A Critical Assessment of the Major Rulings of the International Criminal Tribunal Over the Past Decade: Mens Rea and the International Criminal Tribunal for the Former Yugoslavia' (2003) 37 *New England Law Review* 1015, 1030–33; N Piacente, 'Importance of the Joint Criminal Enterprise Doctrine for the ICTY Prosecutorial Policy' (2004) 2 *Journal of International Criminal Justice* 446; AM Danner and JS Martinez, 'Guilty Associations: Joint Criminal Enterprise, Command Responsibility, and the Development of International Criminal Law' (2005) 93 *California Law Review* 75, 107.

[6] For a detailed account of the ICTY cases in which JCE has been pleaded by the prosecution and/or formed the basis for the judgment, see G Boas, JL Bischoff and NL Reid, *International Criminal Law Practitioner Library Vol I: Forms of Responsibility in International Criminal Law* (Cambridge, Cambridge University Press, 2007) 10–124. The War Crimes Chamber of the Court of Bosnia and Herzegovina has also accepted the applicability of JCE before the court. See A Strippoli, 'National Courts and Genocide: The *Kravica* Case at the Court of Bosnia and Herzegovina' (2009) 7 *Journal of International Criminal Justice* 577, 586–87.

[7] See, eg, Boas et al, above n 6, 28–33.

[8] *Prosecutor v Brima, Kamara, and Kanu*, No SCSL-04-16-T, Trial Chamber II Judgment (20 June 2007) ('*AFRC Trial Judgment*'); *Prosecutor v Norman, Fofana and Kondewa*, No SCSL-03-24-T, Trial Chamber I, Judgment (2 August 2007); *Prosecutor v Brima, Kamara, and Kanu*, No SCSL-04-16-A, Appeals Chamber, Judgment (22 February 2008) ('*AFRC Appeals Judgment*'); *Prosecutor v Sesay, Kallon, and Gbao*, No SCSL-04-15-T, Trial Chamber I, Judgment (2 March 2009) ('*RUF Trial Judgment*'); *Prosecutor v Sesay, Kallon, and Gbao*, No SCSL-04-15-A, Appeals Chamber, Judgment (26 October 2009) ('*RUF Appeals Judgment*'); *Prosecutor v Charles Ghankay Taylor*, No SCSL-03-01-T, Trial Chamber II, Judgment (18 May 2012) ('*Taylor Trial Judgment*'); see also Boas et al, above n 6, 128–33.

[9] See *Prosecutor v Francisco Perreira*, SPSC No 34/2003, Judgment (27 April 2005) 19–20. See also *Prosecutor v Jose Cardoso*, SPSC No 04/2001, Judgment (5 April 2003); *Prosecutor v Domingos de Deus*, SPSC No 2a/2004, Judgment (12 April 2005) at 13; Boas et al, above n 6,133–36.

[10] See, eg *Prosecutor v Thomas Lubanga Dyilo*, No ICC-01/04-01/06, Pre-Trial Chamber I's Decision on the Prosecutor's Application for a Warrant of Arrest, Art 58 (10 February 2006). As we shall see in ch 5, the Prosecutor has since abandoned JCE in favour of the doctrines of co-perpetration and indirect perpetration.

[11] 'Statement of the Co-Prosecutors on the First Introductory Submission in the Extraordinary Chambers in the Courts of Cambodia' (18 July 2007) 3–4, at <www.unakrt-online.org/Docs/Court%20Statements/2007-07-18%20Statement%20of%20Co-Prosecutors-First%20 Submission.pdf>. See also *Order on the Application at the ECCC of the Form of Liability Known as Joint Criminal Enterprise*, No 002/19-09-2007-ECCC-OCIJ, Office of the Co-Investigating Judges (8 December 2009) ('*OCIJ 2009 Order*'); *Decision on the Appeals Against the Co-Investigative Judges Order on Joint Criminal Enterprise (JCE)*, No: 002/19-09-2007-ECCC-OCIJ, Pre-Trial Chamber (20 May 2010) ('*PTC Decision*'); *Judgment, Kaing Guek Eav, alias Duch*, No 001/18-07-2007-ECCC/TC, Trial Chamber (26 July 2010) ('*Duch Judgment*'); *Closing Order*, No 002/19-09-2007-ECCC-OCIJ, Office of the Co-Investigating Judges (15 September 2010) ('*OCIJ Closing Order*'); *Decision on the Applicability of Joint Criminal Enterprise*, No 002/19-09-2007-ECCC-TC, Trial Chamber (12 September 2011) ('*Trial Chamber JCE Decision*').

crimes.[12] Nevertheless, academics remain sceptical about its possibilities and limitations, ranging from an outright denunciation of JCE as a metaphor for 'just convict[ing] everyone'[13] to pleas for curtailing its scope and applicability.[14] Recent years have witnessed the first few rumblings of discontent with JCE within the international criminal law community, where courts such as the ICC[15] and prominent academics[16] now propose the doctrines of indirect perpetration and co-perpetration as doctrinally richer alternatives.

The evolution of JCE has been driven primarily by international tribunals; the ICTY in particular has contributed substantially to developing the elements of the doctrine, while courts such as the SCSL, the ECCC and the STL have introduced variations that depart from the ICTY's explication in significant ways. The chaotic manner in which JCE has matured contributes to the lack of doctrinal sophistication in the debates surrounding the justifications for, and legitimacy of, the doctrine. Moreover, the sheer nebulousness of the doctrine (the confused nomenclature[17] used to refer to the concept is only a surface reflection of its ambiguousness) makes it hard to ascertain whether different tribunals simply interpret JCE differently, or whether its contradictory applications[18] mask deeper

---

[12] See M Milanovic, 'An Odd Couple: Domestic Crimes and International Responsibility in the Special Tribunal for Lebanon' (2007) 5 *Journal of International Criminal Justice* 1139, 1139–40. See also *Interlocutory Decision on the Applicable Law: Terrorism, Conspiracy, Homicide, Perpetration, Cumulative Charging*, Case No STL 11-01/I, Appeals Chamber (26 February 2011).

[13] ME Badar, '"Just Convict Everyone!" – Joint Perpetration: From *Tadić* to *Stakić* and Back Again' (2006) 6 *International Criminal Law Review* 293, 302.

[14] See, eg, H Olásolo, 'Reflections on the Treatment of the Notions of Control of the Crime and Joint Criminal Enterprise in the Stakić Appeal Judgement' (2007) 7 *International Criminal Law Review* 143, 157–61; E van Sliedregt, *The Criminal Responsibility of Individuals for Violations of International Humanitarian Law* (The Hague, TMC Asser Press, 2003) 4–5; Danner and Martinez, above n 5,134–46; JD Ohlin, 'Three Conceptual Problems with the Doctrine of Joint Criminal Enterprise' (2007) 5 *Journal of International Criminal Justice* 69, 89–90.

[15] See *Prosecutor v Lubanga*, Decision on the Confirmation of Charges, No ICC-01/04-01/06, ICC Pre-Trial Chamber I (29 January 2007); *Prosecutor v Germain Katanga and Mathieu Ngudjolo Chui*, No ICC-01/04-01/07, Pre-Trial Decision on the Confirmation of Charges (30 September 2008).

[16] See, eg, K Ambos, 'Joint Criminal Enterprise and Command Responsibility' (2007) 5 *Journal of International Criminal Justice* 159; H van der Wilt, 'Joint Criminal Enterprise: Possibilities and Limitations' (2007) 5 *Journal of International Criminal Justice* 91.

[17] In *Tadić* alone, the Appeals Chamber used the following terms interchangeably to describe the form of liability: common criminal plan, a common criminal purpose, a common design or purpose, a common criminal design, a common purpose, a common design, and a common concerted design. The common purpose was also described, more generally, as being part of a criminal enterprise, a common enterprise, and a joint criminal enterprise; see A Bogdan, 'Individual Criminal Responsibility in the Execution of a "Joint Criminal Enterprise" in the Jurisprudence of the *ad hoc* International Tribunal for the Former Yugoslavia' (2006) 6 *International Criminal Law Review* 63, 80. See also *Prosecutor v Brdanin and Talić*, No IT-99-36-PT, Trial Chamber II Pre-Trial Decision on Form of Further Amended Indictment and Prosecution Application to Amend (26 June 2001).

[18] For the different formulations of the requirements of JCE by the ICTY for instance, see Boas et al, above n 6, 10–124. For debates on whether and to what extent Art 25(3) of the Rome Statute of the International Criminal Court recognises JCE, see K Ambos, 'Individual

disagreements about its fundamental bases. A useful starting point for analysing the appropriateness of JCE for attribution of individual responsibility is a critical analysis of the elements of JCE, including its historical counterparts, and more recent refinements to the doctrine.

II. RESPONSIBILITY FOR COLLECTIVE PARTICIPATION AT THE IMTS

A. Formulating Principles of Liability at Nuremberg

The Nuremberg trials took place against the backdrop of an increasing recognition in international law that criminal responsibility and guilt should be personal rather than collective in nature. Commentators recognise that historically, international law did not distinguish clearly between civil and criminal liability. Individuals could often be held responsible for their association through nationality, domicile or otherwise with an enemy or criminal State, in a manner that resembled criminal liability.[19] This position underwent a gradual change, however, during the nineteenth and twentieth centuries. For instance, modifications were made in the laws of war acknowledging that apart from liabilities flowing from war, no person should be held responsible for the conduct of another and that subjects should not be punished for the acts of their rulers.[20] There was also a spurt in recognition of fundamental human rights at the international level, including the rights of fair trial, presumption of innocence and an emphasis on non-distinction in rights based on certain group characteristics.[21]

At the same time, there were almost no recorded cases of individuals being held criminally accountable by an international body (rather than a sovereign State) for conduct that might loosely be termed an act against the law of nations. Instances of early 'international prosecutions' fall into roughly two categories. The first comprises cases where it was unclear

---

Criminal Responsibility' in O Triffterer (ed), *Commentary on the Rome Statute of the International Criminal Court*, 2nd edn (Baden-Baden, Nomos, 1999) 743, 747–53; Boas et al, above n 6, 125–28; V Militello, 'The Personal Nature of Individual Criminal Responsibility and the ICC Statute' (2007) 5 *Journal of International Criminal Justice* 941, 949–51; G Werle, 'Individual Criminal Responsibility in Article 25 ICC Statute' (2007) 5 *Journal of International Criminal Justice* 953, 958–63.

[19] Q Wright, 'International Law and Guilt by Association' (1949) 43 *The American Journal of International Law* 746, 749–50. See also A Nussbaum, *A Concise History of the Law of Nations* (New York, The Macmillan Company, 1947) 34. For a more detailed historical account of criminal responsibility in international law, see AG Levy, 'Criminal Responsibility of Individuals and International Law' (1945) 12 *University of Chicago Law Review* 313.

[20] Wright, above n 19, citing Grotius, *De Jure Belli as Pacis* (Carnegie Endowment for International Peace 1925) vol ii, ch xxi, sec xii; vol III, ch xi; sec ii, 539, 723. See also G Komarow, 'Individual Responsibility under International Law: The Nuremberg Principles in Domestic Legal Systems' (1980) 29 *ICLQ* 21, 21–23.

[21] Wright, above n 19, 752.

whether the trial was truly international[22] – that is, either whether the body trying the accused could be deemed properly international, or whether the conduct with which the accused was charged could be considered an international crime.[23] The second consists of trials that never materialised due either to lack of political will in pursuing them,[24] or to the proposed punishment having been overridden by amnesty guarantees.[25]

It was in the context of these developments that the International Military Tribunals at Nuremberg (IMT) and Tokyo (IMTFE) were tasked with establishing accountability for crimes committed by the Axis powers during World War II. The political sentiment surrounding the constitution of the IMTs is vital to understanding the principles of criminal responsibility developed for the prosecutions. The Americans, who were instrumental in formulating the theories of liability finally included in the Charter, were heavily influenced by their perception that the atrocities in World War II had been directed by a highly organised bureaucratic apparatus.[26] Their dilemma was to design a theory of liability that would fulfil the popular call for retributive measures against the horrors of Nazism, while at the same time avoiding blanket condemnation of the German

---

[22] Eg, the trial and execution of Peter von Hagenbach in Breisach, Austria, in 1474, is cited by some international lawyers as the earliest instance of international criminal law being applied to an individual. See G Schwarzenberger, *International Law as Applied by International Courts and Tribunals, International Law vol I*, 3rd edn (London, Stevens & Sons Limited, 1957) 462–66; M Cherif Bassiouni, 'The Time Has Come For An International Criminal Court' (1991) 1 *Indiana International & Comparative Law Review* 1, 1. This has been heavily disputed in more recent commentary. See TLH MacCormack, 'Selective Reaction to Atrocity: War Crimes and the Development of International Criminal Law' (1997) 60 *Albany Law Review* 681, 690–91; R Cryer, *Prosecuting International Crimes: Selectivity and the International Criminal Law Regime* (Cambridge, Cambridge University Press, 2005) 18.

[23] Eg, the attempt to prosecute Kaiser Wilhelm II for initiating World War I and offences against 'international morality and the sanctity of treaties'. For a discussion of this, see JW Garner, 'Punishment of Offenders against the Laws and Customs of War' (1920) 14 *American Journal of International Law* 70, 91–92; H Leonhardt, 'The Nuremberg Trial: A Legal Analysis' (1949) 11 *Review of Politics* 449, 459–60; see also Q Wright, 'The Legal Liability of the Kaiser' (1919) 13 *American Political Science Review* 120.

[24] German military personnel alleged to have violated the laws and customs of war during World War I were meant to be tried before allied military tribunals, but the Allies finally asked Germany to try a select number before the Supreme Court of Germany in Leipzig. See M Cherif Bassiouni, 'International Criminal Investigations and Prosecutions: From Versailles to Rwanda' in *International Criminal Law Vol III* (New York, Transnational Publishers, 1999) 33–34, 37; R Bierzanek, 'War Crimes: History and Definition' in *International Criminal Law Vol III* (New York, Transnational Publishers, 1999) 87, 92–93.

[25] The Treaty of Lausanne between the Allies and Turkey signed in 1923 was accompanied by a declaration of amnesty in respect of the attempted extermination of the Armenian people by the Ottoman Government and its agents in 1915. T MacCormack, 'From Sun Tzu to the Sixth Committee: The Evolution of an International Criminal Regime' in TLH MacCormack and GJ Simpson (eds), *The Law of War Crimes: National and International Approaches* (The Hague, Kluwer, 1997) 31, 44–45; Cryer, above n 22, 33.

[26] Memorandum to President Roosevelt from the Secretaries of State and War and the Attorney General, 22 January 1945, in *Report of Robert H Jackson, United States Representative to the International Conference on Military Trials* (Washington, 1949) 4–5.

people as a whole.[27] They did so through two ingenious doctrines first developed by Colonel Murray C Bernays, an inconspicuous young lawyer in the section of Special Projects branch of the US Department of War: conspiracy and liability for membership of criminal organisations.[28]

Quite unsurprisingly, both doctrines were at the centre of controversy in the negotiations leading up to the drafting of the Nuremberg Charter between the four powers, France, the UK, the Soviet Union and the US. Conspiracy, as an inchoate crime, was unknown to most of the civil law world.[29] Subsequent French and Russian re-drafts of the Charter conspicuously failed even to mention conspiracy, an omission criticised by a despairing Justice Jackson on the ground that there were no other acceptable means of reaching large numbers of people, especially those against whom evidence of specific unlawful acts was lacking.[30] A compromise was finally reached and conspiracy, both as an inchoate crime and as a mode of complicity, was included in the Charter of the IMT.[31] However, not only did the Charter fail to provide for a definition of what constitutes conspiracy, it also criminalised only conspiracy (as an inchoate crime) to

---

[27] S Pomorski, 'Conspiracy and Criminal Organisation' in G Ginsburgs and VN Kudriavtsev (eds), *The Nuremberg Trial and International Law* (London, Martinus Nijhoff, 1990) 213, 214.

[28] A Tusa and J Tusa, *The Nuremberg Trial* (London, BBC Books, 1995) 54. For a detailed account of Bernays' proposal and the American version of both doctrines, see ibid, 50–67.

[29] For a slightly surreal and humorous account of the conspiracy debate at the London conference, see B Smith (ed), *The American Road to Nuremberg: The Documentary Record 1944–45* (Stanford, CA, Hoover Institute Press, 1982) 51. See also H-H Jescheck, *Die Verantwortlichkeit der Staatsorgane nach Völkerstrafrecht* (Bonn, Röhrscheid, 1952) 276 (describing conspiracy as an inapposite concept for international criminal law due to its absence in the Continental criminal law tradition). But see KJ Heller, *The Nuremberg Military Tribunals and the Origins of International Criminal Law* (Oxford, Oxford University Press, 2011) 277 (arguing that pre-war German criminal law recognised criminal responsibility for mere agreements to commit certain kinds of violent acts).

[30] *Report of Robert H Jackson*, above n 26, Doc XXXVII, 300.

[31] Nuremberg Rules, in Agreement for the Prosecution and Punishment of the Major War Criminals of the European Axis, 82 UNTS 279, entered into force 8 August 1945. Art 6 of the Charter of the IMT states: 'The following acts, or any of them, are crimes coming within the jurisdiction of the Tribunal for which there shall be individual responsibility: I CRIMES AGAINST PEACE: namely, planning, preparation, initiation or waging of a war of aggression, or a war in violation of international treaties, agreements or assurances, or participation in a common plan or conspiracy for the accomplishment of any of the foregoing; II WAR CRIMES: namely, violations of the laws or customs of war. Such violations shall include, but not be limited to, murder, ill-treatment or deportation to slave labor or for any other purpose of civilian population of or in occupied territory, murder or ill-treatment of prisoners of war or persons on the seas, killing of hostages, plunder of public or private property, wanton destruction of cities, towns or villages, or devastation not justified by military necessity; III CRIMES AGAINST HUMANITY: namely, murder, extermination, enslavement, deportation, and other inhumane acts committed against any civilian population, before or during the war; or persecutions on political, racial or religious grounds in execution of or in connection with any crime within the jurisdiction of the Tribunal, whether or not in violation of the domestic law of the country where perpetrated. Leaders, organizers, instigators and accomplices participating in the formulation or execution of a common plan or conspiracy to commit any of the foregoing crimes are responsible for all acts performed by any persons in execution of such plan.'

commit crimes against peace. Conspiracy to commit war crimes or crimes against humanity was punishable solely as a form of complicity.[32]

The proposal to criminalise membership of certain organisations also met with initial resistance from the Russians on political rather than principled grounds. However, in view of the evidentiary problems confronting prosecutions of suspected offenders, the American proposal in this respect also prevailed: the IMT would be asked to make a declaration of criminality concerning the major Nazi organisations, which would then be binding against individual members of these organisations being prosecuted in national and occupation courts. Further, there would be a presumption of the accused's voluntariness and knowledge of the criminal purposes of the organisation in these proceedings.[33]

B. The Prosecutions' Grand Vision

Despite the IMT prosecution teams' ostensible championing of the principle of individual criminal responsibility over collective accountability,[34] their strategy clearly focused on establishing the existence of a wide-ranging conspiracy, both by the Nazis in Germany[35] and by successive governments in Japan.[36] Holding particular *individuals* accountable for this conspiracy was of secondary importance,[37] and the breadth of the

[32] Pomorski, above n 27, 222–23, 227–28; Elies van Sliedregt, *Individual Criminal Responsibility in International Law* (Oxford, Oxford University Press, 2012) 24. This nevertheless did not prevent the Americans from charging conspiracy for all three crimes in the indictment. Count 1 of the Indictment, labelled 'The Common Plan or Conspiracy', stated, in relevant part: 'All the defendants, with divers other persons, during a period of years preceding 8 May 1945, participated as leaders, organizers, instigators, or accomplices in the formulation or execution of a common plan or conspiracy to commit, or which involved the commission of, Crimes against Peace, War Crimes, and Crimes against Humanity, as defined in the Charter of this Tribunal, and, in accordance with the provisions of the Charter, are individually responsible for their own acts and for all acts committed by any persons in the execution of such plan or conspiracy.' *Trial of the Major War Criminals Before the International Military Tribunal*, vol I (Nuremberg, 1947) 29.

[33] Pomorski, above n 27, 220. See also *Report of Robert H Jackson*, above n 26, Doc XXII, 133. For a discussion of the implications of the legal issues left unclear in the final draft, see C Haensel, 'Nuremberg Problems' in WE Burton and G Grimm (eds), *Nuremberg: German Views of the War Trials* (Dallas, TX, Southern Methodist University Press, 1955) 146.

[34] *Trial of the Major War Criminals*, vol II, above n 32, 102.

[35] See D Bloxham, *Genocide on Trial* (Oxford, Oxford University Press, 2001) 19, citing the statement of Robert H Jackson, lead counsel for the American prosecution, in the Jackson papers, container 191, 'Justice Jacksons's story', fnn 1046–47.

[36] RJ Pritchard (ed), 'Indictment' in *The Tokyo Major War Crimes Trial: The Records of the International Military Tribunal for the Far East*, vol 2 (Lewiston-Lampeter-Queenston, The Edwin Mellen Press, 1998) 1.

[37] See the opening statement of Robert H Jackson, *Trial of the Major War Criminals*, above n 34, vol II 98–99. In the context of the IMTFE, see GF Blewett, US counsel for General Tōjō Hideki: 'Victor's Injustice: The Tokyo War Crimes Trial' (1950) 4 *American Perspective* 282, 287–88; see also RH Minear, *Victor's Justice: The Tokyo War Crimes Trial* (Princeton, NJ, Princeton University Press, 1971) 37, citing S Horwitz, 'The Tokyo Trial' (1950) 466 *International Conciliation* 473, 498.

charges ensured that anyone associated with the leadership or in a government position could be considered part of the conspiracy.[38]

The prosecution thus sought to use the vagueness in some of the terms of the Nuremberg Charter to its advantage. Count 1 of the IMT indictment charged persons who had participated in the formulation or execution of a 'common plan *or* conspiracy' (emphasis added) to commit crimes under the Charter.[39] The concept of a 'common plan' was unknown in any legal system[40] and undefined in the Charter. The Charter also failed to define the concepts of 'group' and 'organisation' in the provisions outlining the individual responsibility of members of criminal organisations.[41] The prosecution interpreted 'group' to mean a looser and more informal structure or relationship than an 'organisation'; both terms, however, implied an 'aggregation of persons associated in some identifiable relationship with a collective general purpose'.[42] The prosecution indicted six separate organisations,[43] while emphasising that they were all interdependent and part of one gigantic apparatus.[44]

In order for an organisation to be declared criminal, the prosecution had to prove the following elements:

(a) the organisation's membership was in general voluntary;
(b) it was designed to perform conduct that was criminal under the Charter;
(c) due to the character of the organisation's activities, the members could be presumed to have knowledge of them; and
(d) that some defendant tried by the Tribunal was a member of the organisation and was guilty of an act on the basis of which the organisation was to be declared criminal.[45]

According to the prosecution, the IMT's adjudication was of a declaratory nature, which left the question of individual guilt to the local courts trying individuals on the basis of the declaratory judgment. The only effect of it was to create a rebuttable presumption of guilt, thus reversing the burden

---

[38] F Biddle, 'The Nurnberg Trial' (1947) 33 *Virginia Law Review* 679, 691; R Wassertrom, 'The Relevance of Nuremberg' (1971) 1 *Philosophy & Public Affairs* 22, 37. It has been remarked that in the case of the IMTFE, the indictments served to condemn an entire epoch and a nation: W Sebald, *With MacArthur in Japan* (New York, WW Norton, 1965) 152, 159, cited from E Kopelman, 'Ideology and International Law: The Dissent of the Indian Justice at the Tokyo War Crimes Trial' (1990–91) 23 *NYU Journal of International Law & Politics* 373, 395.

[39] H Ehard, 'The Nuremberg Trial Against the Major War Criminals and International Law' (1949) 43 *The American Journal of International Law* 223, 226–27.

[40] Ibid, 227.

[41] H Leventhal et al, 'The Nurnberg Verdict' (1947) 60 *Harvard Law Review* 857, 891.

[42] 2 *Nazi Conspiracy and Aggression* (Washington, US Government Printing Office,1946) 17.

[43] *Indictment*, text published by the IMT at Nuremberg as Doc No 1, App B, 35–38.

[44] *History of the United Nations War Crimes Commission and the Development of the Laws of War* (London, HMSO, 1948) 302 ('UNWCC Report'), citing *The Trial of German Major War Criminals – Speeches of the Prosecutors at the Close of the Case against the Indicted Organisations* (London, HMSO, 1946) 61.

[45] UNWCC Report, above n 44, 305.

of proof.[46] The prosecution was unimpressed by arguments that the mere declaration of the organisation's criminality represented the condemnation of its members, and was therefore already a punishment of one kind.[47]

C. The IMT Judgments

i. Criminal organisations

Despite its declaration that collective punishment is reprehensible, the IMT was emphatic that it may declare an organisation to be criminal if satisfied of its criminal guilt. In this endeavour, it would not be deterred by arguments that group criminality was an innovation.[48] The Tribunal was at pains to reconcile this readiness to issue a finding of collective guilt with its statement that all criminal responsibility would be based on the personal guilt of the individual.[49] The Tribunal may have been conscious of the fact that criminal liability for mere membership of a criminal organisation was controversial in the domestic laws of most nations[50] and without precedent in international law.[51] It added various qualifications to the terms of Articles 9[52] and 10[53] to achieve this objective.

First, it narrowed the net of offenders who could be prosecuted by blurring the distinct functions performed by the doctrines of organisational criminality and conspiracy in the prosecution case.[54] The IMT defined a criminal organisation in the following terms: 'A criminal organisation is

---

[46] Ibid, 307.

[47] Haensel, above n 33, 151. *Cf* Biddle, above n 38, 693.

[48] See Biddle, above n 38, 693.

[49] See FB Schick, 'The Nuremberg Trial and the International Law of the Future' (1947) 41 *American Journal of International Law* 770, 787–88.

[50] For a survey of domestic legislation that provided for analogous modes of liability, see UNWCC Report, above n 44, 318–32.

[51] R Woetzel, *The Nuremberg Trials in International Law* (London, Stevens & Sons, 1962) 211. See also Leonhardt, above n 23, 453–54.

[52] IMT Charter, above n 31, Art 9: 'At the trial of any individual member of any group or organization the Tribunal may declare (in connection with any act of which the individual may be convicted) that the group or organization of which the individual was a member was a criminal organization. / After the receipt of the Indictment the Tribunal shall give such notice as it thinks fit that the prosecution intends to ask the Tribunal to make such declaration and any member of the organization will be entitled to apply to the Tribunal for leave to be heard by the Tribunal upon the question of the criminal character of the organization. The Tribunal shall have power to allow or reject the application. If the application is allowed, the Tribunal may direct in what manner the applicants shall be represented and heard.'

[53] Ibid, Art 10: 'In cases where a group or organization is declared criminal by the Tribunal, the competent national authority of any Signatory shall have the right to bring individuals to trial for membership therein before national, military or occupation courts. In any such case the criminal nature of the group or organization is considered proved and shall not be questioned.'

[54] Compare with H Kelsen, 'Will the Judgment in the Nuremberg Trial Constitute a Precedent in International Law?' (1947) 1 *International Law Quarterly* 153, 165–67.

analogous to a criminal conspiracy in that the essence of both is co-operation for criminal purposes. There must be a group bound together and organised for a common purpose.'[55] Secondly, mere membership in the organisation was not criminal; the individual must have had knowledge of the criminal purposes of the organisation. If the accused had been conscripted into the organisation by the State, it would further have to be proved that he was personally implicated in the commission of the criminal conduct.[56] However, he need not have known of the specific criminal acts committed pursuant to the criminal purposes of the group or have been directly connected with them.[57]

In adding these requirements of knowledge and voluntary participation in the criminal purposes of a group, the IMT reformulated the original conception of responsibility for membership of a criminal organisation such that it resembled an extended form of conspiracy liability.[58] Individuals who had joined organisations subscribing to their legitimate aims and without knowledge of their unlawful purposes, could still be prosecuted if they remained members after discovering these criminal purposes.[59] Further, in defining a criminal organisation, the Tribunal stressed that the organisation could be *formed* or used in connection with the commission of conduct denounced under the IMT Charter. The necessary implication of this was that actual commission of crimes by the organisation was not required.[60] This was again similar to conspiracy as an inchoate crime.

The Tribunal went on to limit considerably the kinds of persons who would fall within the net of criminality cast by the organisation. It excluded certain departments and categories of people, such as janitors and secretaries, who played no direct role in the criminal conduct of the organisation.[61] It also declined to make a declaration of criminality against

---

[55] *Trial of the Major War Criminals*, above n 32, 256.

[56] Ibid. The prosecution had already conceded two important qualifications for when an organisation would be considered criminal: (i) its membership must, in general, be voluntary; (ii) information about the criminal conduct of the group must be so widespread or easily available that members' knowledge of the criminal nature could be assumed. See *Trial of the Major War Criminals*, vol VIII, above n 32, 367–68.

[57] Woetzel, above n 51, 203. The Nuremberg Military Tribunals set up by the US to try suspected war criminals in the wake of World War II subsequently endorsed the knowledge standard, and held that knowledge may be inferred from the defendant's position and the nature of the organisation's crimes. See Heller, above n 29, 293–94.

[58] Woetzel, above n 51, 202 citing C Hänsel, *Das Organisationsverbrechen* (München, Biederstein Verlag, 1947) 54–55.

[59] Woetzel, above n 51, 209–10, citing G Rauschenbach, *Der Nürnberger Prozess gegen die Organisationen* (Bonn, L Röhrscheid, 1954) 132–33. Heller refers to the subsequent Nuremberg Military Tribunals' expanded interpretation of the element of voluntariness as effectively rendering the defence of involuntariness redundant. See Heller, above n 29, 292–93.

[60] See UNWCC Report, above n 44, 312; Heller, above n 29, 291.

[61] This had been conceded by the prosecution. See UNWCC Report, above n 44, 302.

groups that were small in size,[62] such as the General Staff and High Command. Here, the Tribunal added the condition that in order to be held responsible, the members should not simply be working alongside each other, but must actually be *conscious* of forming an 'organization'.[63]

ii. Conspiracy at the IMT and the IMFTE

The IMT at Nuremberg accepted the prosecution theory that the Nazi leadership and its associates had been plotting to wage an aggressive war ever since seizing power. It found it unnecessary to determine whether a *single conspiracy* (rather than several conspiracies) to the extent and over the time alleged in the indictment had been proved.[64] This is a surprising omission, given that the kinds of crimes for which an individual can be held guilty by virtue of his participation in the conspiracy are integrally connected to the scale and temporal scope of the conspiracy. The broader the definition of the conspiracy, the greater is the potential responsibility of the individual for acts committed by him and others in its execution.[65]

The IMT mitigated this sweeping pronouncement on conspiracy by subsequent statements narrowing its operation. First, it held that Article 6 of the Charter did not grant any jurisdiction over conspiracies to commit war crimes or crimes against humanity.[66] For crimes against peace, the conspiracy 'must be clearly outlined in its criminal purpose . . . must not be too far removed from the time of decision and action', and must consist of a 'concrete plan to wage war'.[67] The IMT thus avoided the determination that the prosecution would have had them make – that the entire Nazi Government from 1933 onwards was an open conspiracy.[68] Secondly, it set a relatively high standard for judging participation in the conspiracy or common plan: whether the defendants, with knowledge of Hitler's aims, gave him their co-operation.[69] Thus, the individual should have known of the aggressive plan, and have been involved personally in the planning with Hitler.[70] On the other hand, there was no requirement that the participants in the common plan were of equal status; the common plan could be conceived by one person alone and exist even in a

---

[62] The Tribunal stated this as an express reason for making no such declaration in the case of the Reich Cabinet, since there would be no strategic advantage or saving of time and resources compared to individually prosecuting the defendants affiliated to the Cabinet. *Trial of the Major War Criminals*, vol I, above n 32, 275–76.

[63] See Woetzel, above n 51, 199.

[64] *Trial of the Major War Criminals*, vol I, above n 32, 225.

[65] For a similar argument, see Pomorski, above n 27, 236.

[66] *Trial of the Major War Criminals*, vol I, above n 32, 226.

[67] Ibid, 225.

[68] Leventhal et al, above n 41, 871.

[69] *Trial of the Major War Criminals*, vol I, above n 32, 225–26.

[70] On this aspect, and the manner in which it is necessarily implied from the convictions and acquittals in the case of individual defendants, see Leventhal et al, above n 41, 873–81.

dictatorship.[71] Only eight of the 22 defendants were ultimately found guilty of conspiracy.[72]

The IMFTE at Tokyo adopted a broader understanding of conspiracy. It distinguished between the inchoate charge of conspiracy ('naked conspiracy') and conspiracy as a form of complicity ('executed conspiracy').[73] Following the Nuremberg IMT's lead, it dismissed the (inchoate) conspiracy charges to commit crimes against humanity and war crimes.[74] With respect to conspiracy to commit crimes against peace, the IMFTE regarded the prosecution's vision of conspiracy favourably, limiting only the territorial extent of the planned conspiracy.[75] As Arthur Comyns Carr, the British prosecutor at the IMFTE, later observed with no trace of irony:

> The story that unfolded in the judgment is one of a grandiose plot which originated in the late 1920's in the minds of a few officers and civilians, and grew until it became the dominant purpose . . . of every successive government of Japan.[76]

This view of a massive conspiracy by the accused to dominate parts of Asia and the Indian and Pacific Oceans rests on a deeply controversial construction of Japanese history.[77] As noted in Justice Pal's dissent, the conspiracy edifice erected by the prosecution presented a series of discrete events spanning more than a decade, and marked by a combination of foresight, accident and surprise, as a linear historical progression with a calculated object. This represented a hopelessly simplistic and inaccurate judgement on the historical evolution of an entire nation.[78]

---

[71] *Trial of the Major War Criminals*, vol I, above n 32, 226; see also van Sliedregt, above n 32, 25.

[72] Biddle, above n 38, 690–91.

[73] See N Boister, 'The Application of Collective and Comprehensive Criminal Responsibility for Aggression at the Tokyo International Military Tribunal' (2010) 8 *Journal of International Criminal Justice* 425, 430, citing the distinction developed by the Scottish Judge, Lord Patrick, at the IMFTE, in WD Patrick, Member for the United Kingdom, *'Planning' and 'Conspiracy' in Relation to Criminal Trials, and Specially in Relation to the Trial*, 30 January 1948, Papers of William Flood Webb, Series 1, Wallet 14, 3DRL/2481, Australian War Memorial ('Lord Patrick Paper').

[74] RJ Pritchard (ed), 'Judgment of the Tokyo Tribunal' in *The Tokyo Major War Crimes Trial*, vol 101, above n 36, 48451 (*'Tokyo Judgment'*). Inchoate conspiracy, as a separate substantive offence, was also rejected by the subsequent trials conducted by Nuremberg Military Tribunals. See Heller, above n 29, 280.

[75] *Tokyo Judgment*, above n 74, 49763.

[76] AS Comyns Carr, 'The Judgment of the International Military Tribunal for the Far East' (1948) 34 *Transactions of the Grotius Society* 141, 146.

[77] See, eg, AM Danner, 'Beyond the Geneva Conventions: Lessons from the Tokyo Tribunal in Prosecuting War and Terrorism' (2006) 46 *Virginia Journal of International Law* 83, 118; Boister, above n 73, 432; Hosoya Chihiro, 'Question-and-Answer Period' in C Hosoya et al (eds), *The Tokyo War Crimes Trial: An International Symposium* (Tokyo, Kodansha, 1986) 105, 109; JW Dower, *Embracing Defeat: Japan in the Wake of World War II* (New York, Norton, 1999) 463.

[78] For a detailed account of Pal's dissent, see Kopelman, above n 38.

The IMFTE also embraced the doctrine of 'executed' conspiracy, or conspiracy as a form of complicity, in Article 5(c) of the IMFTE Charter.[79] This concept found its way into the judgment by way of a paper circulated by Lord Patrick,[80] who drew upon the common law doctrine of 'joint enterprise'. According to Lord Patrick, the basic form of joint enterprise liability imposed responsibility on the accused for all unlawful acts which fell within the common purpose. The 'parasitical' form of the doctrine, where the accused was additionally responsible for a further unlawful act which was not included in the common purpose but a foreseeable consequence of it, was peculiar to English law. Since the prosecution had charged only the basic form – no count of the indictment included a crime that was not in execution of the conspiracy – the IMFTE did not need to concern itself with the parasitical form.[81]

The majority judgment adopted this version of executed conspiracy. In convicting individual defendants of the crime of conspiracy to wage aggressive war, the judgment deemed it irrelevant whether they were originators of the conspiracy, or parties to it till the very end (indeed, this would have been nearly impossible to prove, given that the conspiracy spanned more than a decade that saw different Cabinets in power).[82] Instead, 'all those who at any time were parties to the criminal conspiracy or who at any time with guilty knowledge played a part in its execution' were declared guilty of the conspiracy to wage aggressive war.[83] The combination of a wide-ranging single grand conspiracy and requirements for minimal conduct by the accused allowed the IMFTE to avoid the difficulties in establishing individual responsibility of the accused for the many and varied actions taken by them individually in the course of the war.[84] While the judgment followed Lord Patrick's lead in omitting to mention responsibility under the parasitic form of the joint enterprise doctrine, it is unclear whether this was merely due to the prosecution's failure to include it specifically in the indictment.[85]

---

[79] Charter of the International Military Tribunal for the Far East, 19 January 1946, TIAS No 1589, 4 Bevans 20 (as amended 26 April 1946, 4 Bevans 27). Art 5(c) states: '*Crimes against Humanity:* Namely, murder, extermination, enslavement, deportation, and other inhumane acts committed against any civilian population, before or during the war, or persecutions on political or racial grounds in execution of or in connection with any crime within the jurisdiction of the Tribunal, whether or not in violation of the domestic law of the country where perpetrated. Leaders, organizers, instigators and accomplices participating in the formulation or execution of a common plan or conspiracy to commit any of the foregoing crimes are responsible for all acts performed by any person in execution of such plan.'

[80] For a detailed account of the injection of 'executed conspiracy' at the IMFTE and Lord Patrick's role, see Boister, above n 73, 435–37.

[81] Lord Patrick paper, above n 73, 3.

[82] Horwitz, above n 37, 507.

[83] *Tokyo Judgment*, above n 74, 49770.

[84] Boister, above n 73, 431; Danner, above n 77, 115.

[85] Boister, above n 73, 437.

Despite the criticisms leveled at the judgments of the IMT and IMFTE, their pronouncements on modes of responsibility, in particular on conspiracy, have been deeply influential. Though advocates of the modern version of the JCE doctrine in international criminal law have been keen to deny any resemblance between JCE and conspiracy liability at IMTs, there is an undeniable connection between the two.[86] The relationship between the doctrines becomes clearer when one considers the ICTY's introduction of JCE into the lexicon of international criminal law.

III. THE APOCALYPTIC MOMENT: *TADIĆ*

The dominant trend in literature on JCE is to signal the ICTY Appeals Chamber's judgment in *Prosecutor v Tadić* as the first enunciation of the JCE doctrine in international criminal law.[87] While this statement is not entirely accurate,[88] *Tadić* was certainly the first case in which an international criminal tribunal clearly established the elements of JCE and its status in customary international law. It is therefore important to analyse *Tadić*'s exposition of JCE in some depth.

A. Brief Factual Background

Dusko Tadić was a member of an armed Serbian group that had attacked the village of Jaskici in Bosnia Herzegovina, killing five Bosnian Muslim men in the village. He was charged with crimes against humanity under Article 7(1) of the ICTY Statute for the killings and other crimes.[89] Although Tadić had been a member of the group and played an active role in the attack, the Trial Chamber had failed to be satisfied beyond reasonable doubt that he had participated in the killings of the five men.[90] The prosecution appealed against this decision, arguing that Tadić should have been held responsible for the killings in accordance with the doctrine of 'common purpose', since the killings were a natural and

---

[86] See E van Sliedregt, *The Criminal Responsibility of Individuals for Violations of International Humanitarian Law* (The Hague, TMC Asser Press, 2003) 107; Danner and Martinez, above n 5, 109, 118–19. Defence counsel before the ICTY have especially emphasised this connection: see MJ Osiel, 'The Banality of Good: Aligning Incentives Against Mass Atrocity' (2005) 105 *Columbia Law Review* 1751, 1791. On the conspiracy underpinning of JCE, see N Piacente, 'Importance of the Joint Criminal Enterprise Doctrine for the ICTY Prosecutorial Policy' (2004) 2 *Journal of International Criminal Justice* 446, 451.

[87] See, eg, Piacente, above n 86, 449.

[88] It is now acknowledged that the ICTY employed the notion of liability for participation in a common criminal plan or enterprise earlier, in *Prosecutor v Furundžija*, No IT-95-17/I-T, Trial Chamber (10 December 1998). See Boas et al, above n 6, 10–14.

[89] *Prosecutor v Tadić*, No IT-94-1-I, Second Amended Indictment (14 December 1995), para 12.

[90] *Prosecutor v Tadić*, No IT-94-1-T, Trial Chamber Judgment (14 July 1997), para 373.

foreseeable consequence of the attack and occurred in the context of a broader policy to ethnically cleanse the region of Prijedor of non-Serbs.[91] As there was no proof that Tadić had personally killed the men, the Appeals Chamber had to decide whether he could be held responsible due to his participation in the acts of the group that committed the killings.[92]

B. Interpretative Stance

The Appeals Chamber analysed Tadić's responsibility under Article 7(1) of the ICTY Statute dealing with modes of participation. It interpreted the term 'commission' in the context of the inviolability of the principle of personal culpability in criminal law,[93] by situating it within the object and purpose of the ICTY Statute,[94] and based on the inherent nature of international crimes.[95] According to the Chamber, the ICTY had a mandate to bring to justice *all* those who were responsible for serious violations of international humanitarian law committed in the former Yugoslavia,[96] regardless of the manner of their participation in these crimes.[97] Thus, an accused who contributed to the commission of a crime enumerated under the Statute in pursuance of a common criminal purpose could, in certain circumstances, also be held responsible.[98] The Chamber seemed to assume that a strict interpretation of 'commission' would allow too many perpetrators to escape justice and defeat the purpose of the Statute.

The Appeals Chamber's approach towards the construction of 'commission' in Article 7(1) adheres to customary rules of treaty interpretation.[99] Nevertheless, it highlights the tension in marrying two very

---

[91] *Prosecutor v Tadić*, No IT-94-1-A, Appeals Chamber Judgment (15 July 1999) ('*Tadić Appeals Judgment*'), para 175.

[92] Ibid, para 183.

[93] Ibid, para 186.

[94] It relied on other provisions of the ICTY Statute and the report of the Secretary General on the ICTY's establishment: ibid, paras 189–90.

[95] Ibid, paras 189–93.

[96] See Art 1 of the Statute of the International Tribunal for the Prosecution of Persons Responsible for Serious Violations of International Humanitarian Law Committed in the Territory of the Former Yugoslavia since 1991, UN Doc S/25704/Add 1 (3 May 1993), adopted by Security Council on 25 May 1993, UN Doc S/RES/827: 'The International Tribunal shall have the power to prosecute persons responsible for serious violations of international humanitarian law committed in the territory of the former Yugoslavia since 1991 in accordance with the provisions of the present Statute.'

[97] *Tadić Appeals Judgment*, above n 91, para 190.

[98] Ibid, para 190.

[99] Art 31(1) of the Vienna Convention on the Law of Treaties, 23 May 1969, 1155 UNTS 331 (entered into force 27 January 1980) states: 'A treaty shall be interpreted in good faith in accordance with the ordinary meaning to be given to the terms of the treaty in their context and in the light of its object and purpose.'

different disciplines of law: international law and criminal law.[100] On the one hand, the teleological approach to treaty interpretation[101] supports a broad, purposive construction of treaty terms; on the other, criminal law statutes are generally construed strictly, where any ambiguity is resolved in favour of the accused.[102] The Vienna Convention on the Law of Treaties (VCLT) provides for uniform rules of treaty interpretation irrespective of the nature of the treaty,[103] but there is room for debate as to whether this is a suitable approach towards treaties that have very different characters.[104] Treaties establishing international criminal tribunals are quite distinct from traditional treaties that were within the contemplation of the drafters of the VCLT; not only do they impose obligations on individuals rather than States, but the nature of the obligations imposed involves a potential severe restriction of the individual's fundamental liberties.[105] There is thus a strong argument to be made that terms such as 'commission' that occur

---

[100] On the hybrid identity of international criminal law, see, eg, A Cassese, *International Criminal Law* (Oxford, Oxford University Press, 2003) 18–19; L Grover, 'A Call to Arms: Fundamental Dilemmas Confronting the Interpretation of Crimes in the Rome Statute of the International Criminal Court' (2010) 21 *European Journal of International Law* 543, 550–51.

[101] There are divergent opinions on whether the dominant aim of treaty interpretation is to give effect to the intention of the contracting parties; whether the interpreter should adhere to the plain text of the treaty; or whether a teleological approach that furthers the object and purpose of the treaty should be favoured. For an analysis of the different approaches, see IM Sinclair, 'The Principles of Treaty Interpretation and their Application by the English Courts' (1963) 12 *ICLQ* 508, 509–10 and references therein.

[102] The application of the principle of strict construction in both the US and the UK has, however, been far from uniform. See JC Jeffries, 'Legality, Vagueness and the Construction of Penal Statutes' (1985) 71 *Virginia Law Review* 189; A Ashworth, 'Interpreting Criminal Statutes: A Crisis of Legality?' (1991) 107 *LQR* 419.

[103] H Waldock, 'Third Report on the Law of Treaties' in *Yearbook of the International Law Commission 1964*, vol II, 57 (New York, United Nations, 1965), UN Doc A/CN.4/SER.A/1964/Add.1; E Schwelb, 'The Law of Treaties and Human Rights' in WM Reisman and BH Weston (eds), *Toward World Order and Human Dignity: Essays in Honor of Myres S McDougal* (New York, The Free Press, 1976) 263, 266–72; M Frankowska, 'The Vienna Convention on the Law of Treaties Before United States Courts' (1988) 28 *Virginia Journal International Law* 281, 285; P Malanczuk, *Akehurst's Modern Introduction to International Law*, 6th rev edn (London, Routledge, 1997) 130.

[104] See, eg, J Wessel, 'Relational Contract Theory and Treaty Interpretation: End-Game Treaties v Dynamic Obligations' (2004) 60 *NYU Annual Survey of American Law* 149; M Toufayan, 'Human Rights Treaty Interpretation: A Postmodern Account of its Claim to "Speciality"' (2005) *NYU Center for Human Rights & Global Justice Working Paper No 2*, at <www.chrgj.org/publications/docs/wp/0502%20Toufayan.pdf>, accessed 10 December 2010; AD McNair, 'The Functions and Differing Legal Character of Treaties' (1930) 11 *British Year Book of International Law* 100, 106; R Matscher, 'Methods of Interpretation of the Convention' in RSt-J Macdonald, R Matscher and H Petzold (eds), *The European System for the Protection of Human Rights* (London, Martinus Nijhoff, 1993) 66.

[105] Publicists and arbitral tribunals commenting on rules of treaty interpretation prior to the drafting of the VCLT were quite emphatic that 'doubtful stipulations should be interpreted in the least onerous sense for the party obligated': *Sambiaggio case* in JH Ralston (ed), *Venezuelan Arbitrations of 1903* (Washington, DC, Government Printing Office, 1904) 689, quoting publicists including Vattel and Pradier-Fodéré; *Aspinwall Case* (4 Moore, *History and Digest of the International Arbitrations to which the United States has been a Party* 3621ff).

in an international criminal law treaty should be construed strictly, and in a manner favourable to the accused.

Moreover, even if the ICTY Statute's object to establish accountability for atrocities committed during the Yugoslavian conflict is a legitimate source for interpreting 'commission' responsibility, it is not obvious that this justifies the imposition of liability on persons acting in pursuance of a common criminal plan. The stipulation that persons acting in pursuance of a common criminal plan must be guilty for their actions assumes that this is in fact the level of culpability imposed by the ICTY Statute. Support for this proposition cannot be adduced from an expanded construction of the very provisions imposing criminal liability but must come from some independent source.[106]

The *Tadić* Chamber also placed great emphasis on the fact that most international crimes are not caused by the actions of discrete individuals; they are 'manifestations of collective criminality':[107]

> Although only some members of the group may physically perpetrate the criminal act . . . the participation and contribution of the other members of the group is often vital in facilitating the commission of the offence in question. It follows that the *moral gravity of such participation is often no less – or indeed no different –* from that of those actually carrying out the acts in question.[108] (emphasis added)

The Chamber thus stressed the moral gravity of an individual's participation in the criminal acts, from which it went on to draw conclusions about his or her criminal responsibility.[109] This is to assume a synonymy at two levels:

(a) between gravity and responsibility; and
(b) between moral and criminal.

Neither of these is tenable without further justification.

Similarly, the assumption that the moral gravity of contributing to the commission of an offence is equal to perpetrating it personally surely merits deeper examination. The Chamber clearly had a hierarchy of responsibility in mind when it stated that holding individuals who make it possible for the physical perpetrator to carry out collective criminal acts liable only as aiders and abettors, understates the degree of their criminal

---

[106] JD Ohlin, 'Three Conceptual Problems with the Doctrine of Joint Criminal Enterprise' (2007) 5 *Journal of International Criminal Justice* 69, 72.

[107] *Tadić Appeals Judgment*, above n 91, para 191.

[108] Ibid.

[109] 'Under these circumstances, to hold criminally liable as a perpetrator only the person who materially performs the criminal act would disregard the role as co-perpetrators of all those who in some way made it possible for the perpetrator physically to carry out that criminal act': ibid, para 192.

responsibility.[110] It is in this context that it distinguished between aiding and abetting and participation in a JCE:[111]

(a) unlike the participant in a JCE, the aider/abettor is always an accessory to the crime perpetrated by the principal;
(b) conviction for aiding and abetting does not require proof of a common plan, which is an essential element of JCE;
(c) an aider/abettor must act specifically to assist or encourage the perpetration of a crime, and his support must have a substantial effect on its perpetration. In contrast, for JCE liability, it is sufficient that the accused's participation is in some way directed to the furthering of the common design;
(d) the aider/abettor must have *knowledge* that his acts assist the commission of a specific crime. This differs from JCE liability, where the accused must have the intent to perpetrate the crime or the intent to further the common design and the *foresight* that crimes beyond this design are likely to be committed.

It is difficult to reconcile this prioritisation of JCE (as commission) over accessorial liability when the Chamber actually requires the aider/abettor to do more than the participant in a common criminal enterprise:[112] while the aider/abettor must act specifically to assist the perpetration of a crime and have a substantial effect on its perpetration, the participant in a JCE need only perform acts that are in some way directed to furthering the common design. The moral compass used by the Chamber to calibrate responsibility therefore remains unclear.

Possibly aware of these insecure foundations, the Appeals Chamber claimed support for this category of collective criminality from customary international law – mainly cases from domestic courts and international legislation.[113]

C. JCE Category I

The first category of cases identified by the Chamber are those where all the perpetrators, acting pursuant to a common design, possess the same criminal intention. The accused must participate voluntarily in one aspect of the common design and intend the object of the common design.[114] To establish the customary international law basis of JCE I, the Chamber relied on cases decided by the Allied Military Courts set up in the after-

---

[110] *Tadić Appeals Judgment*, above n 91, paras 191–92.
[111] Ibid, para 229.
[112] Ambos, above n 16, 171.
[113] *Tadić Appeals Judgment*, above n 91, para 194.
[114] Ibid, para 196.

math of World War II to try individuals for crimes committed during the War.[115] The Chamber's reliance on these cases is questionable on various grounds.

First, some of the cases[116] were decided under the express rules of evidence provided in Regulation 8(ii) of the Royal Warrant of 14 June 1945 (on which the jurisdiction of the British Military Court was based), as amended by the Royal Warrant of 4 August 1945, Army Order 127/1945.[117] Regulation 8(ii) is an evidentiary rule and there is nothing to indicate that it is based on any notion of common design liability. Secondly, for cases which do not rely on this provision, the basis for attribution of liability is unclear – the decisions do not explicitly state the mode of responsibility being applied,[118] or use vague terminology, such as being 'concerned in the commission of the crime' which is capable of multiple meanings, including liability for aiding and abetting.[119] Thirdly, quite a few of the cases cited involve a very small group of people who are familiar with each other and physically present at the commission of the offences.[120] This is a much narrower category of cases than those at which JCE I liability is aimed.

The Appeals Chamber concluded its analysis of JCE I on a surprising note:

> It should be noted that in many post-World War II trials held in other countries, courts took the same approach to instances of crimes in which two or more persons participated with a different degree of involvement. However, they did

[115] For criticism on the lack of accessibility of the judgments, see Danner and Martinez, above n 5, 110, fn 141. Some of these judgments have since been translated and published more widely.

[116] *Trial of Otto Sandrock* ('*Almelo Trial*'), British Military Court, Almelo, 24–26 November 1945, in United Nations War Crimes Commission, *Law Reports of Trials of War Criminals*, vol I (London, HMSO, 1947) 35; *Trial of Franz Schonfeld* ('*Schonfeld*'), British Military Court, Essen, 11–26 June 1946, in United Nations War Crimes Commission, *Law Reports of Trials of War Criminals*, vol XI (London, HMSO, 1949) 64, 71.

[117] This Regulation provides: 'Where there is evidence that a war crime has been the result of concerted action upon the part of a unit or group of men, then evidence given upon any charge relating to that crime against any member of such unit or group, may be received as prima facie evidence of the responsibility of each member of that unit or group for that crime.'

[118] See *Schonfeld*, above n 116, 68–71; *United States v Ohlenforf* ('*Einsatzgruppen Case*'), US Military Tribunal, Judgment in *Trials of War Criminals before the Nuremberg Military Tribunals under Control Council Law No 10*, vol IV (Washington, DC, United States Government Printing Office, 1951) 3. The *Tadić* Chamber relies on a statement of law that was part of the prosecution's closing statement in *Einsatzgruppen* rather than any part of the military court's judgment. See Closing Statement of the Prosecution, 13 February 1948, by Brigadier General Telford Taylor, in *Einsatzgruppen*, 369–83.

[119] *Trial of Gustav Alfred Jepsen*, Proceedings of a War Crimes Trial held at Luneberg, Germany (13–23 August 1946), Judgment of 24 August 1946, 241; *Trial of Feurstein (Ponzano)*, Proceedings of a War Crimes Trial held at Hamburg, Germany (4–24 August 1948), Judgment of 24 August 1948, 7–8. The paragraph cited by the *Tadić Chamber* in support of common design is ambiguous on whether Jepsen was being held responsible for the acts committed by his agents, under his directions and with his active participation, or for being part of the 'common enterprise'.

[120] See Danner and Martinez, above n 5, 111.

not rely upon the notion of common purpose or common design, preferring to refer instead to the notion of co-perpetration.[121]

The distinction drawn by the Chamber between 'common purpose or common design' and 'co-perpetration' is mystifying, given that most of the cases cited by the Chamber would indeed involve acts more akin to a notion of co-perpetration, which was first articulated by the ICTY in *Prosecutor v Furundžija*.[122]

Furundžija, a commander of the Bosnian Croat anti-terrorist police unit, was charged with the war crimes of torture and rape for his interrogation of witnesses A and D, while another member of the police unit, Miroslav Bralo, repeatedly assaulted them and raped witness A before an audience of soldiers.[123] Since the prosecution had not specified the precise form of liability in its indictment, it fell to the ICTY Trial Chamber to ascertain the appropriate mode of liability. The Chamber considered several post-World War II cases dealing with liability for aiding and abetting, and distinguished these from cases dealing with co-perpetration, which involves a group of persons pursuing a common design to commit crimes.[124] It relied on two cases – *Dachau Concentration Camp* (discussed in section III.D. below) and *Auschwitz Concentration Camp* – for this distinction. It also gleaned support from Article 25(3) of the Rome Statute of the International Criminal Court,[125] which distinguishes between participation in a common plan or enterprise on the one hand, and aiding and abetting on the other.[126] The Chamber concluded that two separate modes of liability had crystallised in international criminal law: co-perpetrators who participate in a JCE, and aiders and abettors.[127]

The *Furundžija* Trial Chamber defined common design liability to comprise participation in a JCE (*actus reus*) with the intent to participate

---

[121] *Tadić Appeals Judgment*, above n 91, para 201.

[122] *Furundžija*, above n 88. 'Co-perpetration' liability in the subsequent jurisprudence of the ICTY and the ICC will be discussed in chs 4 and 5.

[123] *Furundžija*, above n 88, paras 127–28.

[124] Ibid, paras 191–210.

[125] Rome Statute of the International Criminal Court, 17 July 1998, UN Doc A/Conf 183/9*, 2187 UNTS 90 (*entered into force 1* July 2002), Art 25(3): 'In accordance with this Statute, a person shall be criminally responsible and liable for punishment for a crime within the jurisdiction of the Court if that person: (a) Commits such a crime, whether as an individual, jointly with another or through another person, regardless of whether that other person is criminally responsible; (b) Orders, solicits or induces the commission of such a crime which in fact occurs or is attempted; (c) For the purpose of facilitating the commission of such a crime, aids, abets or otherwise assists in its commission or its attempted commission, including providing the means for its commission; (d) In any other way contributes to the commission or attempted commission of such a crime by a group of persons acting with a common purpose. Such contribution shall be intentional and shall either: (i) Be made with the aim of furthering the criminal activity or criminal purpose of the group, where such activity or purpose involves the commission of a crime within the jurisdiction of the Court; or (ii) Be made in the knowledge of the intention of the group to commit the crime.'

[126] *Furundžija*, above n 88, paras 211–16.

[127] Ibid, para 216.

(*mens rea*).[128] It further held that the accused would be held guilty as a co-perpetrator (of torture) if he participated in an integral part of the crime (torture) and partook of the purpose behind the crime (torture).[129] While there is no clear distinction made by the Trial Chamber between co-perpetration and JCE liability, the *Furundžija* Chamber actually endorses these two distinct categories of liability (apart from aiding and abetting).[130] Since the accused played an integral role in the torture, the Chamber convicted him as a co-perpetrator.[131] In contrast, due to his lack of personal participation or integral role in the crime of rape, he was held liable only as an accessory.[132] The concept of JCE was not developed any further.

The cases cited by the *Tadić* Appeals Chamber in support of JCE I fit into the concept of co-perpetration articulated in *Furundžija*.[133] In almost all these cases, the accused is not merely part of a large undefined group whose members he may never have met but with whom he is presumed to share a common intention. Rather, he is relatively close to the scene of the crime and provides active assistance.

D. JCE Category II

The category JCE II, labelled as a 'variant' of JCE I,[134] comprises concentration camp cases where crimes are committed by members of military or administrative units, ie by groups of persons acting pursuant to a concerted plan.[135] Whereas the *actus reus* elements are common to all forms of JCE, the *mens rea* differs. For JCE II, the accused must know of the system of ill-treatment and intend to further it. In support of this category, the Chamber relied on two cases decided by the US Military Court sitting in Germany and the British Military Court respectively: *Dachau Concentration Camp*[136] and *Belsen*.[137] Both cases concerned charges against accused who were in important positions in concentration camps, for committing various offences against camp detainees in pursuance of a common design.[138]

---

[128] Ibid, para 249.
[129] Ibid, para 257.
[130] For this analysis, see Boas et al, above n 6, 13–14.
[131] *Furundžija*, above n 88, paras 265, 268.
[132] Ibid, para 273; Boas et al, above n 6, 13.
[133] See Boas et al, above n 6, 18–19.
[134] *Tadić Appeals Judgment*, above n 91, para 203.
[135] Ibid, para 202.
[136] *Trial of Martin Gottfried Weiss* ('*Dachau Concentration Camp*'), General Military Government Court of the United States Zone, Dachau, Germany, 15 November–13 December 1945, United Nations War Crimes Commission, vol XI, 5.
[137] *Trial of Josef Kramer* ('*Belsen Trial*'), British Military Court, Luneberg, 17 September–17 November 1945, United Nations War Crimes Commission, vol II, 1.
[138] *Dachau Concentration Camp*, above n 136, 5, 7; *Belsen Trial*, above n 137, 1.

In *Dachau Concentration Camp*, the crux of the prosecution case was indeed reliance on a common design that required proof of:

(a) a system to ill-treat the prisoners and commit the crimes;
(b) the accused's awareness of the system;
(c) the accused's encouragement and abetment in enforcing this system.[139]

The defence challenged this notion of 'common design' on several counts, the most notable of which was the vagueness of the term and its indistinguishability from a charge of conspiracy.[140] In the course of the trial, relying on *Black's Law Dictionary*, 'common intention' was defined as a community of intention between two or more persons to do an unlawful act.[141]

The Military Court did not find it necessary to distinguish between conspiracy and common design, though from the evidence adduced by the prosecution and the conviction based upon this, it may be surmised that the burden of proof was lower than it would be in a conspiracy charge.[142] There was no evidence to show that the accused had ever come together to form an agreement to kill and ill-treat the detainees; they did not necessarily know each other and were not even all at Dachau at the same time.[143] The conviction was based on the fact that there was a general system of cruelty in place in the camp, which was practised with the active knowledge and participation of the accused. Everyone who took part in this common design was guilty of a war crime, with the differing degrees of participation being reflected in the different sentences imposed.[144] It is difficult, however, to state unreservedly that the court was even conscious of convicting the accused pursuant to a mode of liability that was distinct from conspiracy.

This is also true of *Belsen*, where the prosecution charged the accused with being 'parties to a general conspiracy' (alternative expressions were 'concerted action', 'joint action' or 'unit')' to ill-treat the camp prisoners.[145] There is no explicit statement in the decision on what mode of responsibility was used finally to convict the accused. Further, in his summing up of the prosecution case, the Judge Advocate specified that in assessing responsibility for participation in the administration of the camp, a person's mere presence on the staff would not suffice – there had to be the deliberate commission of a war crime.[146]

The *Tadić* Appeals Chamber relied on these cases to derive the elements of JCE II liability. These consist of 'active participation in the enforcement of a system of repression, *as it could be inferred from the position of authority*

---

[139] *Dachau Concentration Camp*, above n 136, 13.
[140] Ibid, 14.
[141] Ibid.
[142] Ibid.
[143] Ibid.
[144] Ibid.
[145] *Belsen Trial*, above n 137, 108.
[146] Ibid, 120–21.

and the specific functions held by each accused' (emphasis added).[147] In addition, the accused must have known of the nature of the system and have had the intent to further the common design of ill-treatment.[148] The Chamber emphasised that the intent element may be inferred from the accused's position of authority, which can, on its own, indicate an awareness of the common design.[149]

This is a troubling extrapolation from *Dachau Concentration Camp* and *Belsen*. It contradicts the caveat introduced by the Judge Advocate in *Belsen* (one of the only two cases cited by the Chamber) that the mere position on the staff of a concentration camp would be insufficient to establish criminal responsibility. In the *Tadić* Chamber's formulation, a position of authority serves as inferential evidence for establishing both the *actus reus* and the *mens rea* elements of JCE II. This gives the position of the accused far more weight in establishing responsibility than what a fair reading of *Belsen* would indicate. It also casts doubt on the Chamber's claim that JCE II is merely a variant of JCE I. For JCE I, the *mens rea* requirement is that the accused should have intended (along with the co-perpetrators) to perpetrate a certain crime.[150] If this intent element in JCE II may be inferred from the position of the accused in the hierarchy, and if this position can make him liable not only for his own conduct, but also for all crimes that may be part of the concentration camp operation, and despite his lack of express knowledge of these other crimes, then the *mens rea* element in JCE I is watered down to a considerable degree. Indeed, it comes more closely to resemble JCE III.[151]

E. JCE Category III

The category JCE III, also referred to as 'extended JCE' in subsequent ICTY jurisprudence,[152] has proved to be the most controversial category of JCE liability developed by *Tadić*. According to *Tadić*, JCE III comprises cases 'involving a common design to pursue one course of conduct where one of the perpetrators commits an act which, while outside the common design, was nevertheless a natural and foreseeable consequence of the effecting of that common purpose'.[153] To illustrate this definition, the Chamber cited a

---

[147] *Tadić Appeals Judgment*, above n 91, para 203.
[148] Ibid.
[149] Ibid.
[150] Ibid, para 228.
[151] For a similar argument, see S Powles, 'Joint Criminal Enterprise: Criminal Liability by Prosecutorial Ingenuity and Judicial Creativity?' (2004) 2 *Journal of International Criminal Justice* 606, 609–10.
[152] See, eg, *Prosecutor v Blaskić*, No IT-95-14-A, Appeals Chamber Judgment (29 July 2004), para 33.
[153] *Tadić Appeals Judgment*, above n 91, para 204.

case scenario remarkably similar to that in *Tadić*: the responsibility of an accused who shares the common intention of a group to effect ethnic cleansing in a region, in the course of which the victims are killed. Since murder is a foreseeable consequence of the forcible removal of civilians at gunpoint, the accused may be held responsible for the murder as well as for the ethnic cleansing.[154] The accused must have been aware that the actions of the group were most likely to lead to the killing, and have chosen to take that risk; in other words, the mental state is not one of mere negligence but advertent recklessness, or *dolus eventualis*.[155]

The Chamber based its analysis of the requirements for JCE III liability on a series of cases. The first of these involve situations of mob violence, where several participants carry out the common unlawful purpose but the precise role of each perpetrator is unclear, or it is difficult to determine the exact causal connection between individual perpetrators' acts and the harm suffered.[156] The *Tadić* Chamber referred particularly to the *Essen Lynching Case*[157] and *Borkum Island*,[158] cases decided respectively by the British Military Court and the US Military Court. The facts of the two cases are largely similar – they involved German civilians and soldiers being charged with war crimes for having taken part in the repeated assault on, and ultimate death of, British and American prisoners of war.

In the *Essen Lynching Case*, the prosecution had argued that 'every person who, following the incitement to the crowd to murder these men, voluntarily took aggressive action against any one of these three airmen *is guilty in that he is concerned in the killing*'(emphasis added).[159] The accused were all held guilty. The *Tadić* Chamber relied on this conviction to infer that though not all the accused intended to kill, they were nevertheless found guilty for being concerned in the killing. Thus, accused who struck a blow or incited the murder were guilty of murder because they could have foreseen that this would result in the killing of the prisoners.[160] The Chamber's reliance on a summary of the case which fails to state the legal

---

[154] Ibid.

[155] Ibid, para 220. As has been rightly pointed out by some critics, the Chamber uses many different formulations to describe the *mens rea* applicable to JCE III: the consequence not covered in the common plan could be predicted and the accused was indifferent to the risk; *dolus eventualis* (advertent recklessness as described by the Chamber); *culpa* (negligence); and lastly that the crime was foreseeable and the accused willingly took that risk. See M Sassòli and LM Olson, 'The Judgment of the ICTY Appeals Chamber on the Merits in the *Tadić* Case' (2000) 839 *International Review of the Red Cross* 733, 747–48.

[156] *Tadić Appeals Judgment*, above n 91, para 205.

[157] *Trial of Erich Heyer* ('*Essen Lynching Case*'), British Military Court, Essen, 18–19 and 21–22 December 1945, in United Nations War Crimes Commission, *Law Reports of Trials of War Criminals*, vol I (London, HMSO, 1947) 88.

[158] *United States v Kurt Goebell et al* ('*Borkum Island*'), Case No 12-489, Report, *Survey of the Trials of War Crimes Held at Dachau, Germany* (15 September 1948) 2–3.

[159] *Essen Lynching Case*, above n 157, 89, cited in *Tadić Appeals Judgment*, above n 91, para 208.

[160] *Tadić Appeals Judgment*, above n 91, para 209.

basis of the verdict is of dubious value;[161] it is moreover contestable whether the *Essen Lynching* prosecution relied on any theory of common design.[162] On the contrary, it cited several theories of liability in the course of its argument, including holding the accused responsible as accessories before the fact or as principal parties to the crime.[163] Further, even if the court did resort to some notion of common design, it is difficult to see why JCE I cannot be applied to the case – the common design was evidently to kill the prisoners, and the various accused played different roles in that common design with the intent to accomplish this objective.

The same objection may be raised against *Tadić*'s reference to *Borkum Island*.[164] Here, the prosecution had developed a notion of common design which stressed the role of each of the accused as a cog in the wheel of the common design, and their responsibility for the prisoners' murders on the basis of their participation in the violence that led to the killing. The *Tadić* Appeals Chamber acknowledged that this conception was closer to JCE I than JCE III.[165] However, since some of the accused had been found guilty of assault, whereas others had been convicted for murder without any evidence that they had actually killed the prisoners, this must have been on the basis of the latter's ability to predict that the assault would result in the killings.[166] This is a misleading conclusion.[167] One might argue that if JCE III was the basis for convicting some of the accused of murder, it should possibly have been applied to hold everyone in the group guilty of murder rather than assault.

The *Tadić* Chamber then turned to a number of Italian cases dealing with crimes committed during World War II. The first, and possibly the only good case,[168] cited for the proposition that a person may be held criminally responsible for the acts of a group which were not part of the original

---

[161] Danner and Martinez, above n 5, 110–11.

[162] Ibid, 111; see also RC Clarke, 'Return to *Borkum Island*: Extended Joint Criminal Enterprise Responsibility in the Wake of World War II' (2011) 9 *Journal of International Criminal Justice* 839, 851.

[163] *Essen Lynching Case*, above n 157, 90–91.

[164] See, however, Clarke, above n 162, 852–53 discussing *Borkum Island* in light of the post-trial comments by the reviewing military legal officer, whose task was to advise the confirming authority on whether the law was applied correctly.

[165] *Tadić Appeals Judgment*, above n 91, paras 210–11. It is also pertinent to note that in one of its final arguments, the prosecution in fact urged that the Anglo-American doctrine of conspiracy was applicable to the case. See M Koessler, 'Borkum Island Tragedy and Trial' (1956) 47 *Journal of Criminal Law, Criminology and Police Science* 183, 194.

[166] *Tadić Appeals Judgment*, above n 91, paras 212–13.

[167] See also Powles, above n 151, 616.

[168] The relevance of *Aratano*, the next case cited by the *Tadić* Chamber, is even less obvious. If anything, the case deals with exculpatory factors for attributing liability to a group of persons acting together, when the crime committed by one of them goes beyond the intended object. It proves nothing in terms of the standard that should be adopted for attribution of criminal responsibility. The same is true of subsequent Italian cases cited by the *Tadić* Chamber for this proposition. See *Tadić Appeals Judgment*, above n 91, 216–17.

criminal purpose, is *D'Ottavio et al.*[169] In this case, four armed civilians attempted to capture two former Yugoslav prisoners who had escaped from a concentration camp. One of the civilians shot at the prisoners, resulting in their death. The Italian Court of Cassation applied Article 116 of the Italian Criminal Code to uphold the trial court's conviction of the accused for manslaughter.[170] While the result in *D'Ottavio* aligns with an application of JCE III, the legal basis and reasoning are quite different. Unlike *Tadić*, the decision in *D'Ottavio* is based on a mode of liability provided specifically in Article 116 of the Italian Criminal Code. The rationale for liability under Article 116 is the concurrence of independent causes: the cause of a cause is also the cause of the thing caused.[171] This differs from the notion of collective responsibility which is at the heart of all variants of JCE. *D'Ottavio* also applies the causation nexus of foreseeability within the context of a very small closed group of people who work in concert. In contrast, JCE III liability has no ostensible temporal or geographic limitation, and can extend to individuals who had no prior contact with each other and/or were unaware of each other's exact actions.

F. *Tadić*'s Conclusions on JCE

The *Tadić* Chamber concluded that 'the notion of common design *as a form of accomplice liability* is firmly established in customary international law'[172] (emphasis added) and is implicitly included in the ICTY Statute. It further buttressed this claim by citing two international treaties that adopt the notion of common plan[173] – the International Convention for the Suppression of Terrorist Bombing[174] and the Rome Statute of the International Criminal Court.

The Chamber referred to the Terrorist Bombing Convention's[175] distinction between responsibility for acting pursuant to a 'common criminal

---

[169] *D'Ottavio*, Italian Court of Cassation, Criminal Section I, Judgment of 12 March 1947, No 270 (trans A Cassese) in (2007) 5 *Journal of International Criminal Justice* 232 (original pagination retained); see also Powles, above n 151, 616–17.

[170] Art 116 states, in part: '[w]henever the crime committed is different from that willed by one of the participants, also that participant answers for the crime, if the fact is a consequence of his action or omission.' (*D'Ottavio*, above n 169, 3).

[171] See *D'Ottavio*, above n 169, 5.

[172] *Tadić Appeals Judgment*, above n 91, para 220.

[173] Ibid, paras 221–23.

[174] GA Res 164, UN GAOR, 52nd Sess, Supp No 49, at 389, UN Doc A/52/49 (1998), *entered into force* 23 May 2001.

[175] Art 2(3)(c) provides: 'Any person also commits an offence if that person: (c) In any other way contributes to the commission of one or more offences as set forth in paragraph 1 or 2 of the present article by a group of persons acting with a common purpose; such contribution shall be intentional and either be made with the aim of furthering the general criminal activity or purpose of the group or be made in the knowledge of the intention of the group to commit the offence or offences concerned.'

purpose' and liability for aiding and abetting, which is included within 'participating as an accomplice' in an offence. The Chamber recognised that the Convention was not yet in force (it has since entered into force), but argued that its adoption by consensus in the General Assembly could be taken to reflect the legal views of a large number of States.[176] The Chamber's differentiation of common design liability from accomplice liability in the Terrorist Convention contradicts its previous labelling of common design as a form of accomplice responsibility. A similar objection may be levelled against the Chamber's appeal to Article 25 of the Rome Statute, which was directly inspired by Article 2(3)(c) of the Terrorist Bombing Convention. Moreover, since the wording of the common criminal purpose provision in the Rome Statute was adopted as a consensus alternative to the more controversial inclusion of conspiracy,[177] the extent to which the Rome Statute incorporates common criminal purpose liability is unclear.[178]

Finally, the *Tadić* Chamber briefly surveyed national legislation in support of common criminal purpose liability, only to note the lack of any coherent practice among States on this issue.[179] It distinguished between:

(a) jurisdictions that provide for liability for crimes envisaged in the common purpose, regardless of the degree of individual participation; and
(b) jurisdictions that in addition also impute responsibility for crimes that are a foreseeable consequence of the common plan.[180]

Since these jurisdictions embraced differing notions of common purpose, and were not representative of the major legal systems of the world, the Chamber rejected them as a source of general principles of law in international law.[181]

G. The Muddled Legacy of *Tadić*

Tadić is an inventive effort to establish JCE as a mode of individual responsibility that reflects the collective nature of international crimes. The ICTY's interpretative methodology and its elucidation of the elements of JCE echo the driving spirit behind the Nuremberg prosecutions: devising an acceptable solution to enable the prosecution of individuals for crimes of enormous

---

[176] *Tadić Appeals Judgment*, above n 91, para 221.
[177] A Eser, 'Individual Criminal Responsibility' in A Cassese, P Gaeta and JRWD Jones (eds),*The Rome Statute of the International Criminal Court: A Commentary* (Oxford, Oxford University Press, 2002) 767, 802.
[178] Powles, above n 151, 617. This will be discussed in detail in ch 4.
[179] *Tadić Appeals Judgment*, above n 91, para 225.
[180] Ibid, para 224. The Chamber cited Germany and the Netherlands as examples for the former category, and France, Italy, the UK, the US, Australia, Canada and Zambia for the latter.
[181] *Tadić Appeals Judgment*, above n 91, para 224.

proportions, where evidence of specific crimes would be extremely difficult to procure against these individuals. *Tadić*, however, goes beyond the IMT decisions, controversial as they were, in its attempt to prevent impunity for persons who participate in the commission of international crimes. For instance, the IMT verdicts were willing to hold responsible persons who were aware of the object of a collective of which they were part, irrespective of their relationship to the specific criminal acts committed pursuant to this object. Joint Criminal Enterprise resembles this formulation in its flexible understanding of what constitutes participation in the criminal activities of an amorphous collective operating over a significant length of time. However, it does not limit the breadth of this formulation in the manner done by the IMT, for instance in its definition of a conspiracy.[182]

Tadić's reliance on a handful of cases and treaties, that moreover do not support its deductive reasoning, to establish the elements of JCE is also deeply problematic from the point of view of the sources that may legitimately be used to establish customary international law.[183] It is also worth noting that *Tadić* refers primarily to summaries of cases decided by military courts set up by the Allied Powers in the aftermath of World War II, and on domestic prosecutions for war crimes in countries like Italy, to argue that JCE liability has a basis in customary international law. It is debatable whether the Appeals Chamber's analysis, in particular its conclusions on JCE III, could have been strengthened if it had relied on a more in-depth analysis of the case law of the Military Tribunals[184] and had also considered domestic war crimes prosecutions in other jurisdictions, such as Australia and Hong Kong.[185]

For instance, recent literature on the war crimes trials in Australia references the Judge Advocate's directions in some of these cases to argue that concepts similar to JCE III were used to convict the accused.[186] The *Hatakeyama*[187] and *Matsumoto*[188] trials both concern Chinese-Nauruans who

---

[182] See text to nn 66 to 70.

[183] Traditionally, customary international law requires the establishment of two elements: State practice and *opinio juris*. 'State practice refers to general and consistent practice by states, while *opinio juris* means that the practice is followed out of a belief of legal obligation.' AE Roberts, 'Traditional and Modern Approaches to Customary International Law: A Reconciliation' (2001) 95 *American Journal of International Law* 757 and references therein.

[184] See, eg Clarke, above n 162, 854–55, arguing that a perusal of the transcripts and recommendations by the reviewing officers in certain American military trials points to the use of concepts cognate to JCE III. He refers in particular to the cases of *Tashiro* (*United States v Tashiro et al* (US Military Commission, Yokohama, 1948)) and *Rüsselsheim* (*United States v Hartgen et al* (US Military Commission, 1945)).

[185] On Hong Kong, see S Linton, 'Rediscovering the War Crimes Trials in Hong Kong, 1946–48' (2012) 13 *Melbourne Journal of International Law* 1, 32–34.

[186] Clarke, above n 162, 856–58.

[187] Record of Military Court, *Hatakeyama et al*, NAA: A471, 80982, available at National Archives of Australia, at <www.naa.gov.au>.

[188] Record of Military Court, *Matsumoto et al*, NAA: A471, 80728, available at National Archives of Australia, at <www.naa.gov.au>.

were tortured by several accused while in Japanese custody and died. In *Hatakeyama*, the Judge Advocate cited English law, which provides that if several persons combine to carry out an unlawful act, including in the face of opposition, and if one of them kills the victim in its execution, then all are guilty of murder.[189] *Matsumoto* contained reference to a manual on Australian military law, which held each of the accused responsible for all offences committed by any of them in pursuance of a common unlawful purpose. As an example, the text mentioned the responsibility of the occupants of a house who resist the arrest of one of them by a police officer and his assistant, in the course of which the assistant is killed. However, if two individuals plan to commit theft and one of them, unbeknownst to his partner, carries a gun and shoots the victim, the other is not responsible.[190]

However, these cases pose challenges similar to the ones cited by the *Tadić* Chamber for establishing JCE III. It is not clear that the accused are convicted on the basis of the actions performed by one of them as a foreseeable consequence of the common unlawful purpose, rather than due to their joint participation in acts of torture that ultimately result in the victim's death. The Judge Advocates also rely on specific principles of domestic criminal law in England and Australia, which constitute fairly limited evidence of a broader recognition of doctrines similar to JCE III.[191] More importantly, these decisions do not help to establish the exact nature of common purpose liability – that is, whether it is properly regarded as principal or secondary responsibility.

Tadić's concluding observations on JCE as a mode of principal versus accessorial liability mirror this conceptual obscurity. One way to rationalise this doctrinal confusion is to view *Tadic*'s account of JCE against the background of the previously existing unitary model of participation in international criminal law: neither the IMTs, nor the military courts set up by the Allied Powers to conduct war crimes trials distinguished strictly between principal and secondary responsibility.[192] However, *Tadić*'s pronouncements on JCE as a form of 'commission' liability that adequately reflects the degree of the accused's responsibility,[193] as well as the distinction it draws between aiding and abetting on the one hand and JCE on the other,[194] point strongly in favour of JCE having been conceptualised as a

---

[189] *Hatakeyama*, above n 187, 59, citing TR Fitzwalter-Butler and M Garsia, *Archbold's Pleading, Evidence & Practice in Criminal Cases* (London, Sweet & Maxwell, 1943) 1429–30.

[190] *Matsumoto*, above n 188, 17, citing Military Board, *Australian Edition of Manual of Military Law 1941* (Canberra, Commonwealth Government Printer, 1941) 119.

[191] See also Clarke, above n 162, 859–61.

[192] H Olasolo, 'Joint Criminal Enterprise and its Extended Form: A Theory of Co-Perpetration Giving Rise to Principal Liability, a Notion of Accessorial Liability, Or a Form of Partnership in Crime?' (2009) 20 *Criminal Law Forum* 263, 272–74; C Farhang, 'Point of No Return: Joint Criminal Enterprise in *Brdanin*' (2010) 23 *Leiden Journal of International Law* 137, 142.

[193] *Tadić Appeals Judgment*, above n 91, paras 188, 192.

[194] Ibid, para 229.

form of principal liability. This conclusion is borne out by more recent ICTY jurisprudence on JCE[195] which affirms the categorisation of JCE as a form of perpetration.[196] Sentencing practice at the ICTY also supports the inference that aiding and abetting are considered to be less blameworthy forms of participation than modes of commission, including JCE.[197]

Despite these limitations, the framework established by *Tadić* has served as the template for all subsequent discussions on JCE.[198] Notwithstanding the apparent precision of this formulation, though, the devil truly lies in the details. The next chapter will analyse the interpretation and development of the elements of JCE in the jurisprudence of the ICTY and the ICTR.

[195] ICTY decisions following *Tadić* demonstrated the same confusion as to whether it is a form of principal or secondary responsibility. JCE was variously characterised as principal liability (*Prosecutor v Milutinović*, No IT-99-37-AR72, Appeals Chamber Decision on Dragoljub Odjanic's Motion Challenging Jurisdiction – Joint Criminal Enterprise (21 May 2003) para 20; Separate Opinions of Judge Hunt and Judge Shahabuddeen; *Prosecutor v Krnojelac*, No IT-97-25-A, Appeals Chamber Judgment (17 September 2003) paras 73–74); accessorial responsibility (*Prosecutor v Brdanin and Talić*, No IT-99-36/1, Trial Chamber Decision on Motion by Momir Talić for Provisional Release (28 March 2001) paras 43–44; *Prosecutor v Krnojelac*, No IT-97-25-T, Trial Chamber Judgment (15 March 2002) para 77); or even both (*Prosecutor v Kvocka*, No IT-98-30/1-T, Trial Chamber Judgment (2 November 2001) paras 248, 249, 271, 273, 284). For a succinct statement of the contrary pronouncements post-*Tadić*, see C Damgaard, *Individual Criminal Responsibility for Core International Crimes* (Berlin, Springer-Verlag, 2008) 193–212.

[196] See, eg, *Prosecutor v Vasiljević*, No IT-98-32-A, Appeals Chamber Judgment (25 February 2004) paras 95, 102; *Prosecutor v Krstić*, No IT-98-33-A, Appeals Chamber Judgment (19 April 2004) paras 134, 137, 266–69; *Blaskić Appeals Judgment* (n 203) para 33; *Prosecutor v Kvocka*, No IT-98-30/1-A, Appeals Chamber Judgment (28 February 2005) para 79; *Prosecutor v Šljivančanin*, No IT-95-13/1-A, Appeals Chamber Judgment (5 May 2009) para 407.

[197] *Vasiljević Appeals Judgment* (n 247) paras 181–82; *Krstić* (n 247) paras 266, 275; *Prosecutor v Sainović*, No IT-05-87-T, Trial Chamber Judgment (26 February 2009) paras 1209, 1211. See B Hola et al, 'International Sentencing Facts and Figures: Sentencing Practices at the ICTY and ICTR' (2011) 9 *Journal of International Criminal Justice* 411, 417; van Sliedregt, above n 32, 78–79; B Burghardt, 'Modes of Participation and their Role in a General Concept of Crimes under International Law' in C Burchard et al (eds), *The Review Conference and the Future of the International Criminal Court* (Alphen aan den Rijn, Kluwer Law International, 2010) 81, 90.

[198] Boas et al, above n 6, 34 and footnotes therein.

3

Elements of Joint Criminal Enterprise at the ICTY

I. ACTUS REUS

A. Plurality of Persons

S INCE JCE IS a form of participation in crimes that are collective in nature, JCE liability cannot exist unless the accused acts along with a number of other persons towards the perpetration of a crime.[1] This does not imply that the accused must physically perpetrate the crime.[2] There is no minimum or maximum number of persons who may constitute this plurality.[3] Neither does it need to be organised in any military or political structure.[4]

It may be recalled that in nearly all the decisions relied on by the *Tadić* Appeals Chamber, the number of persons forming the plurality was relatively small. They were moreover familiar with each other and physically present at the time of commission of the crime.[5] The plurality element in JCE liability is not limited in any such manner, and subsequent ICTY jurisprudence uses JCE in the context of large-scale and wide-ranging enterprises to establish the liability of individuals in leadership positions.[6]

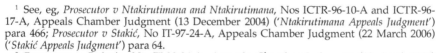

---

[1] See, eg, *Prosecutor v Ntakirutimana and Ntakirutimana*, Nos ICTR-96-10-A and ICTR-96-17-A, Appeals Chamber Judgment (13 December 2004) (*'Ntakirutimana Appeals Judgment'*) para 466; *Prosecutor v Stakić*, No IT-97-24-A, Appeals Chamber Judgment (22 March 2006) (*'Stakić Appeals Judgment'*) para 64.

[2] *Prosecutor v Brđanin*, No IT-99-36-A, Appeals Chamber Judgment (03 April 2007) (*'Brđanin Appeals Judgment'*) para 410.

[3] Even two persons are sufficient for JCE liability to ensue: *Prosecutor v Kvocka*, No IT-98-30/1-T, Trial Chamber Judgment (2 November 2001) para 307; *Prosecutor v Brđanin*, No IT-99-36-T, Trial Chamber Judgment (1 September 2004) para 262 (*'Brđanin Trial Judgment'*); *Prosecutor v Mpambara*, No ICTR-01-65-T, Trial Chamber Judgment (11 September 2006) para 13.

[4] See, for instance, *Prosecutor v Tadić*, No IT-94-1-A, Appeals Chamber Judgment (15 July 1999) (*'Tadić Appeals Judgment'*) para 227; *Ntakirutimana Appeals Judgment*, above n 1, para 466; *Stakić Appeals Judgment*, above n 1, para 64.

[5] This statement of course does not apply to JCE II, where there is an organised system of repression in place.

[6] See, eg, the application of JCE in *Brđanin Appeals Judgment*, above n 2; *Prosecutor v Sainović*, No IT-05-87-T, Trial Chamber Judgment (26 February 2009); *Prosecutor v Krajisnik*, No IT-00-39-A, Appeals Chamber Judgment (17 March 2009) (*'Krajisnik Appeals Judgment'*); E van Sliedregt, *Individual Criminal Responsibility in International Law* (Oxford, Oxford University Press, 2012) 136.

The amorphous nature of the plurality element has consequences for the specificity required in pleading JCE. The indictment may contain the identities of the individuals constituting the JCE, but if that is not possible, simply stating the category or group to which they belong suffices.[7] This can be problematic, given that JCE charges tend to cover a fairly broad range of crimes committed across an extensive territory over a long period of time. For instance, X may be charged for his participation in a JCE that involved the forcible transfer of population in region Y of a country. The plurality element can encompass all the groups that were in some way involved in the transfer – members of the dominant ethnic group, the militia of the country, armed groups and even civilians. Recent decisions of the ICTY have attempted to temper the scope of vague and wide-ranging JCE charges by the prosecution. The prosecution must now specify the period of operation of the enterprise, its goals and objectives, the nature of the accused's participation in the common purpose, and the general identity of the participants and intended victims.[8]

B. The Existence of a Common Plan, Design or Purpose

The second important physical element of JCE is the existence of a common plan, design or purpose, which amounts to or involves the commission of a crime provided for in the Statute (of the criminal tribunal in question).[9] A common plan has been defined as an arrangement or understanding between the accused and one or more persons that a crime will be committed.[10] The ICTY has consistently held that there is no requirement for the common plan or agreement to have been reached at any particular point in time; it can arise extemporaneously[11] and may even materialise after the conduct constituting the crime has already commenced.[12]

---

[7] See *Prosecutor v Simic et al*, No IT-95-9-T, Trial Chamber Judgment (17 October 2003) ('*Simic Trial Judgment*') para 145; *Brdanin Trial Judgment*, above n 3, para 346; *Prosecutor v Simba*, No ICTR-01-76/T, Trial Chamber Judgment (13 December 2005) para 389; *Krajisnik Appeals Judgment*, above n 6, para 156; *Prosecutor v Popović et al*, No IT-05-88-T, Trial Chamber II Judgment (10 June 2010) ('*Popović Trial Judgment*') para 1023.

[8] *Prosecutor v Simić et al*, No IT-95-9-A, Appeals Chamber Judgment (28 November 2006) para 22; *Brdanin Appeals Judgment*, above n 2, para 430; *Popović Trial Judgment*, above n 7, para 1024.

[9] *Tadić Appeals Judgment*, above n 4, para 227; *Stakić Appeals Judgment*, above n 1, para 64.

[10] *Simic Trial Judgment*, above n 7, para 158; *Prosecutor v Blagojevic and Jokic*, No IT-02-60-T, Trial Chamber Judgment (17 January 2005) para 699. See further references at G Boas, JL Bischoff and NL Reid, *International Criminal Law Practitioner Library Vol I: Forms of Responsibility in International Criminal Law* (Cambridge, Cambridge University Press, 2007) 37.

[11] *Tadić Appeals Judgment*, above n 4, para 227; *Prosecutor v Vasiljević*, No IT-98-32-A, Appeals Chamber Judgment (25 February 2004) ('*Vasiljević Appeals Judgment*') paras 100, 109; *Stakić Appeals Judgment*, above n 1, para 64.

[12] *Prosecutor v Krnojelac*, No IT-97-25-T, Trial Chamber Judgment (15 March 2002) ('*Krnojelac Trial Judgment*') para 80.

Furthermore, the common plan or agreement need not be express. Its existence may be inferred from all the circumstances.[13] In *Blagojevic and Jokic*, the ICTY established the existence of an understanding to commit murder and persecution at Srebrenica from the fact that over 7,000 male Bosnian Muslims were detained, murdered and buried in a span of five days. This could not have been accomplished without considerable planning and co-ordination amongst JCE members.[14]

The establishment of the common plan based on circumstantial evidence can prove controversial, and the outcome may vary depending on the factual assessment by the court. This is amply demonstrated by the case of *Gotovina*, where the Trial Chamber upheld the existence of a JCE aimed at the permanent removal of the Serb civilian population from the Krajina region by force or threat of force, which amounted to and involved persecution (deportation, forcible transfer, unlawful attacks against civilians and civilian objects, and discriminatory and restrictive measures), deportation and forcible transfer.[15] These events took place during and after the military offensive 'Operation Storm' launched in August 1995, with artillery attacks on towns and villages in the Krajina region. Some of these attacks constituted unlawful, indiscriminate attacks on civilians and civilian objects, and resulted in the deportation of approximately 20,000 civilians.[16]

The Trial Chamber relied on a series of events in order to reach this conclusion on the object of the JCE, including transcripts of a meeting of Croatian leaders at Brioni and the preparation of 'Operation Storm'; crimes committed by the Croatian military and police against the remaining Serb civilian population and property in the aftermath of 'Operation Storm'; and the Croatian leadership's policies on the return of Croatian displaced persons and refugees, and discriminatory property laws targeting the Serb minority.[17] Nonetheless, the *Gotovina* Appeals Chamber overturned the Trial Chamber's decision on JCE on the basis that it rested primarily on the unlawfulness of the artillery attacks. According to the Appeals Chamber, since the attacks could not be characterised as unlawful and indiscriminate, this also vitiated the finding on the existence of the JCE.[18] Strongly worded dissents were filed by Judges Agius and Pocar, questioning the majority's analysis of the unlawfulness of the attacks[19]

[13] Ibid, para 80; *Vasiljević Appeals Judgment*, above n 11, para 100; *Stakić Appeals Judgment*, above n 1, para 64.

[14] *Prosecutor v Blagojevic and Jokic*, above n 10, para 721.

[15] *Prosecutor v Gotovina et al*, No IT-06-90-T, Trial Chamber Judgment (15 April 2011) ('*Gotovina Trial Judgment*') paras 2314–15.

[16] Ibid, paras 2305, 2309–10.

[17] Ibid, paras 1756–58, 1843–46, 1970–2098, 2304–12.

[18] *Prosecutor v Gotovina*, No IT-06-90-A, Appeals Chamber Judgment (16 November 2012) ('*Gotovina Appeals Judgment*') paras 91–96.

[19] Ibid, Dissenting Opinion of Judge Agius, paras 18–46; Dissenting Opinion of Judge Pocar, paras 9–18.

and its reduction of the JCE analysis to these attacks despite the additional evidence adduced by the Trial Chamber.[20]

Special considerations apply for establishing the existence of a common plan in the case of JCE II. Instead of an agreement, the entire system of repression is treated as the common plan.[21] The ICTY has not been rigorous in construing this condition. In *Krnojelac*, the Appeals Chamber held that as long as the accused is involved in the system of ill-treatment, it is less important to prove that he had an agreement with other JCE members.[22] The applicable standard of liability is whether the accused 'knew of the system and agreed to it, without it being necessary to establish that he had entered into an agreement with . . . the principal perpetrators of the crimes'.[23]

These are potentially different criteria for liability. An accused may be involved in a system in various ways – through indirect assistance, express approval by way of words or moral support, or direct physical contribution to the crimes. The extent of this involvement can also vary. For instance, a photographer who is periodically brought into a prison camp to take pictures of certain prisoners can be involved in the system of repression without any exact knowledge of why he is taking the photographs, or whether the prisoners are being subjected to ill-treatment (even if he may have his suspicions). Should this suffice for liability under JCE II? The second standard – agreeing to the system – is perhaps an even lesser form of involvement. In the Chamber's formulation, it appears to connote mere acquiescence (coupled with knowledge) in the system of repression. Thus, if the accused is aware of the system, does he have a positive obligation to take action actively to denounce or dissociate himself from the system? If so, does this duty vary depending upon his position in the system?

Recent decisions of the ICTY show its discomfort with a broad interpretation of the common plan. For instance, in *Krajisnik*, the Trial Chamber expressly stated that a common objective alone does not transform a group of persons into a plurality. Instead, persons in the criminal enterprise must act jointly, or in concert, to achieve this common objective.[24]

---

[20] Ibid, Dissenting Opinion of Judge Agius, paras 49–50; Dissenting Opinion of Judge Pocar, paras 21–30.

[21] *Prosecutor v Krnojelac*, No IT-97-25-A, Appeals Chamber Judgment (17 September 2003) ('*Krnojelac Appeals Judgment*') para 97; *Prosecutor v Kvocka*, No IT-98-30/1-A, Appeals Chamber Judgment (28 February 2005) ('*Kvocka Appeals Judgment*') paras 118–19.

[22] *Krnojelac Appeals Judgment*, above n 21, para 96.

[23] *Krnojelac Appeals Judgment*, ibid, para 97. On the Chamber's confusing use of the concept of agreement, see JD Ohlin, 'Joint Intentions to Commit International Crimes' (2011) 12 *Chicago Journal of International Law* 693, 697–98.

[24] *Prosecutor v Krajisnik*, No IT-00-39-T, Trial Chamber Judgment (27 September 2006) para 884. The Trial Chamber cited some instances of how this acting in concert could be ascertained (paras 1081–82): 'Whether the perpetrator was a member of, or associated with, any organised bodies connected to the JCE; whether the crimes committed were consistent with

The Chamber nevertheless failed to clarify the nature of this joint action and, on the facts of the case, did not focus on establishing the exact nature of the relationship between the accused and other JCE participants.[25]

The most significant attempt to qualify the extent of common purpose is the Trial Chamber's decision in *Brdanin*, where the accused, who was a high-level political figure within the Serbian Democratic Party (SDS) and within the ARK (an area within the planned Bosnian Serb State), was charged with acts pursuant to a JCE that included the leadership of the SDS, political figures within the ARK, members of the army (VRS), and the Serb paramilitary forces and others. The alleged purpose of the JCE was the permanent forcible removal of Bosnian Muslim and Croat inhabitants from the territory of the planned Bosnian Serb State. According to the *Brdanin* Trial Chamber, in order to establish JCE liability, there must be an understanding between the accused and the *physical perpetrators* of the crime to commit that particular crime, or a crime that is a natural and foreseeable consequence of the crime agreed upon.[26] It is not sufficient to show an agreement between the accused and the person in control of a military or similar unit committing the crime.[27] This mutual understanding or arrangement to commit a crime can be established through direct evidence, or it may be inferred from the fact that the accused and the physical perpetrators acted in unison to implement the common plan, though only when this is the sole inference possible from the evidence.[28] A necessary implication of this definition of an agreement is that the physical perpetrator must be a member of the JCE.[29] The Chamber also cautioned that given the extraordinarily broad nature of the case and the structural remoteness of the accused from the commission of the crimes, JCE may not be an appropriate mode of liability to describe the accused's responsibility.[30]

the pattern of similar crimes by JCE members against similar kinds of victims; whether the perpetrator acted at the same time as members of the JCE, or as persons who were tools or instruments of the JCE; whether the perpetrator's act advanced the objective of the JCE; whether the perpetrator's act was ratified implicitly or explicitly by members of the JCE; whether the perpetrator acted in cooperation or conjunction with members of the JCE at any relevant time; whether any meaningful effort was made to punish the act by any member of the JCE in a position to do so; whether similar acts were punished by JCE members in a position to do so; whether members of the JCE or those who were tools of the JCE continued to affiliate with the perpetrators after the act; finally – and this is a non-exhaustive list – whether the acts were performed in the context of a systematic attack, including one of relatively low intensity over a long period.' See also *Prosecutor v Dordević*, No IT-05-87/1, Trial Chamber Judgment (23 February 2011) para 1862; *Gotovina Trial Judgment*, above n 15, para 1954.

[25] *Krajisnik Trial Judgment*, above n 24, paras 1086–88; Boas et al, above n 10, 102–03.
[26] *Brdanin Trial Judgment*, above n 3, paras 344, 347 (emphasis added).
[27] Ibid, para 347.
[28] Ibid, paras 352–53.
[29] *Brdanin Appeals Judgment*, above n 2, paras 389–91.
[30] *Brdanin Trial Judgment*, above n 3, para 355.

Brdanin has evoked mixed reactions: on the one hand, the requirement of an agreement between the physical perpetrators of the crime and the accused reinforces JCE's adherence to the concept of liability based on shared criminal intent;[31] on the other hand, this criterion makes it difficult to convict high-level individuals who are physically remote from the commission of the crime.[32] It has been suggested that high-level accused can still be held responsible by reconfiguring the attribution of liability through a maze of multiple and overlapping JCEs.[33] In this structure, two separate JCEs are envisaged – one between the high-level accused, and the other between the actual physical perpetrators of the crimes. If a non-physical perpetrator, such as a military commander who is part of the subsidiary JCE, has a dual role as a Minister in the senior JCE, then crimes committed by physical perpetrators of the subsidiary JCE can be attributed to all the members of the senior JCE, as long as the actions of the subsidiary JCE are in pursuance of the plan formulated by the senior JCE. The relevant agreement is not between the physical perpetrators of the crime and the high-level offender but between the accused and any member of the subsidiary JCE.[34] In this situation, the criminal plan of the subsidiary JCE is subsumed by and narrower than the senior JCE.[35]

Construing JCE in this fashion, however, turns it into an amalgam of superior responsibility (which is typically a form of omission liability for failing to prevent or punish the criminal conduct of subordinates) and conspiracy liability. The attribution of responsibility is predicated upon a vertically defined command structure, which differs from JCE's emphasis on a mutual understanding between individuals. The connection between the various members of the criminal plan gets attenuated even further: the other members of the senior JCE may have undertaken no further actions pursuant to the policy and yet be held responsible for crimes pursuant to a subsidiary JCE's plan, which may be quite far removed from their initial policy. The concern that limiting JCE liability in the manner suggested by the *Brdanin Trial Judgment* would make it difficult to prosecute high-level accused is understandable, but it cannot be taken as a decisive argument for accepting a mode of liability that appears to stretch its own notion of common plan beyond recognition.

[31] A Cassese, 'The Proper Limits of Individual Responsibility under the Doctrine of Joint Criminal Enterprise' (2007) 5 *Journal of International Criminal Justice* 109, 126; E van Sliedregt, 'Joint Criminal Enterprise as a Pathway to Convicting Individuals for Genocide' (2007) 5 *Journal of International Criminal Justice* 184, 200–01.

[32] K Gustafson, 'The Requirement of an 'Express Agreement' for Joint Criminal Enterprise Liability' (2007) 5 *Journal of International Criminal Justice* 134, 144–45. See also A O'Rourke, 'Joint Criminal Enterprise and Brdanin: Misguided Over-correction' (2006) 47 *Harvard International Law Journal* 307.

[33] Gustafson, above n 32. For criticism of Gustafson's position, see Boas et al, above n 10, 89, stating that this is a specious construct for the attribution of liability.

[34] Gustafson, above n 32 146–48.

[35] Ibid, 149.

The inappropriateness of using purely teleological arguments for determining the validity of a theory of individual criminal responsibility was acknowledged by the *Brdanin* Appeals Chamber,[36] which nonetheless rejected the limits on JCE imposed by the Trial Chamber. In order to do this, it relied heavily on the Separate Opinion of Judge Bonomy in *Prosecutor v Milutinović*,[37] on whether 'commission' responsibility through participation in a JCE is possible if the physical perpetrator is not a JCE member.[38] Judge Bonomy considered this question under three headings: tribunal jurisprudence, international case law and general principles of criminal law.

According to Judge Bonomy, this issue had not been specifically addressed in any ICTY decision. Moreover, nothing in previous case law suggested that a JCE participant cannot be liable for commission where the physical perpetrator of the crime is a non-member *but acts as an instrument of the JCE*.[39] Judge Bonomy introduces a completely new element into the ways in which a person can be held responsible as a JCE member: not only the accused but no member of the JCE needs to commit the *actus reus* of the crime in question. As long as any member of the JCE can be held responsible for using someone outside the JCE to commit the crime, all JCE members become liable for its commission. He also fails to specify the kind of relationship that must exist between the JCE members and the physical perpetrators of the crime. What must be the level of control exercised by JCE members over the physical perpetrators? Should they completely dominate the latter's actions, or simply use them in some way to execute the plan, for example through implicit approval of their conduct? If only one member of the JCE has a connection with different groups of physical perpetrators committing a series of different crimes under the common plan, can the other members be held responsible, even if they are unaware of the method of execution of the plan and do not lend it any further support?

In drawing support from international case law, Judge Bonomy referenced two cases decided by the Military Tribunals established under Control Council Law No 10 – the *Justice case*[40] and the *RuSHA case*[41] – both of which held the accused liable for their connection with the common

---

[36] *Brdanin Appeals Judgment*, above n 2, para 421. See also a similar teleological argument in O'Rourke, above n 32, 323.

[37] *Prosecutor v Milutinović*, No IT-05-87-PT, Trial Chamber Decision on Ojdanić's Motion Challenging Jurisdiction (22 March 2006).

[38] Ibid, Separate Opinion of Judge Bonomy, para 1.

[39] Ibid, Separate Opinion of Judge Bonomy, para 13.

[40] *United States v Altstoetter* ('*Justice case*'), US Military Tribunal, Judgment, 3–4 December 1947 in *Trials of War Criminals before the Nuernberg Military Tribunals under Control Council Law No 10*, vol III (Washington, DC, United States Government Printing Office, 1951).

[41] *United States v Greifelt* ('*RuSHA case*'), US Military Tribunal, Judgment, 10 March 1948, in *Trials of War Criminals before the Nuernberg Military Tribunals under Control Council Law No 10*, vol V (Washington, DC, United States Government Printing Office, 1950).

criminal plan of racial discrimination, even though the *actus reus* was per-petrated by physical perpetrators who simply carried out their orders. The state of mind of the actual physical perpetrators was never in issue.[42] Excessive reliance on these decisions is inappropriate, however, given that the whole point of JCE is to hold the accused liable as principals rather than accessories, a distinction that was blurred in the judgments of the tribunals acting under Control Council Law No 10. The indictments in these two cases charged the accused as principals as well as accessories, and the judgments did not distinguish between various modes of respon-sibility in their opinions.[43]

Judge Bonomy also drew support from general principles of criminal law common to most legal systems of the world. In most common law jurisdictions, the distinction between principals and accessories is nomi-nal, and accessories before the fact especially (persons who order, counsel, or otherwise aid or abet a crime) are as culpable as principal perpetrators.[44] Civil law jurisdictions hold an accused who uses an innocent agent to com-mit a crime liable as a principal.[45] Judge Bonomy concluded that most legal systems impose liability on an accused who is not the physical perpetrator of the crime, as long as his conduct causes some element of the *actus reus*. The mental state of the actual physical perpetrator is irrelevant.[46]

These statements again deserve more nuanced consideration than Judge Bonomy offered them. One of the main reasons why JCE liability has been developed by courts and is charged so frequently by prosecutors is that accessorial forms of participation are considered an inadequate reflection of the true role of the accused in the crime.[47] The accused in a JCE is not simply *liable in the same way* as the principal; *he is the principal*. Even if accessories and principals are punished equally in some domestic jurisdiction, these are still conceptually distinct categories, and this dis-tinction is relevant for liability for international crimes.

In addition to Judge Bonomy's opinion, the *Brdanin* Appeals Chamber also took into account two previous ICTY decisions[48] to conclude that in

---

[42] *Milutinović*, above n 37, Separate Opinion of Judge Bonomy, paras 18–21, 25.

[43] See especially *Justice Case*, above n 40, 1063. It is also worth noting that the *Justice case* and *RuSHA case*, by themselves, are insufficient to establish customary international law. See van Sliedregt, above n 6, 163. For reliance on the *Justice case* to establish liability under JCE for crimes physically committed by other persons, see also *Prosecutor v Rwamakuba*, No ICTR-98-44-AR72.4, Appeal Chamber's Decision on Interlocutory Appeal Regarding Application of Joint Criminal Enterprise to the Crime of Genocide (22 October 2004) paras 18–24.

[44] *Milutinović*, above n 37, Separate Opinion of Judge Bonomy, para 29, citing the law in Scotland, England, the US and Australia.

[45] Ibid, Separate Opinion of Judge Bonomy, para 28, citing the law in Germany, France, Poland, Argentina and Colombia.

[46] Ibid, Separate Opinion of Judge Bonomy, para 30.

[47] See, eg, *Tadić Appeals Judgment*, above n 4, para 192.

[48] *Prosecutor v Krstić*, No IT-98-33-T, Trial Chamber Judgment (2 August 2001) ('*Krstić Trial Judgment*') paras 601, 611, 613, 617–18, 644–45; *Stakić Appeals Judgment*, above n 1, paras 68–70, 75, 81, 84, 95–96, 98. These decisions had held only political and military leaders

order to establish JCE liability, it is not important whether the physical perpetrator of the crime is a JCE member but whether 'the particular crime in question forms part of the common purpose'. This may be inferred from various circumstances, including whether some member of the JCE closely co-operated with the physical perpetrator to further the common criminal purpose. It is not essential that the latter knows of the existence of the JCE.[49] Regardless of whether the physical perpetrator is a JCE member, an express agreement between him and the JCE members is not necessary.[50] The crime must be imputable to a JCE member who, in using the physical perpetrator, acts according to the common plan.[51] The determination of this connection depends on the individual facts of the case. If a JCE member explicitly or implicitly requests, instigates, orders, encourages or otherwise avails himself of a non-JCE member to commit the crime, this is indicative of the requisite link.[52]

The most important factor is the existence of a criminal purpose that is not merely the same but common to all the persons acting together within the enterprise. Even if the contribution of the accused to this purpose is not substantial, it must be significant for the crimes for which he is found responsible.[53] This common plan is moreover fluid in its criminal means; the accused may be held responsible for crimes that were initially not part of the plan if leading JCE members have information about additional crimes committed due to an expansion of the criminal objective, and do not prevent their recurrence.[54]

These are two potentially irreconcilable criteria. According to the first standard, if the common criminal purpose consists of ethnically cleansing a certain territory, which involves the crimes of forced movement, forced labour and sexual violence, even if the accused's contribution is not substantial for ethnic cleansing, it must be significant for the crime of forced movement for which he is held responsible. This partly defeats the rationale for JCE liability which seeks to hold the accused responsible for *all* the crimes that are part of the common criminal purpose (to which he contributes). The second standard makes an accused liable for crimes that were

responsible as JCE members, even though the crimes in question had been carried out by low-level perpetrators who were not members of the JCE. *Brdanin Appeals Judgment*, above n 2, paras 408–9.

[49] *Brdanin Appeals Judgment*, above n 2, para 410; *Dordević*, above n 24, para 1866.
[50] *Brdanin Appeals Judgment*, above n 2, paras 415–18.
[51] Ibid, para 413; *Dordević*, above n 24, para 1866.
[52] *Krajisnik Appeals Judgment*, above n 6, para 226; *Dordević*, above n 24, para 1866.
[53] *Brdanin Appeals Judgment*, above n 2, para 430. The *Brdanin* Appeals Chamber's rejection of the requirement of an express agreement between the physical perpetrator and a JCE member, and its holding that the physical perpetrator does not need to be a member of the JCE, has been affirmed in subsequent decisions and now constitutes established ICTY jurisprudence. See, eg, *Popović Trial Judgment*, above n 7, para 1029; *Dordević*, above n 24, para 1866; *Gotovina Trial Judgment*, above n 15, para 1953.
[54] *Krajisnik Trial Judgment*, above n 24, para 1098.

not even part of the initial plan, as long as leading members of the JCE approve of the expansion of the common criminal plan through these additional crimes. In this situation, the accused's contribution towards these additional crimes is not likely to be significant, yet he will still be responsible for them, not because of his own conduct but because of the conduct of leading JCE members.

The notion of a 'fluid' common plan, where crimes that are not initially part of the plan (unlawful detentions, killings, inhumane treatment) are accepted by JCE members and are thus regarded as an expansion of the means of achieving the objectives of the JCE (forcible transfer and deportation),[55] is also troubling. Using this logic, the accused can be convicted under JCE I rather than under JCE III (the further crimes are a natural and foreseeable consequence of the planned JCE crimes), which undermines the shared intent requirement for JCE I and elides the distinction between JCE I and JCE III.[56] The *Krajisnik* Appeals Chamber attempted to distinguish between this fluid JCE I category and JCE III on the basis that in the case of the former, the accused is responsible for crimes after they have become part of the common objective, and not beforehand (on the basis that they were a natural and foreseeable consequence under JCE III).[57] It also demanded a more rigorous factual evaluation of when and how leading JCE members became aware of the expanded crimes, and if they failed to take preventative measure and persisted in their implementation.[58] The Appeals Chamber overturned the Trial Chamber's conviction on the basis of a fluid JCE I due to its failure to determine at what point exactly the expanded crimes came to form part of the common plan.[59]

Despite these safeguards, the creation of a fluid JCE I category leads to an expansion in the scope of JCE liability. As the Appeals Chamber notes, there is no clarity on who is regarded as a 'leading JCE member'[60] – an acceptance of the expanded crimes by zealous mid-level participants who go beyond the policy formulated initially by political or military leaders may thus form part of the fluid plan, for which the latter can be responsible under JCE I. Moreover, the broader the definition of the initial expanded JCE, the easier it is to build a case for even further crimes under JCE III occurring as a natural and foreseeable consequence of this evolving JCE I.

---

[55] Ibid, paras 1098, 1126, 1182; see also *Popović Trial Judgment*, above n 7, para 1028; *Dordević*, above n 24, para 1862.
[56] Van Sliedregt, above n 6, 137.
[57] *Krajisnik Appeals Judgment*, above n 6, paras 164–67.
[58] Ibid, para 172.
[59] Ibid, paras 173–77.
[60] Ibid, para 172.

C. The Participation of the Accused in the Common Plan

The third physical element of JCE is the participation of the accused in the common design, involving the perpetration of one of the substantive crimes contained in the relevant law.[61] The accused need not physically commit any crime in order to fulfil this element.[62] The extent of participation required is in fact lower than that needed for aiding and abetting. In the latter case, the accused must perform acts specifically directed to encourage, assist or lend support to another person in the perpetration of a specific crime.[63] Participation for JCE merely requires the accused to have performed some act that is *in some way directed to the furtherance of the common plan or purpose*.[64] As commentators have noted, this turns the traditional distinction between accessory (aiding and abetting) and principal (JCE) liability on its head, by requiring more from the aider/abettor than from the perpetrator.[65] This act may even be in the form of an omission that contributes to the common criminal purpose.[66]

Recent decisions of the ICTY present a confused picture as to whether a substantial contribution is required. In *Kvocka*, the Appeals Chamber partially overruled the Trial Chamber's determination[67] that the accused's participation must be substantial.[68] The Appeals Chamber held that the fact that the accused can easily be replaced, and that the criminal purpose can therefore be achieved without his participation, is of little relevance.[69] There are, however, special cases where proof of a substantial contribution becomes necessary.[70] For instance, opportunistic visitors who are not staff members in a detention camp, but who enter the camp and commit

---

[61] *Tadić Appeals Judgment*, above n 4, para 227; *Stakić Appeals Judgment*, above n 1, para 193.

[62] *Kvocka Appeals Judgment*, above n 21, para 99; *Stakić Appeals Judgment*, above n 1, para 64; *Mpambara Trial Judgment*, above n 3, para 13.

[63] *Vasiljević Appeals Judgment*, above n 11, para 102; *Prosecutor v Blaskić* , No IT-95-14-A, Appeals Chamber Judgment (29 July 2004) paras 45, 50; *Kvocka Appeals Judgment*, above n 21, para 33.

[64] *Tadić Appeals Judgment*, above n 4, para 229; *Vasiljević Appeals Judgment*, above n 11, para 102; *Dordević*, above n 24, para 1863.

[65] K Ambos, 'Joint Criminal Enterprise and Command Responsibility' (2007) 5 *Journal of International Criminal Justice* 159, 171. See also, V Haan, 'The Development of the Concept of Criminal Enterprise at the International Criminal Tribunal for the Former Yugoslavia' (2005) 5 *International Criminal Law Review* 167, 201; G Werle, 'Individual Criminal Responsibility in Article 25 ICC Statute' (2007) 5 *Journal of International Criminal Justice* 953, 962.

[66] *Kvocka Appeals Judgment*, above n 21, para 187; *Mpambara Trial Judgment*, above n 3, para 24; *Krajisnik Trial Judgment*, above n 24, para 885; *Dordević*, above n 24, para 1863.

[67] *Prosecutor v Kvocka*, No IT-98-30/1-T, Trial Chamber Judgment (2 November 2001) ('*Kvocka Trial Judgment*') paras 309, 311 (holding that the accused's participation must be 'significant', ie, it must make the enterprise 'efficient or effective' and enable 'the system to run more smoothly or without disruption'.

[68] *Kvocka Appeals Judgment*, above n 21, para 187.

[69] Ibid, para 193.

[70] Ibid, paras 187, 97.

crimes, will be held liable for participation in a JCE only if they make a substantial contribution to the overall effect of the camp.[71]

The absence of the requirement of a substantial contribution on the part of the accused does not sit well with the notion of equal culpability that lies at the heart of JCE liability. The accused in a JCE is held not simply responsible, but equally responsible, as the other participants for all acts carried out pursuant to the common criminal plan.[72] It is difficult to see how this can be reconciled with anything except a significant contribution on the part of the accused. The exception carved out for opportunistic visitors only further confuses the issue. On what basis can one distinguish between a low-level cook in the detention camp, who prepares food for the prisoners and is aware of the activities that are carried out in the camp, and an opportunistic visitor who is not a staff member but enters the camp to commit crimes? The Appeal's Chamber's reasoning makes the cook liable regardless of a substantial contribution, since it is not necessary that he is irreplaceable or that the camp's purpose cannot not be accomplished without his participation. Is it simply because the cook is a staff member? If so, this standard disturbingly begins to resemble guilt by mere association.

Kvocka's ruling has influenced subsequent ICTY jurisprudence, which requires that while it is not necessary that the accused makes a substantial contribution to the plan, it must be significant for the specific crime with which he is charged.[73] Some judgments go further in stating that this contribution should be significant for the common plan as a whole,[74] but incorrectly cite previous ICTY case law which only mandates significant contribution to the crime (and not to the common plan) for this proposition.

II. *MENS REA* FOR JCE I

The primary distinction between the various categories of JCE lies in their mental rather than physical elements. While the *mens rea* requirements for JCE I are relatively uncontroversial, those required for JCE II and JCE III have invited much comment (see sections III. and IV. below).

---

[71] Ibid, para 599.

[72] For an insightful discussion of imposition of equal culpability and the philosophical problems with this, see JD Ohlin, 'Three Conceptual Problems with the Doctrine of Joint Criminal Enterprise' (2007) 5 *Journal of International Criminal Justice* 69, 85–88.

[73] See, eg, *Brdanin Appeals Judgment*, above n 2, para 430; *Krajisnik Appeals Judgment*, above n 6, paras 675–76; *Popović Trial Judgment*, above n 7, para 1027.

[74] See, eg, *Prosecutor v Boskoski*, No IT-04-82-T, Trial Chamber II Judgment (10 July 2008) para 395; *Dordević*, above n 24, para 1863 ('What is important is that the conduct contributes to the common purpose, not the nature of the conduct charged'); *Prosecutor v Haradinaj*, No IT-04-84bis-T, Trial Chamber II Judgment (29 November 2012) para 619.

A. Voluntary Participation

In order for the accused to incur liability under the first category of JCE, he must voluntarily participate in some aspect of the common criminal plan or design and intend the criminal result.[75] The ICTY has not clarified how this element of voluntariness is to be construed.

B. Shared Intent

All participants in the JCE must share the intent to commit the crime that is the object of the common criminal plan, regardless of the extent of their actual physical contribution towards the achievement of the plan.[76] Theoretically, this standard requires the prosecution to prove the state of mind of every single person who is alleged to be a JCE member. In practice, however, the prosecution has only been required to demonstrate that each of the persons charged and (if not one of those charged) the principal offenders shared the intent required for the crime that is the object of the criminal plan.[77]

It is important to note that the element of shared intent does not greatly limit the operation of JCE I liability, given that JCE members can act through physical perpetrators who need not be JCE members, and will thus not need to 'share' the intent.[78] One might envisage a scenario where X1 (a high-ranking civilian leader), X2 (the head of the national police) and X3 (a military commander) develop a common plan to ethnically cleanse a certain territory by ordering killings, deportations, torture and rape. They implement these plans through unit leaders under their authority, Y1, Y2 and Y3. These unit leaders use low-level members of the military, police and civilians under their control to commit the crimes of murder, rape and torture. The physical perpetrators are unaware of the full extent of the crimes planned, or of the policy behind their commission. In this scenario, JCE members can still be convicted under JCE I for the crimes committed in execution of the common plan of ethnic cleansing, even though the physical crimes are perpetrated by offenders who did not intend, know or foresee that these crimes were directed towards the object of ethnic cleansing.

---

[75] *Tadić Appeals Judgment*, above n 4, para 196; *Vasiljević Appeals Judgment*, above n 11, para 119; *Blagojevic and Jokic*, above n 10, para 703.

[76] Cassese, above n 31, 111. See also *Tadić Appeals Judgment*, above n 4, para 196; *Kvocka Appeals Judgment*, above n 21, para 82; *Stakić Appeals Judgment*, above n 1, para 65.

[77] *Krnojelac Trial Judgment*, above n 12, para 83; *Simic Trial Judgment*, above n 7, para 160.

[78] See text to nn 48 to 50 above; see also Boas et al, above n 10, 54, alluding to but not quite following this conundrum to its logical conclusion.

It has been suggested that in addition to shared intent, *dolus eventualis* (advert recklessness)[79] is sufficient to hold members of a JCE liable under the first category.[80] The example given is that of a group of servicemen who decide to deprive civilians of sustenance to force them to build a bridge for military operations. If some of these civilians die, the servicemen are responsible not only for a JCE to commit the war crime of intentionally starving civilians, but also for murder, since the death was a natural and foreseeable consequence of the common criminal plan.[81] This proposition simultaneously employs different standards of *mens rea*. *Dolus eventualis* in civil law systems has no strict equivalent in the common law, and requires a volitional element of identification and approval with the ultimate evil result which common law concepts such as recklessness lack.[82] While the additional requirement of 'advertence' approximates this standard, it is still different from the much lower standard of mere awareness of the natural and foreseeable consequences of one's act.

The example also presupposes a relatively small group of people with comparable knowledge of the scale and extent of the crimes and roughly equal participation in the conduct that constitutes the crime. This situation makes it easier to evaluate the natural and foreseeable consequence of the common criminal plan. The extent of foreseeability possessed by a minor participant with little awareness of the scope of the common criminal plan is, however, quite different, which makes it difficult to attribute responsibility to him under JCE I.

III. *MENS REA* REQUIREMENTS FOR JCE II

A. Personal Knowledge of the System

In order for the accused to be held responsible for participation in an institutionalised common criminal plan, he must have personal knowledge of

---

[79] The ICTY Trial Chamber in *Stakić* discussed the requirement of *dolus eventualis* in the following terms: 'The technical definition of *dolus eventualis* is the following: if the actor engages in life-endangering behaviour, his killing becomes intentional if he "reconciles himself" or "makes peace" with the likelihood of death. Thus, if the killing is committed with "manifest indifference to the value of human life", even conduct of minimal risk can qualify as intentional homicide. Large scale killings that would be classified as reckless murder in the United States would meet the continental criteria of *dolus eventualis*.' *Prosecutor v Stakić*, No IT-97-24-T, Trial Chamber Judgment (31 July 2003) para 587. The Appeals Chamber went on to hold that this was equivalent to 'advertent recklessness': *Stakić Appeals Judgment*, above n 1, paras 99–103.
[80] Cassese, above n 31, 109.
[81] Ibid, 111–12.
[82] GP Fletcher and JD Ohlin, 'Reclaiming Fundamental Principles of Criminal Law in the Darfur Case' (2005) 3 *Journal of International Criminal Justice* 539, 554; M Bohlander, *Principles of German Criminal Law* (Oxford, Hart Publishing, 2009) 63–65.

the system of ill-treatment.[83] The ICTY has not defined the term 'system', but JCE II's application to internment or concentration camp cases[84] suggests that it refers to a closed hierarchical organisational structure set up for a specific purpose. Some ICTY judgments have formulated the *mens rea* requirement a little differently: the accused must have knowledge of the criminal nature of the system.[85]

The accused's knowledge of the criminal nature of the system may be inferred from the circumstances surrounding his participation in it, for instance his position and functions in the system, the amount of time spent by him in the system, and any contact he has with other members of the system.[86] Awareness of the crimes may also be inferred from the accused's observance of the effects of such crimes and reports made to him by other people.[87] The accused's position of authority, even a *de facto* one, is a factor indicating his awareness of the system's purpose.[88]

While the circumstances of the accused may legitimately be taken into account to infer his knowledge of the crimes, it is important to do so with caution.[89] An institutionalised system of ill-treatment on a large scale may depend on functional division of labour between various persons involved in the system. For instance, in a large concentration camp, different parts of the camp may be deliberately isolated. X, the driver of prisoners to the camp, may have no contact with the camp cook Y, or with Z who documents the prisoners who enter the camp. They all may at times hear rumours about the crimes committed in the camp, but their own status rigidly restricts them to the performance of a particular isolated function within the camp. In this situation, the validity of inferring knowledge of the full scale of crimes in the camp from mere continued participation in the camp's activities and hearsay is suspect.

---

[83] *Tadić Appeals Judgment*, above n 4, para 228; *Krnojelac Appeals Judgment*, above n 21, para 32; *Vasiljević Appeals Judgment*, above n 11, para 101.

[84] See *Amicus Curiae* Brief of Professor Antonio Cassese and members of the *Journal of International Criminal Justice on Joint Criminal Enterprise Doctrine*, Case File No 001/18-07-2007-ECCC/OCIJ (PTC 02) (27 October 2008) para 24; H van der Wilt, 'Joint Criminal Enterprise: Possibilities and Limitations' (2007) 5 *Journal of International Criminal Justice* 91, 96.

[85] *Kvocka Appeals Judgment*, above n 21, para 198.

[86] *Kvocka Trial Judgment*, above n 67, para 324; *Kvocka Appeals Judgment*, above n 21, paras 201, 203.

[87] *Kvocka Trial Judgment*, above n 67, para 384.

[88] *Tadić Appeals Judgment*, above n 4, para 228; *Kvocka Trial Judgment*, above n 67, para 324; *Kvocka Appeals Judgment*, above n 21, paras 174, 202; *Stakić Appeals Judgment*, above n 1, para 65.

[89] The inference of knowledge on part of the accused from his position of authority within the system of ill-treatment has been particularly criticised as reversing the burden of proof with regard to knowledge and intent. See Haan, above n 65, 190; van Sliedregt, above n 31, 184, 188. In his survey of trials conducted by the Nuremberg Military Tribunals, Heller notes that they rejected the claim that the accused's knowledge might be inferred from his position in the Nazi hierarchy. See KJ Heller, *The Nuremberg Military Tribunals and the Origins of International Criminal Law* (Oxford, Oxford University Press, 2011) 284.

B. Intent to Further the Criminal Purpose

The accused must intend to further the system of ill-treatment.[90] Except in the case of special intent crimes,[91] there is no further requirement that he intends to commit the specific crime with which he is charged. Though ICTY jurisprudence consistently refers to JCE II as a 'variant of the first category',[92] this mental element distinguishes it from JCE I, which requires the accused to share the intent for the crime that is the object of the JCE.[93] The mental elements for JCE I and JCE II are the same only in the case of special intent crimes. In cases where the crimes charged pursuant to the JCE require special intent, such as the crime of persecution, the accused must also meet the additional requirements imposed by the crime, such as the intent to discriminate on political, religious or racial grounds.[94] Thus, mere proof of intent to further the criminal system does not satisfy the mental element. It has been suggested that the specific intent of the accused to commit a special intent crime may be used to infer his further intent to support the system of ill-treatment.[95] Caution must be exercised against drawing such a conclusion in all cases. X may intend to commit the crime of persecution, without intending to further the crimes of forced labour or sexual violence that may also be part of the system of ill-treatment.

The intention to advance the system of ill-treatment may be deduced from two factors: knowledge of the plan and participation in its advancement.[96] The threshold of participation required is fairly low. The accused need not have displayed any enthusiasm or initiative, or have derived any personal satisfaction from his participation.[97] Marginal members of

---

[90] *Krnojelac Appeals Judgment*, above n 21, paras 89, 94, 96; Boas et al, above n 10, 59–63, citing and interpreting *Tadić Appeals Judgment*, above n 4, para 228. Against *Prosecutor v Brdanin and Talić*, No IT-99-36-PT, Trial Chamber II pre-Trial Decision on Form of Further Amended Indictment and Prosecution Application to Amend (26 June 2001); *Krnojelac Trial Judgment*, above n 12, para 78.

[91] 'Special intent of a crime, is the specific intention, required as a constitutive element of the crime, which demands that the perpetrator clearly seeks to produce the act charged': *Prosecutor v Akayesu*, No ICTR-96-4-T, Trial Chamber Judgment (2 September 1998) para 498. This has been termed a 'purpose based' interpretation of intent. See C Kress, 'The Darfur Report and Genocidal Intent' (2005) 3 *Journal of International Criminal Justice* 562, 566.

[92] *Tadić Appeals Judgment*, above n 4, para 203; *Vasiljević Appeals Judgment*, above n 11, para 98; *Kvocka Appeals Judgment*, above n 21, para 82. See also *Amicus Curiae* Brief of Professor Antonio Cassese, above n 84, para 24.

[93] For this careful analysis, see Boas et al, above n 10, 62–63. For a different source of challenge to JCE II as a variant of JCE I, see K Ambos, *Amicus Curiae* concerning Criminal Case File No 001/18-07-2007-ECCC/OCIJ (PTC 02) (27 October 2008) 13–15.

[94] *Kvovka Trial Judgment*, above n 67, para 288; *Kvocka Appeals Judgment*, above n 21, paras 110–11.

[95] Boas et al, above n 10, 68.

[96] *Kvocka Trial Judgment*, above n 67, para 271; *Kvocka Appeals Judgment*, above n 21, para 243.

[97] *Krnojelac Appeals Judgment*, above n 21, para 100; *Kvocka Appeals Judgment*, above n 21, paras 106, 242.

the system, such as individuals providing medical treatment or food to the detainees in a prison camp, may be considered indispensable cogs in the criminal system, as the system cannot be sustained without their willing participation in the performance of administrative duties.[98]

The combination of low *mens rea* and participation requirements for JCE II gives rise to concerns as to its legitimacy as a form of principal responsibility. If the accused does not need to intend to commit the particular crime in question, and may incur liability simply through the performance of administrative duties, it is difficult to see how this mode of participation differs from aiding and abetting.[99] Indeed, the latter requires substantial contribution,[100] whereas for JCE II, the accused may only discharge a task of some consequence in the institution.[101]

IV. *MENS REA* REQUIREMENTS FOR JCE III

A. Intent to Participate in and Further Criminal Purpose

In order to incur liability under JCE III, the accused must possess the intent to participate in the JCE, and to further – individually and jointly – the criminal purpose of the enterprise.[102] These two elements overlap with the mental elements of JCE I and JCE II liability. The intent to participate in the JCE is analogous to the JCE I's requirement of voluntary participation in an aspect of the common criminal plan. The intent to further the common criminal purpose is similar to the general intent to further the system of ill-treatment in JCE II.[103]

B. The Accused's Foresight and Voluntary Assumption of Risk

Liability under JCE III arises where one or more members of the JCE commit crimes that go beyond the common purpose. The accused is responsible for these additional crimes only if they were a natural and foreseeable consequence of the realisation of the plan and the accused willingly took this risk.[104] According to the standard in *Tadić*, two conditions need to be fulfilled for liability to ensue. First, the rapes and murders should be

---

[98] *Amicus Curiae* Brief of Professor Antonio Cassese, above n 84, paras 24–25.
[99] *Amicus Curiae* Brief of Kai Ambos, above n 93, paras 13–14.
[100] *Tadić Appeals Judgment*, above n 4, para 229.
[101] *Amicus Curiae* Brief of Professor Antonio Cassese, above n 84, para 25.
[102] *Tadić Appeals Judgment*, above n 4, paras 220 and 228: *Kvocka Appeals Judgment*, above n 21, para 83: *Stakić Appeals Judgment*, above n 1, para 65.
[103] Boas et al, above n 10, 69.
[104] Ambos, above n 65, 160–61.

objectively as well as subjectively foreseeable,[105] that is, not only should the accused be able to predict that these crimes may be committed in the course of the forcible expulsion, but the same must also have been foreseeable to a reasonable person in his position.[106] Secondly, for subjective foreseeability, the crime must be foreseen to be likely; for objective foreseeability, the crime should merely be seen as possible.[107] That is, the accused must know that the actions of the group are *likely* to result in rapes and murders, and it should be objectively foreseeable that rapes and murders *might* be committed by one or more members of the group.[108]

Subsequent ICTY Chambers have used different standards. In *Brđanin*, the Trial Chamber lowered the subjective foreseeability standard[109] such that the accused need only have been aware that the rapes and murders were a 'possible' rather than a 'predictable' consequence of the common plan. The *Krstić* Trial Chamber, on the facts of the case, applied the test that the accused should have foreseen the crimes as an 'inevitable' outcome of the common plan,[110] while quoting *Brđanin*'s standard of the crime as a 'possible' consequence.[111] *Brđanin* and *Krstić* also failed to specify the degree of probability required for objective foreseeability.[112] The *Kvočka* Appeals Chamber introduced yet another standard: the prosecution must prove that 'the accused had sufficient knowledge such that the additional crimes were a natural and foreseeable consequence to him'.[113] Thus, the crimes must be objectively foreseeable, and the accused must know that these additional crimes normally occur in the given enterprise.[114] This formulation has been modified in subsequent judgments which conflate the objective and subjective foreseeability elements by

---

[105] Against Cassese, who supports a standard of mere objective foreseeability on the ground that participants in large-scale atrocities may be expected to be particularly alert to the consequences of their actions; the gravity of the crimes makes the maximum penalty within the bounds of legality desirable; and the level of culpability of the accused may be taken into account at the sentencing stage. See Cassese, above n 31, 123. One might conversely argue that it is the very scale of atrocities committed in armed conflict situations that makes foreseeability of another person's conduct exceptionally difficult.

[106] *Tadić Appeals Judgment*, above n 4, paras 220, 228. See Boas et al, above n 10, 72.

[107] *Tadić Appeals Judgment*, above n 4, paras 220, 232. See Boas et al, above n 10, 73–74.

[108] *Tadić Appeals Judgment*, above n 4, paras 220, 232. See Boas et al, above n 10, 73–74.

[109] *Brđanin and Talić Pre-trial Decision*, above n 90, para 31; *Gotovina Appeals Judgment*, above n 18, para 90. See S Darcy, 'Imputed Criminal Liability and the Goals of International Justice' (2007) 20 *Leiden Journal of International Law* 377, 383.

[110] *Krstić Trial Judgment*, above n 48, para 616.

[111] Ibid, para 613; *Prosecutor v Krstić*, No IT-98-33-A, Appeals Chamber Judgment (19 April 2004) para 149.

[112] *Brđanin and Talić Pre-trial Decision*, above n 90, para 31; *Krstić Trial Judgment*, above n 48, para 613. Other ICTY cases have also quoted the correct standard as the one in *Brđanin*. See, eg, *Vasiljević Appeals Judgment*, above n 11, para 101; *Ntakirutimana Appeals Judgment*, above n 1, para 467.

[113] *Kvočka Appeals Judgment*, above n 21, para 86. See also *Krajisnik Trial Judgment*, above n 24, para 882; *Prosecutor v Limaj*, No IT-03-66-T, Trial Chamber Judgment (30 November 2005) para 512.

[114] Ambos, above n 65, 175.

requiring that the accused must have 'sufficient knowledge that the additional crimes were a natural and foreseeable consequence', that is, it must be 'reasonably foreseeable on the basis of the information available to the accused that the crime or underlying offence would be committed'.[115] Ironically, the contrary standards on foreseeability applied by tribunals make the conviction unforeseeable.[116]

The category JCE III may also be used to hold JCE members liable for crimes that are committed by direct perpetrators who are not JCE members. Thus, when the direct perpetrator commits a crime which is a natural and foreseeable consequence of the JCE, the accused is responsible if he possesses the requisite intent for the common criminal purpose and if:

(a) it was foreseeable that the additional crime might be committed by an individual used by him or another JCE member to carry out the crimes that are part of the common purpose; and

(b) he willingly took that risk, that is, he was aware that the additional crime was a possible consequence of the implementation of the common purpose.[117]

Consider a slightly modified version of the example used in JCE I. X1 (the high-ranking civilian leader), X2 (the head of the national police) and X3 (the military commander), all belonging to ethnic group Alpha, develop a common plan to remove members of ethnic group Beta permanently from a region by launching artillery attacks on towns and villages in that territory and by forcible transfers of civilians. They implement these plans through unit leaders of the military (Y1) and special police (Y2). These unit leaders use low-level members of the military (A1 to A100) and police (B1 to B100) to carry out the shellings and to deport civilians using physical force. In the course of the attacks, Y2 takes the initiative to recruit armed groups of civilians belonging to Alpha (C1 to C100) to facilitate the deportations through force and intimidation. In the course of these deportations, C1 to C100 commit rapes and killings.

Under the mental requirements outlined, it is possible to hold X1 and X2 liable for the rapes and killings, as long as it was foreseeable that individuals used by Y2 to carry out the forcible transfers might commit rapes and killings, and provided they knew that these crimes were a possible consequence of the forced expulsions.[118] Thus, JCE members may find themselves liable as principals for a vast array of additional crimes that are perpetrated by different groups of physical perpetrators used by one

---

[115] *Dordević*, above n 24, para 1865; see also *Prosecutor v Milutinović*, No IT-05-87-T, Trial Chamber Judgment (26 February 2009) para 111.

[116] Ambos, above n 65, 174; see also Fletcher and Ohlin, above n 82, 550.

[117] *Brdanin Appeals Judgment*, above n 2 para 411; *Boskoski*, above n 74, para 397; *Dordević*, above n 24, para 1867.

[118] See Darcy, above n 109, 383. For a similar analysis, see C Farhang, 'Point of No Return: Joint Criminal Enterprise in *Brdanin*' (2010) 23 *Leiden Journal of International Law* 137, 154–55.

or more of them to effectuate the crimes that form part of the common purpose.[119]

The only exception to this expansion of responsibility is for specific intent crimes like genocide, where it will be necessary to prove that the accused knew that the crimes amounting to genocide might be committed, and with genocidal intent.[120] It bears emphasising, though, that JCE III is a form of principal rather than accomplice liability, which makes the accused liable as *perpetrators*, to the same degree as the individuals who have committed the rapes and murders with genocidal intent, and despite the fact that the former did not act with the *mens rea* required for genocide.[121] This is a serious concern for specific intent crimes like genocide,[122] but is also problematic in the case of general intent crimes, where the foreseeability standard places on a par individuals who deliberately commit the crime with the intent proper to it and those who only entertain the lesser *mens rea* of foreseeability.[123]

Cassese acknowledges these objections to JCE III, but adopts a contrary position. He asserts that the application of JCE III is necessitated by public policy considerations that society must be protected against criminals who band together in illegal enterprises.[124] He relies on English law justifications for convictions in cases of joint enterprises, where the accused is held criminally liable for the harm he foresees resulting from the crime he encouraged, but where it would be impossible to prove the specific intention required for the crime.[125] However, considerations of public policy also counsel respect for the principle of personal culpability, and Cassese

---

[119] For a sophisticated analysis of how such a scenario presents problems about the criteria by which to 'link' horizontally the JCE members to each other, and link them vertically with the physical perpetrators, see JD Ohlin, 'Second-Order Linking Principles: Combining Vertical and Horizontal Modes of Liability' (2012) 25 *Leiden Journal of International Law* 771, 774–76.

[120] *Prosecutor v Brdanin*, No IT-99-36-A, Appeals Chamber Decision on Interlocutory Appeal (19 March 2004) para 10. Prior to 2004, the ICTY had held that the notion of genocide as a 'natural and foreseeable consequence' of an enterprise that did not have genocide as its aim was not compatible with the *dolus specialis* element for genocide (*Stakić Trial Judgment*, above n 79, para 530; *Prosecutor v Brdanin*, No IT-99-36-T, Trial Chamber Decision on Motion for Acquittal Pursuant to Rule 98 *bis* (28 November 2003) paras 30, 57. However, current jurisprudence rejects this requirement on the basis that it confuses the *mens rea* element for the crime of genocide with that required by the mode of participation (*Brdanin Interlocutory Decision*, para 6). See also *Prosecutor v Milosević*, No IT-54-02-T, Trial Chamber's Decision on Motion for Judgment of Acquittal (16 June 2004) para 291; *Popović*, above n 7, para 1031). On the requirement of *dolus eventualis*, see generally DL Nersessian, *Genocide and Political Groups* (Oxford, Oxford University Press, 2010) 36–38.

[121] On this point, see Haan, above n 65, 200.

[122] See van Sliedregt, above n 6, 139.

[123] S Powles, 'Joint Criminal Enterprise: Criminal Liability by Prosecutorial Ingenuity and Judicial Creativity?' (2004) 2 *Journal of International Criminal Justice* 606, 612; Ambos, above n 65, 168–69. Cassese acknowledges this concern but argues that there are factors that counter or outweigh it. See Cassese, above n 31, 117–23.

[124] Cassese, above n 31, 117–18.

[125] *R v Powell and English* [1999] 1 AC 1.

provides no scale with which to rank these principles. Moreover, since JCE III is a mode of principal liability, his reliance on accessorial joint enterprise liability in English law,[126] which is in any case fairly controversial among scholars,[127] is misplaced.

Cassese's next argument also meets with the same problem. He relies on the intuitive notion that since the common criminal plan is a *sine qua non* for the 'extra crime', the accused's culpability consists in his foreseeability of the extra crime (because of his participation in the initial plan) and his failure to prevent or dissociate himself from it.[128] While a sophisticated legal system can calibrate the different degrees of responsibility of the accused and the principal offender, international criminal law lacks the maturity to make these gradations. Instead, the difference in levels of culpability may appropriately be taken into account at the sentencing stage.[129] Cassese's position misses the *raison d'être* for the introduction of JCE liability: that it matters not only what we hold someone responsible for, but also *how* we hold them responsible. The accused in JCE III is clearly culpable to some extent; the rationale for delineating modes of liability is to reflect the differences in the degrees of culpability between different categories of accused. The solution to international criminal law's immaturity as a discipline cannot lie in running roughshod over these distinctions at the level of imposition of responsibility.[130]

The problems with the justification for JCE III have not gone unnoticed by other international tribunals. While the ICTY has been at the forefront of developments in the JCE doctrine, having championed it aggressively since its inception, tribunals such as the Extraordinary Chambers in the Courts of Cambodia and the Special Tribunal for Lebanon have developed their variants on JCE, including JCE III, which depart from the ICTY's formulation in important respects. JCE has also been jettisoned sometimes in favour of new forms of commission responsibility. The following chapter discusses these developments in commission responsibility at other international and hybrid criminal tribunals.

---

[126] Ibid.

[127] This will be considered in detail in Part Three.

[128] Cassese, above n 31, 119–20; see also Judge Shahabuddeen's defence of JCE III liability on the basis that the secondary party (in a JCE) shares the intent of the primary offender, due to his willingness to take the risk associated with the commission of the additional offence. M Shahabuddeen, 'Judicial Creativity and Joint Criminal Enterprise' in S Darcy and J Powderly (eds), *Judicial Creativity at the International Criminal Tribunals* (New York, Oxford University Press, 2010) 184, 197.

[129] Cassese, above n 31, 120–22.

[130] On this point, see Fletcher and Ohlin, above n 82, 539, 550. Fletcher and Ohlin go so far as to state that JCE III liability is equivalent to strict liability, which is slightly overstating the case.

4

Variants of JCE and Other Forms of Commission at the Ad Hoc *Tribunals*

I. THE EVOLUTION OF JCE AT THE *AD HOC* TRIBUNALS

A. Special Court for Sierra Leone

THE SPECIAL COURT for Sierra Leone (SCSL) purports to follow the ICTY's lead on the elements of JCE, but has in practice embraced an even more flexible approach to identifying the contours of JCE liability. The most troubling departure from ICTY jurisprudence has been the SCSL's rejection of the necessity for an inherently criminal objective. Initially, in the *AFRC* case, the Trial Chamber dismissed the JCE pleading in the indictment on the basis that the common purpose of taking 'any actions necessary to gain and exercise political power and control over the territory of Sierra Leone' was not inherently criminal.[1] This was overturned by the Appeals Chamber which ruled that

> the requirement that the common plan, design or purpose of a joint criminal enterprise is inherently criminal means that it must either have as its objective a crime within the Statute, *or contemplate crimes* within the Statute as the means of achieving its objective.[2] (emphasis added)

Thus, even though the ultimate objective of the common plan alleged in the indictment – gaining and exercising political power and control over the territory of Sierra Leone – may not be criminal, the means to achieve this contemplated by the accused, such as unlawful killings, forced labour, and physical and sexual violence, were crimes within the SCSL Statute.[3]

The *AFRC* Appeals Chamber's standard of the accused's 'contemplation' of crimes as a means of achieving the non-criminal JCE objective arguably expands the limits of JCE in a manner unsupported by ICTY jurisprudence. Contemplating a crime may potentially be likened to involving, or amounting to, a crime, which does not pose any challenges

---

[1] *Prosecutor v Brima, Kamara, and Kanu*, No SCSL-04-16-T, Trial Chamber II Judgment (20 June 2007) ('*AFRC Trial Judgment*') paras 67–69.
[2] *Prosecutor v Brima, Kamara, and Kanu*, No SCSL-04-16-A, Appeals Chamber, Judgment (22 February 2008) ('*AFRC Appeals Judgment*') para 80.
[3] Ibid, paras 82–84.

as such. However, another way to read the requirement is that the accused must merely foresee the crimes as a possible result of accomplishing the JCE's non-criminal objectives.[4] This undermines the shared criminal intent for a common purpose that is a prerequisite for JCE liability.[5] The SCSL has abandoned the requirement of a 'necessary relationship between the objective of a common purpose and its criminal means'; it suffices that the 'latter are contemplated to achieve the former'.[6] Thus, if the accused co-operates with other individuals who share the common (lawful) objective of gaining political power over territory, and each of them independently foresees the possibility that crimes may be committed in the accomplishment of this lawful objective, they can all be held liable for the commission of crimes pursuant to a common criminal enterprise.[7]

This new JCE standard not only abandons the distinction between JCE I and JCE III, but also unduly stretches the bounds of JCE III liability.[8] This is demonstrated in the SCSL's conviction of Revolutionary United Front (RUF) commander Augustine Gbao under JCE I, despite the determination that he lacked the shared intent to commit all the crimes that were within the common criminal purpose.[9] Instead, his liability was based on the fact that he shared the (non-criminal) common objective to control parts of the country's territory, and intended or could foresee that other JCE members or individuals used by them might commit crimes in this pursuit.[10]

Some other aspects of the SCSL's JCE jurisprudence also appear to downplay the limitations on the scope and application of JCE introduced by the ICTY. For instance, in the *RUF* case, the Trial Chamber held that the criminal enterprise is 'divisible as to participants, time and location . . . [and] as to the crimes charged as being within or the foreseeable consequence of the purpose of the joint enterprise'.[11] The prosecution need demonstrate only

---

[4] C Rose, 'Troubled Indictments at the Special Court for Sierra Leone: The Pleading of Joint Criminal Enterprise and Sex-Based Crimes' (2009) 7 *Journal of International Criminal Justice* 353, 362–63. See also W Schabas, 'Special Court for Sierra Leone Rejects Joint Criminal Enterprise' (*The Trial of Charles Taylor*, 25 June 2007), at <www.charlestaylortrial.org/expert-commentary/professor-william-schabas-on-afrc-decision> accessed 13 December 2010.

[5] W Jordash and P van Tuyl, 'Failure to Carry the Burden of Proof: How Joint Criminal Enterprise Lost its Way at the Special Court for Sierra Leone' (2010) 8 *Journal of International Criminal Justice* 591, 603.

[6] *Prosecutor v Sesay, Kallon, and Gbao*, No SCSL-04-15-A, Appeals Chamber, Judgment (26 October 2009) ('*RUF Appeals Judgment*') para 296.

[7] Jordash and van Tuyl, above n 5, 603–04.

[8] *RUF Appeals Judgment*, above n 6, Dissenting Opinion of Justice Fisher, paras 17–19; Jordash and van Tuyl, above n 5, 607–08.

[9] *Prosecutor v Sesay, Kallon, and Gbao*, No SCSL-04-15-T, Trial Chamber I, Judgment (2 March 2009) ('*RUF Trial Judgment*') paras 2010–14, 2040, 2048, 2060, 2019; *RUF Appeals Judgment*, above n 6, Dissenting Opinion of Justice Fisher, paras 14–16; Jordash and van Tuyl, above n 5, 606–07.

[10] *RUF Trial Judgment*, above n 9, paras 2010–14, 2048, 2060, 2019; *RUF Appeals Judgment*, above n 6, paras 486, 492; *RUF Appeals Judgment*, above n 6, Dissenting Opinion of Justice Fisher, paras 17–19; Jordash and van Tuyl, above n 5, 607.

[11] *RUF Trial Judgment*, above n 9, para 354.

that the enterprise existed during some part of the time period charged in the indictment. Further, due to the fluid nature of the means used to accomplish the enterprise's objective, the indictment might specify only one (and not all) of the crimes that is used to accomplish this objective as being within the enterprise, or a foreseeable consequence of it.[12] This is a disturbingly low threshold, especially in the context of a JCE which does not need a shared common criminal intent.

In addition, the SCSL has embraced the *Brdanin* Appeals Chamber's holding that the physical perpetrator does not need to be a JCE member.[13] It has not, however, been rigorous in establishing the link between any specific JCE member and his control over the physical perpetrators who commit the crimes for which all other JCE members are held responsible.[14] In the *RUF* case, for instance, the Trial Chamber held that the physical perpetrators of the crimes – low-ranking AFRC and RUF Commanders, and rank-and-file fighters – were sufficiently connected to 'one or more members' of the JCE, primarily based on circumstantial evidence and the widespread and systematic nature of the crimes.[15]

Recently, there are indications that the SCSL is seeking to rein in such an expanded application of JCE. In the *Taylor* Trial Judgment, the Chamber rejected the JCE charges due to the lack of a common plan between Taylor and other alleged JCE participants. The prosecution had been inconsistent in its pleading on JCE.[16] In its final trial brief, the prosecution alleged the existence of a common plan between Taylor and members of the AFRC and the RUF, involving 'the use of criminal means, a campaign of terror encompassing the Indictment crimes, in order to achieve the ultimate objective of the JCE, to forcibly control the population and territory of Sierra Leone and to pillage its resources, in particular diamonds.'[17] Thus, the campaign of terror including the indictment crimes was a *means* to achieve the *purpose* or *objective* of controlling Sierra Leone's territory and population, and pillaging its resources. However, the Trial Chamber recharacterised the means alleged by the prosecution as the *purpose* of the JCE, by holding that the common purpose was 'a campaign to terrorize

---

[12] Ibid.

[13] Ibid, paras 263, 266; *RUF Appeals Judgment*, above n 6, para 400; *Prosecutor v Charles Ghankay Taylor*, No SCSL-03-01-T, Trial Chamber II, Judgment (18 May 2012) ('*Taylor Trial Judgment*') para 464.

[14] W Jordash and S Martin, 'Due Process ad Fair Trial Rights at the Special Court: How the Desire for Accountability Outweighed the Demands of Justice at the Special Court for Sierra Leone' (2010) 23 *Leiden Journal of International Law* 585, 602–06.

[15] *RUF Trial Judgment*, above n 9, para 1992. See also *RUF Appeals Judgment*, above n 6, paras 417–18; Jordash and Martin, above n 14, 602–06.

[16] For a detailed account of the various versions of the JCE alleged by the prosecution, see J Easterday, 'Initial Reflections on JCE and Terrorism in the *Taylor* Judgment' (*IntLawGrrls*, 30 April 2012), at <www.intlawgrrls.com/2012/04/initial-reflections-on-jce-and.html# more> accessed 19 August 2013.

[17] *Prosecutor v Taylor*, No SCSL-03-01-T, Prosecution Final Trial Brief (08 April 2011) para 574.

the civilian population of the Republic of Sierra Leone, of which the crimes charged in . . . the Indictment were either an integral part, or a fore-seeable consequence thereof'.[18] The Chamber held that while Taylor had provided military, logistical, and financial support to the RUF/AFRC, this was not in the context of a common plan to terrorize the civilian popula-tion. The RUF/AFRC and Taylor simply had common interests and mutual enemies, and his support to their operations was based on con-verging military and trading benefits.[19]

If the Chamber had accepted the prosecution's dual objectives of con-trolling Sierra Leone's territory and plundering its resources, it is possible that the evidence relied on by the Chamber would have been sufficient to establish that the indictment crimes were a foreseeable consequence of this shared (non-criminal) purpose. The Chamber's narrowing of the common purpose thus serves to limit the potential liability under a more expansive JCE charge; nevertheless, it fails to recognise the error in charg-ing the accused under JCE I for a crime that he does not intend but merely foresees as a consequence of a lawful shared objective.

B. Extraordinary Chambers in the Courts of Cambodia

The Extraordinary Chambers in the Courts of Cambodia (ECCC) is the only international tribunal to have expressly rejected JCE III on the basis that it does not have a firm foundation in customary international law.[20] Joint Criminal Enterprise has a long and troubled history at the ECCC. The first significant pronouncement on its application was the 2009 JCE Order by the Office of the Co-Investigating Judges (OCIJ) in Case 002, which relied on the reasoning and sources in *Tadić* to hold that JCE was a recognised mode of liability in customary international law.[21] Since the ECCC possessed the indicia of an international court, and the existence of JCE in customary international law satisfied the tests of foreseeability and

---

[18] *Taylor Trial Judgment*, above n 13, para 6892, relying on *Prosecutor v Taylor*, No SCSL-2003-01-T-752, Decision on Urgent Defence Motion Regarding a Fatal Defect in the Prosecution's Second Amended Indictment Relating to the Pleading of JCE (27 February 2009) paras 70–76; *Prosecutor v Taylor*, No SCSL-2003-01-T, Appeals Chamber Decision on Defence Notice of Appeal and Submissions Regarding The Majority Decision Concerning the Pleading of JCE in the Second Amended Indictment (1 May 2009). See also J Easterday, 'Joint Criminal Enterprise in the *Taylor* Judgment' (*IntLawGrrls*, 9 August 2012), at <www.intlawgrrls.com/2012/08/joint-criminal-enterprise-in-charles.html> accessed 19 August 2013.

[19] *Taylor Trial Judgment*, above n 13, paras 6894–99.

[20] *Decision on the Appeals Against the Co-Investigative Judges Order on Joint Criminal Enterprise (JCE)*, No: 002/19-09-2007-ECCC-OCIJ, Pre-Trial Chamber (20 May 2010) ('*PTC Decision*') para 83; *Decision on the Applicability of Joint Criminal Enterprise*, No 002/19-09-2007-ECCC-TC, Trial Chamber (12 September 2011) ('*Trial Chamber JCE Decision*') para 35.

[21] *Order on the Application at the ECCC of the Form of Liability Known as Joint Criminal Enterprise*, No 002/19-09-2007-ECCC-OCIJ, Office of the Co-Investigating Judges (8 December 2009) ('*OCIJ 2009 Order*') paras 13, 21.

accessibility to the accused, the ECCC was justified in applying JCE in Case 002.[22] However, JCE was a specifically international mode of participation, developed to capture the unique features of international crimes where the individuals who bore the greatest responsibility were often far removed from their physical commission. Thus, applying the French doctrine of autonomous legal 'regimes', the OCIJ held that JCE was limited to international crimes, and did not extend to Cambodian national crimes under the ECCC law.[23]

This ruling was partially overturned by the Pre-Trial Chamber, which confirmed that the ECCC was authorised to apply JCE I and JCE III which were firmly established in customary international law, but was unable to find similar support for JCE III.[24] The basic concept of JCE (JCE I and JCE II) required a shared *mens rea* for the crime and contribution to its commission. This concept had traditional civil law counterparts, including in the 1956 Cambodian Penal Code which was applicable during the temporal jurisdiction of the ECCC.[25] The basic form of JCE could be likened to liability for 'co-perpetration' under Cambodian criminal law, even though it had broader application to situations where the accused was more remote from the physical perpetration of the *actus reus* of the crime. Actions that fell outside the common purpose, however, could only be punishable as 'complicity' under Cambodian law.[26]

In its analysis of JCE I and JCE II, the Pre-Trial Chamber did not confine itself to the sources cited in *Tadić* but also relied on post-World War II cases decided under Control Council No 10, in particular the *Justice* case and the *RuSHA* case.[27] It dismissed *Tadić*'s reliance on international instruments and case law to establish JCE III, holding that these either did not mention the extended form of JCE,[28] or failed to indicate the precise mode of liability being applied.[29] Moreover, the Italian judgments cited by *Tadić* were decisions by domestic courts applying domestic law, and were not appropriate precedents to establish customary international law.[30]

The Pre-Trial Chamber also rejected the contention that the OCIJ Order incorrectly restricted the application of JCE to the domain of international crimes. It noted that Article 29 of the ECCC Law on modes of responsibility did not distinguish between domestic crimes defined in Article 3(new) of the Law and international crimes provided for in Articles 4 to 7. Domestic forms of co-perpetration recognised in the applicable law and

---

[22] Ibid, paras 19–21.
[23] Ibid, para 22.
[24] *PTC Decision*, above n 20, paras 57–58, 69, 83.
[25] Ibid, para 41.
[26] Ibid.
[27] Ibid, paras 57, 65–69.
[28] Ibid, para 78.
[29] Ibid, paras 79–81.
[30] Ibid, para 82.

JCE were thus both forms of commission under Article 29. However, the parties had failed to demonstrate any error in the holding that JCE, which was a form of liability recognised in customary international law, should apply only to international crimes.[31]

The Pre-Trial Chamber's JCE Decision breaks new ground in rejecting the customary international law basis of JCE III through a sophisticated and critical analysis of the sources referenced in *Tadić*. The decision is nonetheless open to the same criticism as *Tadić* – a broader survey of war crimes prosecutions in countries such as Australia and Hong Kong (which moreover pre-date the ECCC's temporal jurisdiction) may have yielded more support for the existence of JCE III. The decision also does not provide any rationale for the confinement of JCE to international crimes under the ECCC Law. The failure to cite any justification for this limitation is particularly troubling, given that there is no proper basis for relying on the French concept of autonomous legal 'regimes' to interpret ECCC Law. Further, Article 29 of the ECCC Law itself makes no such demarcation between domestic and international crimes.[32] This is in contrast to the Statute for the SCSL, which explicitly provides that individual criminal responsibility for domestic crimes under Article 5 will be determined by applying principles of the domestic law of Sierra Leone.[33] One might argue that the application of uniquely international forms of responsibility that have no equivalent in domestic law to prosecute purely domestic crimes violates the legality principle.[34] The Chamber, however, makes no such determination.

In July 2010, the Trial Chamber affirmed the Pre-Trial Chamber's reasoning on JCE I and JCE II in its first judgment in the case of *Duch*,[35] but refrained from commenting on JCE III since the co-prosecutors had relied on it only in the alternative in their Final Trial Submissions.[36] This was followed by the Office of the Co-Investigating Judges' Closing Order of September 2012 in Case 002, where the OCIJ, on the facts of the case, considered JCE I to be the most suitable form of liability for characterising the conduct of the accused.[37]

---

[31] Ibid, para 102.

[32] See K Gustafson, 'ECCC Tackles JCE: An Appraisal of Recent Decisions' (2010) 8 *Journal of International Criminal Justice* 1323, 1330.

[33] Statute of the Special Court for Sierra Leone, 16 January 2002, 2178 UNTS 138, 145, Art 6(5).

[34] For a similar argument in the context of the Special Tribunal for Lebanon, see M Milanovic, 'An Odd Couple: Domestic Crimes and International Responsibility in the Special Tribunal for Lebanon' (2007) 5 *Journal of International Criminal Justice* 1139, 1142, 1144.

[35] *Judgment, Kaing Guek Eav, alias Duch*, No 001/18-07-2007-ECCC/TC, Trial Chamber (26 July 2010) ('*Duch Judgment*') paras 505–12.

[36] Ibid, para 513.

[37] *Closing Order*, No 002/19-09-2007-ECCC-OCIJ, Office of the Co-Investigating Judges (15 September 2010) ('*OCIJ Closing Order*') para 1541.

The OCIJ established that senior leaders of the Democratic Kampuchea (DK) regime, who were members of the Communist Party of Kampuchea (CPK), had a common purpose to

> implement rapid socialist revolution in Cambodia through a 'great leap forward' and to defend the Party against internal and external enemies, by whatever means necessary. The purpose itself was not entirely criminal in nature but its implementation resulted in and/or involved the commission of crimes within the jurisdiction of the ECCC.[38]

The CPK leaders designed and implemented five policies to achieve this purpose: population movements from urban to rural areas; establishment of co-operatives and work sites; 're-education' of bad elements and enemies; targeting of groups perceived as opposed to the revolution; and regulation of marriage. These policies resulted in or involved the commission of crimes by JCE members and non-members, that comprised several counts of crimes against humanity, genocide and war crimes including murder, extermination, torture, wilful killings and causing serious injury, deportations, imprisonments, persecution, other inhumane acts, enslavement, unlawful confinements and rape.[39] The members of the JCE included members of the Standing Committee (including accused Nuon Chea and Ieng Sary), members of the Central Committee (including accused Khieu Samphan); heads of CPK Ministries (including accused Ieng Thirith), zonal and sector secretaries, and heads of military divisions.[40]

The common purpose determination by the OCIJ is susceptible to the same criticism as that levelled against SCSL jurisprudence. The OCIJ links the accused to the crimes in a series of moves: the accused shared the (non-criminal) purpose to achieve a socialist revolution and defend the Party against enemies; the accused designed policies that were not necessarily criminal by nature to attain these ends, the execution of which resulted in or involved international crimes; further, the accused were held responsible under JCE I (and not JCE III) for their contribution to this purpose. The OCIJ thus repeats the problems with the SCSL's acceptance of the accused's contribution to a non-criminal purpose, where he merely foresees the commission of the crimes. This formula does not meet JCE I's requirement of a shared intent to commit a criminal offence. Indeed, the OCIJ's standard is potentially broader than the SCSL's, since the common plan may only 'result in' the crimes being committed. It is unclear what, if any, *mens rea* the accused must possess towards these crimes.

The Trial Chamber's 2011 Decision on the Applicability of JCE limited the OCIJ's definition of common purpose by citing SCSL jurisprudence that the common plan must at least 'contemplate crimes' as the means of

---

[38] Ibid, para 1524.
[39] Ibid, para 1525.
[40] Ibid, para 1529.

achieving the non-criminal objective,[41] but this only means that the problems with the SCSL's common purpose standard will also be manifested in ECCC jurisprudence. The Chamber also examined the sources in *Tadić* and additional post-World War II cases to confirm that JCE III was not recognised in customary international law,[42] and that State practice did not yield any uniform concept that would form part of general principles of law.[43] The final decision, though, on whether JCE III is applicable at the ECCC will rest with the Supreme Court Chamber, which has yet to pronounce on this matter.[44]

C. Special Tribunal for Lebanon

The Special Tribunal for Lebanon (STL) examined the application of JCE in detail in its *Interlocutory Decision on the Applicable Law*.[45] The decision is interesting, in that the Appeals Chamber upheld the applicability of JCE, which is specifically an international mode of participation, to the substantive crimes under the STL Statute which are governed by domestic Lebanese law. The Chamber justified this holding on the basis that under Article 2 of the Statute, the application of Lebanese law, including 'criminal participation', was subject to other provisions of the Statute, and Article 3 specifically recognised international forms of responsibility.[46] Thus, the issue of whether Lebanese law or international criminal law was applicable must be evaluated on a case-by-case basis. If there was no conflict between the two, Lebanese law should apply; in the event of a conflict, the law that favoured the accused should govern.[47]

The Chamber also confirmed that JCE may be applied as a form of international responsibility under Article 3, which matched the language in the ICTY and ICTR Statutes that had been interpreted to include JCE.[48] Moreover, JCE, unlike the doctrine of 'perpetration by means' applied by the ICC, was recognised in customary international law.[49] The Chamber disagreed with the ECCC Pre-Trial Chamber's reasoning that JCE III

---

[41] *Trial Chamber JCE Decision*, above n 20, para 17.

[42] Ibid, paras 30–35.

[43] Ibid, para 37.

[44] See JL Watkins and RC DeFalco, 'Joint Criminal Enterprise and the Jurisdiction of the Extraordinary Chambers in the Courts of Cambodia' (2010) 63 *Rutgers Law Review* 193, 198.

[45] *Interlocutory Decision on the Applicable Law: Terrorism, Conspiracy, Homicide, Perpetration, Cumulative Charging*, Case No STL 11-01/I, Appeals Chamber (26 February 2011) ('*STL Interlocutory Decision*').

[46] Ibid, para 210.

[47] Ibid, para 211. Gillett and Schuster call this a 'procedural' rather than 'substantive' answer. See M Gillett and M Schuster, 'Fast-Track Justice: The Special Tribunal for Lebanon Defines Terrorism' (2011) 9 *Journal of International Criminal Justice* 989, 1014.

[48] *STL Interlocutory Decision*, above n 45, para 256.

[49] Ibid, paras 253, 256.

lacked a firm basis in customary international law, arguing that unlike the ECCC, the STL's jurisdiction permitted it to consider jurisprudence and legal developments starting from the 1990s.[50] This is not a particularly convincing argument, given that the ICTY jurisprudence on JCE, including *Tadić*, relies primarily on cases decided before the temporal jurisdiction of the ECCC to establish its customary international law status.

The Appeals Chamber partially departed from ICTY jurisprudence to hold that the better approach was that JCE III should not be applied to special intent crimes such as terrorism.[51] Since the accused did not need to share the primary offender's intent for a conviction under JCE III, it would be anomalous to hold him responsible as a co-perpetrator of a special intent crime unless he possessed the requisite *dolus specialis*.[52] Thus, for special intent crimes such as terrorism, where Lebanese law would uphold a conviction on the basis of *dolus eventualis* alone, JCE III would be more favourable to the rights of the accused, and might apply in the event of a conflict between the two.[53]

The exclusion of special intent crimes from the scope of JCE III, while a welcome development in restricting the scope of JCE III, also gives rise to some contradictions. As the Appeals Chamber notes, it is anomalous to equate the perpetrator of a special intent crime with someone who simply possesses the foreseeability (and not the shared intent) for the crime. It is difficult to see why this reasoning is not equally applicable to general intent crimes, where the accused under JCE III may similarly lack the intent to commit the crime that the primary offender possesses.[54] The Chamber also assumes that special intent crimes such as terrorism and genocide can easily be distinguished from other crimes on the basis of the *dolus specialis* requirement. However, a whole host of offences in international criminal law, such as the crimes against humanity of torture and murder, the war crimes of wilfully killing or causing serious injury, and intentional attacks against civilian population or objects, may also be said to require 'special intent'.[55] The restriction of JCE III to general intent crimes may thus considerably limit its scope in a manner unintended by the Appeals Chamber, and may even result in more confusion as to which crimes fall within its scope.

[50]   Ibid, para 239, fn 360.

[51]   Ibid, para 249.

[52]   Ibid, para 248. The SCSL has since followed the STL's lead in holding that JCE III cannot be used to convict the accused for special intent crimes, since he lacks the *dolus specialis* required of the perpetrator in these cases. *Taylor Trial Judgment*, above n 13, para 468.

[53]   *STL Interlocutory Decision*, above n 45, para 262.

[54]   Gillett and Schuster, above n 47, 1016–17.

[55]   JD Ohlin, 'Joint Intentions to Commit International Crimes' (2011) 12 *Chicago Journal of International Law* 693, 711–12.

II. NEW FORMS OF COMMISSION AT THE *AD HOC* TRIBUNALS

A. Co-perpetration and Indirect Perpetration at the ICTY and ICTR

While JCE has been the most popular tool for charging commission responsibility at the ICTY, alternative doctrines of criminal liability, namely 'co-perpetration' and 'indirect perpetration', have been conspicuously championed by judges influenced by the Continental legal system, particularly the criminal law of Germany.

The first ICTY judgment to apply the theory of co-perpetration was that of the *Stakić* Trial Chamber, which held that before resorting to JCE, it would give preference to 'a more direct reference to "commission" responsibility, such as co-perpetration'.[56] The Chamber relied on German scholar Claus Roxin to define the key factor as the joint control of the perpetrators over the act. Thus, the perpetrators can realise their plan only in so far as they work together towards its accomplishment, whereas each can individually ruin the plan if he fails to carry out his part.[57] The Trial Chamber set out the physical and mental elements of co-perpetration as consisting of:

(a) an explicit agreement or tacit understanding to reach;
(b) a common goal through;
(c) co-operation; and
(d) joint control over the criminal conduct;[58]
(e) the accused's awareness of the substantial likelihood that crimes will result from co-operation ensuing from the same degree of control over the common acts; and
(f) the accused's awareness that his role is essential for the common goal's fulfilment.[59]

The *Stakić* Trial Chamber acknowledged that even though its concept of perpetration overlapped in part with the definition of JCE, the Chamber's conception was both closer to what most legal systems recognised as commission and avoided introducing modes of liability that were not contemplated in the ICTY Statute.[60] This conclusion is far from satisfactory. Not only is it entirely unclear what the Chamber meant by suggesting that co-perpetration is a more direct mode of responsibility as compared to JCE, it also fails to clarify the relationship between co-perpetration and

---

[56] *Prosecutor v Stakić*, No IT-97-24-T, Trial Chamber Judgment (31 July 2003) ('*Stakić Trial Judgment*') para 438.
[57] Ibid, para 440.
[58] Ibid.
[59] Ibid, para 442.
[60] Ibid, paras 440–41 and fnn 945–49.

JCE.[61] Additionally, the breadth of sources relied on by the Chamber leaves much to be desired.[62]

It is thus not altogether surprising that *Stakić*'s parsimonious account of co-perpetration led to the confused indictment in *Milutinović*, where the prosecution argued that under the concept of *indirect co-perpetration* in *Stakić*, an accused will be liable 'if he has an agreement with others, plays a key role in the agreement and one or more participants used others to carry out crimes'.[63] The *Milutinović* Trial Chamber rejected this mode of responsibility, holding that the source cited by the *Stakić* Trial Chamber (Roxin) did not support its definition of the physical elements, and that it could not find any evidence for these elements in customary international law.[64] Further, neither Roxin nor *Stakić* made mention of participants to the agreement using individuals outside the agreement to commit the crimes.[65] Given that the prosecution put forward an entirely different form of perpetration responsibility than the one accepted in *Stakić*, albeit one that is endorsed by the control theory and by Roxin, the *Milutinović* Trial Chamber rightly did not find its claim supportable by *Stakić*. On the same day, the *Stakić* Appeals Chamber set aside the portions of the *Stakić* Trial Chamber's decision dealing with co-perpetration on the ground that the latter lacked support in customary international law and in ICTY jurisprudence.[66]

Judge Schomburg sought to remedy some of the problematic aspects of *Stakić* in his Separate Opinion in the *Gacumbitsi Appeals Judgment*. He reiterated the core physical elements of co-perpetration set out in *Stakić*, while relying not only on Roxin, but also on the penal codes of Colombia, Paraguay and Finland in support of these elements.[67] He also put forward indirect perpetration or perpetration by means as a distinct mode of responsibility that was well established in several legal systems around the world.[68] In order to be liable for indirect perpetration, the accused

---

[61] JCE I has been likened to co-perpetration by the ICTY as well as in academic literature: *Prosecutor v Tadić*, No IT-94-1-A, Appeals Chamber Judgment (15 July 1999) ('*Tadić Appeals Judgment*') paras 198, 201; *Prosecutor v Babic*, No IT-03-72, Appeals Chamber Judgment on Sentencing Appeals (18 July 2005) para 38; K Ambos, 'Joint Criminal Enterprise and Command Responsibility' (2007) 5 *Journal of International Criminal Justice* 159, 170.

[62] The Chamber cited Claus Roxin almost exclusively in support of the elements of the doctrine. See *Stakić Trial Judgment*, above n 56, para 441 and fn 950.

[63] *Prosecutor v Milutinović*, No IT-05-87-PT, Trial Chamber Decision on Ojdanić's Motion Challenging Jurisdiction (22 March 2006) para 7.

[64] On this point, see also *Prosecutor v Gacumbitsi*, No ICTR-2001-64-A, Appeals Chamber Judgment (7 July 2006) ('*Gacumbitsi Appeals Judgment*'), Separate Opinion of Judge Shahabuddeen, para 51.

[65] *Milutinović*, above n 63, paras 37, 39, 40–42.

[66] *Prosecutor v Stakić*, No IT-97-24-A, Appeals Chamber Judgment (22 March 2006) ('*Stakić Appeals Judgment*') paras 62–63.

[67] *Gacumbitsi Appeals Judgment*, above n 64, Separate Opinion of Judge Schomburg, para 17 and fn 29.

[68] Ibid, Separate Opinion of Judge Schomburg, fn 30 and paras 18–21.

must have used the physical perpetrator of the crime as a mere instrument for the commission of the crime. The attribution of criminal liability was based on the accused's control over the conduct and the will of the physical perpetrator.[69]

Judge Schomburg concluded that indirect perpetration was particularly apposite as a theory of international criminal responsibility, as it served to bridge the gap between the crime and individuals who should be considered the main perpetrators due to their involvement in and control over the crimes.[70] This had also been recognised in Article 25(3)(a) of the Rome Statute establishing the International Criminal Court, which provided for liability through co-perpetration as well as indirect perpetration.[71] Judge Schomburg acknowledged that these modes of liability overlapped to a great extent with JCE, the main difference consisting in the key element of attribution: while JCE is based primarily on the common state of mind of the perpetrators (subjective criterion), co-perpetration and indirect perpetration also depend on whether the perpetrator exercises control over the criminal act (objective criterion).[72] He suggested that these doctrines should be harmonised in the jurisprudence of the *ad hoc* tribunals better to reflect the notion of 'commission' in different national legal systems.[73]

In yet another Separate Opinion in *Milan Martić*,[74] Judge Schomburg pushed for the acceptance of co-perpetration as a mode of responsibility for international crimes, arguing that it reflected the accused's true position as a high-ranking principal perpetrator. In contrast, JCE trivialised his guilt by holding him guilty as a mere member of a criminal group.[75] Under JCE, the individual's criminal liability was derived from his group membership, which was counterproductive for the ICTY's mandate of achieving peace and reconciliation.[76] Category JCE III especially lacked specificity and any objective criteria for imposition of criminal responsibility.[77]

---

[69] Ibid, Separate Opinion of Judge Schomburg, para 18, citing C Roxin, *Täterschaft und Tatherrschaft*, 8th edn (Berlin, de Gruyter Recht, 2006) 142–274 and K Ambos, 'Individual Criminal Responsibility' in O Triffterer (ed), *Commentary on the Rome Statute of the International Criminal Court*, 2nd edn (Baden-Baden, Nomos, 1999) 743, marginal note 9.

[70] *Gacumbitsi Appeals Judgment*, above n 64, Separate Opinion of Judge Schomburg, para 21.

[71] For this, he also cited the observations of the ICC Pre-Trial Chamber I interpreting Art 25(3). See *Prosecutor v Thomas Lubanga Dyilo*, Decision Concerning Pre-Trial Chamber I's Decision of 10 February 2006 and the Incorporation of Documents into the Record of the Case against Mr Thomas Lubanga Dyilo, ICC-01/04-01/06, 24 February 2006, Annex I: Decision on the Prosecutor's Application for a Warrant of Arrest, Art 58, para 96.

[72] *Gacumbitsi Appeals Judgment*, above n 64, Separate Opinion of Judge Schomburg, para 22 and fn 41.

[73] Ibid, Separate Opinion of Judge Schomburg, paras 22, 24.

[74] *Prosecutor v Milan Martić*, No IT-95-11-A, Appeals Chamber Judgment (8 October 2008) ('*Martić Appeals Judgment*').

[75] Ibid, Separate Opinion of Judge Schomburg, para 2.

[76] Ibid, Separate Opinion of Judge Schomburg, para 5.

[77] Ibid, Separate Opinion of Judge Schomburg, paras 3, 7 and 9.

These attempts to introduce the doctrines of co-perpetration and indi-rect perpetration into ICTY jurisprudence, however, failed to dethrone JCE as the preferred mode of commission liability at the *ad hoc* tribunals. Part of the reason for this is that, *Gacumbitsi* notwithstanding, the opin-ions lack any detailed examination of the elements of these doctrines. While the physical elements that must be present to constitute these modes of liability are relatively precise, the mental elements are quite ambiguous. For instance, the *Stakić* Trial Chamber's holding that the accused must be aware of the substantial likelihood that crimes will occur is scarcely sufficient to establish responsibility for special intent crimes such as genocide. It is also unclear whether each of the accused charged as co-perpetrators should share the relevant mental state, or whether only a specific defendant's state of mind is in question.[78] Moreover, the opinions do not succeed in clarifying the distinction between the doctrines of co-perpetration and indirect perpetration. Thus, an international criminal lawyer unacquainted with the doctrines' background in German criminal law would be hard pressed to be able to distinguish between the two.

B. Commission Through 'Integral' Participation at the ICTR and ICTY

Yet another attempt to widen the concept of 'commission' beyond physi-cal perpetration of the crime has emerged primarily in ICTR case law. In *Gacumbitsi*, the Appeals Chamber held that in the context of the crime of genocide, conduct other than physical killings could be considered 'direct' participation in the *actus reus*.[79] The accused was present at Nyarubuye Parish, and directed and supervised the massacre by separating the Tutsi refugees so that they could be killed. His action was 'as much an integral part of the genocide as were the killings which it enabled',[80] and could not be adequately captured by the modes of 'ordering' or 'instigation'.[81] Judge Guney filed a strong dissent, challenging the majority's creation of an entirely new form of commission beyond physical perpetration and JCE,[82] and arguing that the accused's actions could easily have been analysed through the lens of JCE.[83]

While *Gacumbitsi* was confined to the crime of genocide, in *Seromba* the ICTR applied the new form of commission to both genocide and extermina-

---

[78] For a similar point, see ME Badar, '"Just Convict Everyone!" – Joint Perpetration: From *Tadić* to *Stakić* and Back Again' (2006) 6 *International Criminal Law Review* 293, 297.

[79] *Gacumbitsi Appeals Judgment*, above n 64, para 60; see also *Prosecutor v Rukundo*, No ICTR-2001-7-T, Trial Chamber II Judgment (27 February 2009) paras 562–63; *Prosecutor v Kalimanzira*, No ICTR-05-88-A, Appeals Chamber Judgment (20 October 2010) para 219.

[80] *Gacumbitsi Appeals Judgment*, above n 64, paras 60–61.

[81] Ibid, para 61.

[82] *Gacumbitsi Appeals Judgment*, above n 64, Dissenting Opinion of Judge Guney, paras 3–6.

[83] Ibid, Dissenting Opinion of Judge Guney, para 7.

tion as a crime against humanity.[84] It applied the standard of whether Seromba's actions were 'as much an integral part of the genocide as were the killings which [they] enabled', and whether Seromba had approved and embraced as his own the decision to commit the crime.[85] The Chamber found that Seromba had accepted the decision of the communal authorities to destroy the Nyange church, resulting in the death of 1,500 Tutsi refugees. He had also encouraged the bulldozer driver to destroy the church, going so far as to point out its weak side.[86] It was irrelevant that Seromba had not physically driven the bulldozer, since he exercised complete influence over the driver who accepted Seroma as the only authority.[87] Seromba's actions were thus an integral part of the genocide and his responsibility was that of a perpetrator of the crime.[88]

In Judge Liu's dissent, he distinguished between the nature and degree of involvement of the accused in *Gacumbitsi* and *Seromba*; unlike Gacumbitsi, Seromba had not actively directed or supervised the massacre.[89] Judge Liu criticised the majority for applying a form of 'commission' without specifying the criteria for this approach. Indeed, this novel form of participation partially resembled various other modes of liability, including JCE, co-perpetration and indirect perpetration, without fully satisfying the conditions for any of them.[90] The elements of the new form of commission were also vague and unsupported by existing jurisprudence. Any act, including one that aided and abetted the commission of the offence, could technically be considered an 'integral' part of the crime. The judgment also failed to clarify whether the determination that Seromba approved and embraced as his own the decision to destroy the church was based on the cumulative effect of all his actions, or on his individual acts in directing the driver.[91]

Subsequent ICTR judgments reveal the problems in applying a vague 'integral role' standard to distinguish between perpetration and accessorial responsibility. The *Munyakazi* Trial Chamber convicted Munyakazi for committing genocide on the basis of his active involvement in the attacks on Shangi and Mibilizi parishes, resulting in the deaths of Tutsi refugees.[92]

---

[84] *Prosecutor v Seromba*, No ICTR-2001-66-A, Appeals Chamber Judgment (12 March 2008) ('*Seromba Appeals Judgment*') paras 161, 190.

[85] Ibid, para 161; see also *Prosecutor v Munyakazi*, No ICTR-97-36A-T, Trial Chamber I Judgment (5 July 2010) para 430.

[86] *Seromba Appeals Judgment*, above n 84, paras 164–70.

[87] Ibid, para 171.

[88] Ibid.

[89] Ibid, Dissenting Opinion of Judge Liu, paras 4–5.

[90] Ibid, Dissenting Opinion of Judge Liu, paras 6–8.

[91] Ibid, Dissenting Opinion of Judge Liu, paras 14–15. Badar and Karsten argue that it is the mental element of approval and embracing the act that distinguishes this form of commission liability from aiding and abetting. See ME Badar and N Karsten, 'Current Developments at the International Criminal Tribunals (2008)' (2009) 9 *International Criminal Law Review* 227, 233.

[92] *Prosecutor v Munyakazi*, No ICTR-97-36A-T, Trial Chamber I Judgment (5 July 2010) ('*Munyakazi Trial Judgment*') paras 491, 496.

Though it could not establish that Munyakazi had personally committed any of the killings,[93] the Chamber based his responsibility on his leadership position at the crimes sites, where he had led the assailants, issued instructions and supervised key aspects of the crimes.[94]

In contrast, in *Kalimanzira*, the Appeals Chamber rejected the prosecution's argument that the accused should be responsible for commission rather than aiding and abetting. Kalimanzira had lured Tutsi refugees to Kabuye Hill, provided armed reinforcements for the attack on them and possessed the genocidal intent.[95] Nonetheless, he did not supervise and direct the killings, and his actions were better characterised as aiding and abetting the genocide.[96] It is difficult to reconcile this decision with the court's earlier holding in *Ndindabahizi*, where it convicted the accused for having 'committed' the crime of extermination.[97] Ndindabahizi's acts were fairly similar to those of Kalimanzira – he had contributed to creating the conditions for the killings of Tutsis on Gitwa Hill by distributing weapons and transporting and urging attackers, thus implying his official approval of the attack.[98]

One way to limit the integral role criterion is to adopt the narrower application in *Gacumbitsi* and *Munyakazi*, where the accused actually directs or supervises the crimes and his authority and influence over the perpetrators contributes significantly to their commission.[99] This stricter interpretation, however, resembles indirect co-perpetration in *Stakić*, without having the criterion of control as an anchoring device.[100]

As the *ad hoc* tribunals near the end of their life, it is unlikely that they will radically alter their jurisprudence on commission responsibility to adopt indirect perpetration and co-perpetration directly as distinct modes of participation. However, as the following chapter demonstrates, these doctrines have acquired increasing importance in international criminal law with their incorporation into the jurisprudence of the ICC.

---

[93]   Ibid, para 491.

[94]   Ibid, paras 134, 365, 366, 376, 380, 386, 387, 416, 417, 422, 423, 491, 496; *Prosecutor v Munyakazi*, No ICTR-97-36A-A, Appeals Chamber Judgment (28 September 2011) para 136.

[95]   *Prosecutor v Kalimanzira*, No ICTR-05-88-A, Appeals Chamber Judgment (20 October 2010) ('*Kalimanzira Appeals Judgment*') paras 219–20.

[96]   Ibid.

[97]   *Prosecutor v Ndindabahizi*, No ICTR-2001-71-I, Trial Chamber I Judgment (15 July 2004) para 485.

[98]   Ibid.

[99]   This is also the case in ICTY jurisprudence which adopts the new form of commission. See *Prosecutor v Lukić and Lukić*, No IT-98-32/1-T, Trial Chamber III Judgment (20 July 2009) paras 898, 908–09 (convicting the accused for commission of murder)

[100]   On the similarity between the concept of commission in *Gacumbitsi* and *Munyakazi* on the one hand and indirect co-perpetration and co-perpetration on the other, see B Goy, 'Individual Criminal Responsibility before the International Criminal Court: A Comparison with the *ad hoc* Tribunals (2012) 12 *International Criminal Law Review* 1, 37; FZ Giustiniani, 'Stretching the Bounds of Commission Liability: The ICTR Appeal Judgment in *Seromba*' (2008) 6 *Journal of International Criminal Justice* 783, 795.

5

'Perpetration' at the International Criminal Court

I. THE ROME STATUTE AND MODES OF PARTICIPATION

I N CONTRAST TO the Statutes of the *ad hoc* tribunals, the Rome Statute of the International Criminal Court (ICC) contains a detailed provision on modes of criminal responsibility. Article 25(3) of the Rome Statute, in relevant part, states:

3. In accordance with this Statute, a person shall be criminally responsible and liable for punishment for a crime within the jurisdiction of the Court if that person:

(a) Commits such a crime, whether as an individual, jointly with another or through another person, regardless of whether that other person is criminally responsible;

(b) Orders, solicits or induces the commission of such a crime which in fact occurs or is attempted;

(c) For the purpose of facilitating the commission of such a crime, aids, abets or otherwise assists in its commission or its attempted commission, including providing the means for its commission;

(d) In any other way contributes to the commission or attempted commission of such a crime by a group of persons acting with a common purpose. Such contribution shall be intentional and shall either:

(i) Be made with the aim of furthering the criminal activity or criminal purpose of the group, where such activity or purpose involves the commission of a crime within the jurisdiction of the Court; or

(ii) Be made in the knowledge of the intention of the group to commit the crime . . .

Article 25(3) represents an amalgam of various modes of participation based on a number of domestic and international sources. Paragraph (a) on 'commission' draws on German criminal law;[1] paragraphs (b) and (c)

---

[1] Jessberger and Geneuss note that given that the Rome Statute represents the first instance where indirect perpetration was explicitly recognised in an international criminal law instrument, it is surprising that there was little debate preceding its inclusion, precluding reliance on the *travaux préparatoires* as a guide to interpretation of Art 25(3). What is clear, though, from the express wording of Art 25(3)(a), is that it recognises criminal responsibility for the acts of an

on various forms of accessorial responsibility are inspired by international treaty law and domestic criminal law; the text of paragraph (d) on contribution to a common purpose is taken from Article 2(3)(c) of the 1997 International Convention for the Suppression of Terrorist Bombing, and resembles joint enterprise liability in English common law.[2]

The first decision of the ICC Pre-Trial Chamber on modes of liability[3] came in the wake of intense speculation over what form of commission responsibility is included under Article 25(3). In *Lubanga*, the Pre-Trial Chamber noted different approaches – objective, subjective and 'control' – to distinguish between parties to a crime. Article 25(3) provided for responsibility for the acts of an 'innocent agent', and was thus incompatible with the objective approach where the perpetrator must physically contribute to an objective element of the crime.[4] The subjective approach required the perpetrators to share the common intent to commit the crime, regardless of the extent of their contribution to its commission. This approach resembled JCE liability, and was encompassed by Article 25(3) (d) as a *residual form of accessory liability* which was not covered under concepts such as ordering, soliciting, aiding and abetting.[5] In contrast, the third approach of 'control' over the crime was expressly included in the provision of liability for indirect perpetration in Article 25(3)(a) of the Rome Statute.[6] The notion of 'co-perpetration' in the same Article must therefore cohere with this criterion for differentiating between principals and accessories.[7] Thus, only persons who had control over the crime by virtue of the essential tasks assigned to them for the commission of the crime, and who were aware of having such control, could be considered joint or co-perpetrators.[8]

agent, irrespective of whether the agent himself is culpable or innocent (eg, when he is a minor). See F Jessberger and J Geneuss, 'On the Application of a Theory of Indirect Perpetration in *Al Bashir*: German Doctrine at the Hague?' (2008) 6 *Journal of International Criminal Justice* 853, 857.

[2] E van Sliedregt, *Individual Criminal Responsibility in International Law* (Oxford, Oxford University Press, 2012) 64–65.

[3] *Prosecutor v Lubanga*, Decision on the Confirmation of Charges, No ICC-01/04-01/06, ICC Pre-Trial Chamber I (29 January 2007) ('*Lubanga Confirmation of Charges*').

[4] Ibid, paras 328, 333.

[5] Ibid, paras 329, 334–38.

[6] Ibid, paras 328–35, 338–39.

[7] Ibid, paras 331–32, 349–50.

[8] Ibid, paras 330–32, 341. The Pre-Trial Chamber has since endorsed the 'control' theory in a series of decisions dealing with the confirmation of charges against the accused. See, eg, *Prosecutor v Bemba Gombo*, No ICC-01/05-01/08, Decision Pursuant to Article 61(7)(a) and (b) of the Rome Statute on the Charges of the Prosecutor Against Jean-Pierre Bemba Gombo, Pre-Trial Chamber I (15 June 2009) para 349; *Prosecutor v Abu Garda*, No ICC-02/05-02/09, Corrigendum of the Decision on the Confirmation of Charges, Pre-Trial Chamber I (8 February 2010) para 152; *Prosecutor v Abdallan Banda and Saleh Jerbo*, No ICC-02/05-03/09, Corrigendum of the Decision on the Confirmation of Charges, Pre-Trial Chamber I (7 March 2011) para 126; *Prosecutor v Ruto, Kosgey and Sang*, No ICC-01/09-01/11, Decision of the Confirmation of Charges Pursuant to Article 61(7)(a) and (b) of the Rome Statute, Pre-Trial

The Pre-Trial Chamber thus set out a distinctive approach to modes of participation through the invocation of different approaches to parties to a crime: it used the 'control theory' as the doctrinal basis not only for paragraph (a), but also for the entire scheme of liability under Article 25; further, it embraced a clear division between principal and accessorial modes of participation, and put JCE, which it likened to common purpose liability under paragraph (d), in the latter category.[9] As van Sliedregt notes, the drafting history of Article 25(3) suggests no such single coherent doctrinal grounding for the modes of liability as a whole. It is also questionable whether the terms of the Statute embrace any hierarchical ordering of participation, where 'accessorial modes of liability' in paragraphs (b)–(d) are deemed less serious than commission responsibility under paragraph (a).[10]

The ICC has nonetheless upheld the proposition that the modes of liability in Article 25(3) are arranged according to a 'value oriented hierarchy of participation in a crime', and control over the crime decreases with each paragraph.[11] Article 25(3)(d) has thus been interpreted as a residual form of secondary responsibility, which comes into play when the accused's contributions cannot be encapsulated within paragraphs (a)–(c).[12] In order to be liable under Article 25(3)(d), the following elements must be present:

(a) a crime within the Court's jurisdiction is committed or attempted;
(b) a group of persons acting with a common purpose committed or attempted to commit this crime; and
(c) the individual contributed to the crime in any way other than those set out in Article 25(3)(a)–(c) of the Statute;
(d) the contribution was intentional; and
(e) the contribution was made either with the aim of furthering the group's criminal activity or purpose, or in the knowledge of the group's intention to commit the crime.[13]

While Article 25(3)(d) states only that the accused must contribute in 'any other way', in the *Mbarushimana* arrest warrant decision, the Pre-Trial Chamber held that contributions must reach a certain threshold of significance for liability, lest every person who is a member of a community, such as a grocer or utility provider, and who contributes an infinitesimal amount

---

Chamber II (23 January 2012) para 291; *Prosecutor v Muthaura, Kenyatta and Ali*, No ICC-01/09-02/11, Decision of the Confirmation of Charges Pursuant to Article 61(7)(a) and (b) of the Rome Statute, Pre-Trial Chamber II (23 January 2012) para 296.

[9] Van Sliedregt, above n 2, 84–85.

[10] Ibid, 85–86; JD Ohlin, E van Sliedregt and T Weigend, 'Assessing the Control-Theory' (2013) 26 *Leiden Journal of International Law* 725, 744–45.

[11] *Prosecutor v Callixte Mbarushimana*, No ICC-01/04-01/10, Decision of the Confirmation of Charges, Pre-Trial Chamber II (16 December 2011) para 279.

[12] Ibid, para 278; *Ruto, Kosgey and Sang*, above n 8, para 354.

[13] *Ruto, Kosgey and Sang*, above n 8, para 351.

to the criminal activity, becomes responsible.[14] Relying on the *ad hoc* tribunals' jurisprudence on JCE, the Chamber held that the contribution to the commission of a crime by a group acting with a common purpose must be at least significant. The significance of the contribution is to be assessed on a case-by-case basis, depending on the nature of the accused's conduct and the context of the crime.[15] Even contributions made to the crime after it has been committed may count as significant if the group and the accused agreed upon them prior to the crime's commission.[16]

The *mens rea* requirements under Article 25(3)(d) have posed some difficulty in interpetration.[17] According to the Pre-Trial Chamber, the element of 'intentional' contribution to the commission or attempted commission of the crime should be interpreted in light of the definition of 'intent' in Article 30, and separately from the two-pronged requirements under Article 25(3)(d)(i) and (ii), to save them from redundancy.[18] The accused should therefore act intentionally, that is, he should mean to engage in the conduct that contributes to the crime, and with the awareness that it contributes to the activities of the group. In addition, the contribution should be made either with the aim of furthering the group's criminal activity or purpose, or in the knowledge of the group's intention to commit the crime. It is thus not necessary that the accused possesses the intent to commit any specific crime.[19]

The relationship between Article 25(3)(d) and JCE remains unclear.[20] The Pre-Trial Chamber has noted that while both JCE and Article 25(3)(d)

---

[14] *Mbarushimana*, above n 11, paras 276–77. See JD Ohlin, 'Three Conceptual Problems with the Doctrine of Joint Criminal Enterprise' (2007) 5 *Journal of International Criminal Justice* 69, 78–80 (identifying the problem of minor contributions being captured by Art 25(3)(d), based on the wording of the paragraph. However, Ohlin does not seem to consider Art 25(3) (d) as accessorial in nature, since he goes on to argue that this provision makes equally liable the person who makes the greatest contribution as well as the person who makes the smallest contribution to the criminal enterprise. Arguably, the first category of persons would be charged under Art 25(3)(a) rather than Art 25(3)(d)).

[15] *Mbarushimana*, above n 11, paras 283–85. See also *Ruto, Kosgey and Sang*, above n 8, para 354 (holding that there is no requirement for a 'substantial' contribution under Art 25(3)(d)).

[16] *Mbarushimana*, above n 11, para 287.

[17] B Goy, 'Individual Criminal Responsibility before the International Criminal Court: A Comparison with the *Ad Hoc* Tribunals (2012) 12 *International Criminal Law Review* 1, 67–70; K Ambos, 'Individual Criminal Responsibility' in O Triffterer (ed), *Commentary on the Rome Statute of the International Criminal Court*, 2nd edn (Baden-Baden, Nomos, 1999) 743, 762. Clark argues that despite the difference in the literal drafting of the two mental states in Art 25(3)(d), the drafters perhaps did not really intend different results, or else these offences may be of different gravity. See RS Clark, 'Drafting a General Part to a Penal Code: Some Thoughts Inspired by the Negotiations on the Rome Statute of the International Criminal Court and by the Court's First Substantive Law Discussion in the *Lubanga Dyilo* Confirmation Proceedings' (2008) 19 *Criminal Law Forum* 519, 548.

[18] *Mbarushimana*, above n 11, para 288.

[19] Ibid, paras 288–89.

[20] Several commentators have previously grappled with fitting JCE into the structure of Art 25. See, eg, Jessberger and Geneuss, above n 1, 865 (predicting that the ICC may be willing to interpret accessory liability under Art 25(3)(d) as a 'little cousin' of JCE); T Weigend,

contemplate actions that are performed pursuant to a common plan, and require contributions that are less substantial than those needed for liability for aiding and abetting, they are also sufficiently dissimilar doctrines.[21] For instance, the accused need not be a member of the group acting with the common purpose to be liable under Article 25(3)(d),[22] whereas JCE liability is contingent on group membership. It is also difficult to accommodate JCE III within the structure of Article 25(3)(d), as the threshold *mens rea* requirement of knowledge is already higher than JCE III's acceptance of *dolus eventualis*.[23]

II. THE ICC'S JURISPRUDENCE ON PERPETRATION

The ICC has developed a rich and complex jurisprudence on the concept of perpetration under Article 25(3)(a) that is distinct from the *ad hoc* tribunals' jurisprudence on commission responsibility, and that includes the doctrines of co-perpetration and indirect perpetration.

A. Indirect Perpetration and Co-perpetration

The ICC first specified the objective and subjective elements of co-perpetration in the *Lubanga Decision on Confirmation of Charges*, and these have formed a template for subsequent iterations of the elements by the Pre-Trial Chamber. The objective elements consist of, first, an agreement or a common plan between two or more persons. This plan may be implicit and should include an element of criminality, even though

---

'Intent, Mistake of Law and Co-Perpetration in the *Lubanga* Decision on Confirmation of Charges' (2008) 6 *Journal of International Criminal Justice* 471, 478 (remarking that Art 25(3)(d) 'cracks open the door' on JCE); L Engvall, 'The Future of Extended Joint Criminal Enterprise – Will the ICTY's innovation meet the standards of the ICC?' (2007) 76 *Nordic Journal of International Law* 241, 258 (arguing that JCE may be split between para (a) and para (d) of Art 25). See generally, V Militello, 'The Personal Nature of Individual Criminal Responsibility and the ICC Statute' (2007) 5 *Journal of International Criminal Justice* 941, 949–51; Goy, above n 17, 69–70; van Sliedregt, above n 2, 146.

[21] *Mbarushimana*, above n 11, para 282.

[22] Ibid, 272–75.

[23] K Ambos, 'Joint Criminal Enterprise and Command Responsibility' (2007) 5 *Journal of International Criminal Justice* 159, 172–73; van Sliedregt, above n 2, 146. There is nonetheless some academic support for Art 25(3)(d) being accorded an expansive interpretation to include JCE III situations. See A Cassese, 'The Proper Limits of Individual Responsibility under the Doctrine of Joint Criminal Enterprise' (2007) 5 *Journal of International Criminal Justice* 109, 132 (suggesting that 'knowledge' could include 'foresight' and 'voluntary taking of risk' of a criminal action by members of the criminal group); Ohlin, above n 14, 85 (noting that it is plausible to argue that if the accused makes a contribution with the aim of furthering the *criminal purpose* of the group, it is certainly possible that he was unaware of the conduct with which he is charged but could have foreseen its possibility).

it need not be directed specifically at the commission of a crime.[24] The second required objective element is co-ordinated essential contribution by each perpetrator resulting in the realisation of the objective elements of the crime. This contribution is not limited to the execution stage and may be at any stage of the crime.[25] The Pre-Trial Chamber has identified essential contributions to include activating mechanisms by leaders that lead to automatic compliance with their orders and the commission of the crime, such as designing an attack, and providing institutional, financial and logistical support.[26]

While there has been little dispute about the objective elements required for co-perpetration in the jurisprudence of the ICC, the manner in which some of the elements have been fleshed out, in particular in the Trial Chamber's first-ever judgment in the *Lubanga* case,[27] gives rise to some concerns. Lubanga was the founder and leader of the Forces Patriotiques pour la Libération du Congo (FPLC), the military wing of a political group in the Democratic Republic of Congo (DRC) called the Union of Congolese Patriots (UPC). The organisation's goal was to gain control over the Ituri district in the DRC, for the purpose of which Lubanga and his co-perpetrators built an army that included child soldiers.[28] Lubanga was convicted as a co-perpetrator under Article 25(3)(a) for the crime of using, conscripting or enlisting children.[29] The Trial Chamber drew heavily on the Pre-Trial Chamber's jurisprudence while detailing the elements of co-perpetration liability. It broadly concurred with the Pre-Trial Chamber's analysis of the objective elements required for co-perpetration, while adding that though it was not essential for the common plan to be intrinsically criminal, it must include an element of criminality, that is, its implementation should embody 'a sufficient risk that, if events follow the

[24] *Lubanga Confirmation of Charges*, above n 3, paras 343–45; *Prosecutor v Germain Katanga and Mathieu Ngudjolo Chui*, No ICC-01/04-01/07, Pre-Trial Decision on the Confirmation of Charges (30 September 2008) paras 522–23; *Muthaura, Kenyatta and Ali*, above n 8, paras 399–400; *Banda and Jerbo*, above n 8, paras 129–35; *Ruto, Kosgey and Sang*, above n 8, paras 301–04; *Abu Garda*, above n 8, paras 160, 163–232.

[25] *Lubanga Confirmation of Charges*, above n 3, paras 346–48; *Katanga and Ngudjolo*, above n 24, paras 524–26; *Muthaura, Kenyatta and Ali*, above n 8, paras 401–06; *Banda and Jerbo*, above n 8, paras 136–49; *Ruto, Kosgey and Sang*, above n 8, paras 305–12; *Abu Garda*, above n 8, paras 160, 180–232.

[26] See, eg *Katanga and Ngudjolo*, above n 24, paras 524–26 (giving examples of essential contribution as activating mechanisms by leaders that lead to automatic compliance with their orders, including designing an attack, supplying ammunition and co-ordinating the activities of troops); *Muthaura, Kenyatta and Ali*, above n 8, paras 401–06 (stating that the contribution was essential, since in the absence of activating mechanisms by the accused which included giving orders for the commission of the crimes, and institutional, financial and logistical support, the common plan to commit the crimes would have been frustrated).

[27] *Prosecutor v Thomas Lubanga Dyilo*, No ICC-01/04-01/06, Trial Chamber I Judgment (14 March 2012) ('*Lubanga Judgment*').

[28] Ibid, paras 1136, 1351–56.

[29] Rome Statute of the International Criminal Court, 17 July 1998, UN Doc A/Conf 183/9*, 2187 UNTS 90 (*entered into force 1 July 2002*), Art 8(2)(e)(vii).

ordinary course, a crime will be committed'.[30] As Ambos argues, this is an unnecessarily confused formulation which does not sufficiently exclude the possibility of a plan that is predominantly non-criminal and that does not necessarily include a concrete crime.[31] The Chamber also vacillates between an objective and a subjective risk requirement. Initially, it emphasises that under Article 30 of the Rome Statute, which defines intent, the co-perpetrators must be (subjectively) aware of the risk that the implementation of the plan will result in the crime.[32] This is undoubtedly the correct approach, but is diluted in subsequent formulations where it is replaced by the (objective) requirement that the plan's implementation 'will result in the commission of the relevant crime in the ordinary course of events'.[33]

The Trial Chamber also affirmed the second objective element of co-ordinated essential contribution by the co-perpetrators.[34] Some Pre-Trial Chambers have defined an essential contribution such that the accused's failure to carry it out would result in the frustration of the execution of the crime.[35] While the Trial Chamber did not formally adopt this standard, it seemed to have used it in its factual assessment of Lubanga's responsibility.[36] The Trial Chamber nonetheless failed adequately to consider a crucial ambiguity in the Pre-Trial Chamber's Confirmation Decision. In the Pre-Trial Chamber, since there was no direct evidence that Lubanga was involved in the recruitment of child soldiers, the Chamber based his responsibility for this crime on his 'essential role' in the common plan between him and some leaders of the FPLC to broaden the base of their army.[37] The Pre-Trial Chamber held that the implementation of this plan, which targeted young recruits, entailed the objective risk that children under 15 years of age would be recruited.[38] Lubanga's key role in the overall co-ordination of the FPLC demonstrated that he had joint control

---

[30] *Lubanga Judgment*, above n 27, paras 984–87.

[31] K Ambos, 'The First Judgment of the International Criminal Court (*Prosecutor v Lubanga*): A Comprehensive Analysis of the Legal Issues' (2012) 12 *International Criminal Law Review* 115, 139–40.

[32] *Lubanga Judgment*, above n 27, para 986.

[33] Ibid, paras 1018, 1136. Indeed, Wirth argues that the Chamber replaces the subjective risk requirement with an objective one. See S Wirth, 'Co-Perpetration in the Lubanga Trial Judgment' (2012) 10 *Journal of International Criminal Justice* 971, 986.

[34] *Lubanga Judgment*, above n 27, paras 999–1000, 1003–05.

[35] See, eg *Lubanga Confirmation of Charges*, above n 3, paras 342, 347; *Katanga and Ngudjolo*, above n 24, para 525; *Muthaura, Kenyatta and Ali*, above n 8, para 404; *Ruto, Kosgey and Sang*, above n 8, paras 301–04; *Abu Garda*, above n 8, paras 163–232; *Banda and Jerbo*, above n 8, paras 126, 136.

[36] Wirth, above n 33, 987 (arguing that the standard of the power to frustrate the commission of the crime should be rejected, as the word 'crime' is ambiguous). With respect, this author disagrees, since its absence would weaken significantly the basis for mutual attribution of the physical acts to the co-perpetrators.

[37] See *Lubanga Confirmation of Charges*, above n 3, para 377.

[38] Ibid.

as a co-perpetrator over the implementation of the plan.[39] This part of the decision has been criticised on the basis that Lubanga's key role in the leadership of the FPLC and its activities does not support the inference that his contribution was essential for the specific crime of the recruitment of child soldiers.[40] The criticism is certainly valid and stems from the Pre-Trial Chamber's failure to clarify what it deems as the object of essential contribution – that is, the specific crime or the common plan.

The Trial Chamber simply stated that the accused must have provided an 'essential contribution to the common plan that resulted in the commission of the relevant crime'.[41] In its factual assessment of Lubanga's responsibility, the Chamber determined that as President and Commander-in-Chief of the FPLC/UPC, Lubanga played an essential role in the organisation. He had ultimate control over military matters, and played a key role in planning military operations and providing logistical support.[42] However, while the Chamber was persuaded that Lubanga was actively involved in the recruitment of troops for the military operations, it could not establish that he personally recruited children. Nonetheless, it was certain that he was informed of children being recruited, and condoned the policy and played an active role in its implementation.[43] He visited the Rwampara recruitment camp, where he witnessed and addressed recruits below 15 years of age.[44] Along with other UPC officials, he also employed children as bodyguards and security escorts.[45] Thus, Lubanga's position within the FPLC/UPC, his authority over the co-perpetrators who were involved with the day-to-day recruitment operations, combined with his active involvement in rallies and visits to recruit troops, and his personal guard which included child soldiers, demonstrated the essential nature of his contribution to the common plan.[46] The Chamber concluded that all this evidence proved that Lubanga and his co-perpetrator made co-ordinated essential contributions to the common plan which resulted in the recruitment and use of child soldiers.[47]

The Trial Chamber, like the Pre-Trial Chamber, fails to resolve the ambiguity of the object of the essential contribution. A strict construction of 'essential contribution to the common plan that resulted in the commission of the relevant crime' would entail that the accused's contribution need not be essential for the crime itself. The factual assessment by the Chamber devotes more attention to Lubanga's essential overall role in the

[39] Ibid, paras 383, 398.
[40] See Weigend, above n 20, 486–87.
[41] *Lubanga Judgment*, above n 27, paras 1006, 1018
[42] Ibid, paras 1169, 1222.
[43] Ibid, para 1234.
[44] Ibid, para 1245.
[45] Ibid, para 1262.
[46] Ibid, para 1270.
[47] Ibid, para 1271.

UPC/FPLC and does not emphasise sufficiently how it was in addition essential to the recruitment of the child soldiers, which should have formed the main focus of the analysis.

The subjective elements of co-perpetration were also first laid down in the Pre-Trial Chamber's *Lubanga* decision, but there has been a significant amount of controversy about the requirements in subsequent decisions. According to the *Lubanga* Pre-Trial Chamber, the first subjective element is the accused's fulfilment of all subjective elements of the crime with which he is charged, including the specific intent for crimes such as genocide. For most crimes under the jurisdiction of the ICC, this would mean meeting the 'intent' and 'knowledge' requirements in Article 30(1) of the Rome Statute.[48] The second subjective element is that all co-perpetrators must be mutually aware of and accept that the execution of the common plan may result in the realisation of the objective elements of the crime. If there is a substantial likelihood that the objective elements of the crime would occur, this mutual acceptance may be inferred from the co-perpetrators' awareness of this likelihood and their decision to implement the plan despite such awareness. If, on the other hand, the risk is low, the co-perpetrators must have expressly accepted that implementing the plan would result in the realisation of the objective elements of the crime.[49] The third subjective factor is the accused's awareness of the factual circumstances enabling him jointly to control the crime – that is, that his role is essential in the implementation of the common plan and that he can frustrate its realisation by failing to perform his function.[50]

The second subjective element outlined by the Pre-Trial Chamber is unconvincing for several reasons. The Chamber inferred that the co-perpetrators mutually accept that the execution of the plan may result in the realisation of the objective elements of the crime in low-risk cases from their express acceptance of this result.[51] As an example of this express

---

[48] *Lubanga Confirmation of Charges*, above n 3, paras 349–60. See also *Katanga and Ngudjolo*, above n 24, paras 527–32; *Bemba*, above n 8, para 351; *Muthaura, Kenyatta and Ali*, above n 8, paras 410–17; *Ruto, Kosgey and Sang*, above n 8, paras 333, 338–47; *Abu Garda*, above n 8, para 161; *Banda and Jerbo*, above n 8, paras 150–57.

[49] *Lubanga Confirmation of Charges*, above n 3, paras 361–65; *Katanga and Ngudjolo*, above n 24, paras 533–37.

[50] *Lubanga Confirmation of Charges*, above n 3, paras 366–67; *Bemba*, above n 8, para 351; *Banda and Jerbo*, above n 8, paras 150, 160–61; *Abu Garda*, above n 8, para 161. The last subjective element has mostly been dropped by Pre-Trial Chamber Confirmation Decisions which combine co-perpetration and indirect perpetration into indirect co-perpetration as a mode of responsibility. In this new formulation, the last subjective element for indirect co-perpetration is that the perpetrator must be aware of the factual circumstances that enable him to exercise joint control over the crime's commission through another person. See *Katanga and Ngudjolo*, above n 24, paras 533–37; *Muthaura, Kenyatta and Ali*, above n 8, para 410; *Ruto, Kosgey and Sang*, above n 8, para 292. The Lubanga Trial Chamber mentions it (*Lubanga Judgment*, above n 27, para 1008) but does not finally apply the standard (*Lubanga Judgment*, above n 27, para 1013): see Ambos, above n 31, 148.

[51] See *Lubanga Confirmation of Charges*, above n 3, para 354, fn 436.

acceptance, the Chamber pointed to when 'killing is committed with "manifest indifference to the value of human life"'; on the other hand, intent was absent when the actor perceived a non-substantial risk but believed that his expertise would prevent the realisation of the offence.[52] However, it is difficult to see how 'manifest indifference' in the first case can imply 'acceptance' of the victim's death, apart from treating this as an acceptance of the risk of death (which in the Chamber's formulation is not sufficient to prove intent in low-risk cases). In contrast, one might say in the second case that the actor 'accepts the risk' and is simply mistaken about his ability to prevent the risk, the level of his expertise or both.[53]

The second element as defined by the *Lubanga* Pre-Trial Chamber also incorporates the *mens rea* of *dolus eventualis*, which is unlikely to meet the 'intent' and 'knowledge' test required under Article 30 of the Rome Statute. This is precisely the ground on which it was challenged and ultimately rejected by the *Bemba* Pre-Trial Chamber.[54] The *Bemba* Pre-Trial Chamber reformulated the second subjective element to require that the co-perpetrators must be mutually aware that the implementation of the plan will result in the commission of the crime, and should nonetheless carry out their actions either with the purpose to commit the material elements of the crime, or with the awareness that their fulfilment will, in the ordinary course of things, be a 'virtually certain consequence' of their actions.[55] The *Lubanga* Trial Chamber also rejected the *dolus eventualis* standard as incompatible with Article 30's requirement of intent or knowledge.[56] Thus, the co-perpetrators must 'know the existence of a risk that the consequence will occur', that is, they must be aware that the consequence will occur 'in the ordinary course of events'.[57] This is clearly the more logical interpretation of Article 30[58] and a more suitable subjective requirement for co-perpetration liability under the Rome Statute.

In the decision on confirmation of charges in *Katanga and Ngudjolo*, the Pre-Trial Chamber endorsed and expanded upon the notion of control and liability under Article 25(3)(a) developed in *Lubanga*.[59] In *Katanga and Ngudjolo*, however, the Chamber focused on the elements of liability for joint perpetration through another person. The Chamber saw no merit in the defence's argument that the phrase 'jointly with another or through another person' can include either 'co-perpetration' or 'indirect perpetra-

---

[52] See ibid, para 355, fn 437.
[53] See Weigend, above n 20, 483.
[54] *Bemba*, above n 8, paras 352–69.
[55] Ibid, para 370. See also *Ruto, Kosgey and Sang*, above n 8, paras 334–36 (concurring with the rejection of *dolus eventualis*); *Banda and Jerbo*, above n 8, para 159 (determining that the accused were mutually aware that the implementation of the common plan would result, in the ordinary course of events, in the fulfilment of the material elements of the crime).
[56] *Lubanga Judgment*, above n 27, para 1011.
[57] Ibid, para 1012.
[58] See also Ambos, above n 31, 149–50; van Sliedregt, above n 2, 47.
[59] See *Katanga and Ngudjolo*, above n 24, paras 480–86.

tion' but not 'indirect co-perpetration'.[60] It then set out the objective elements for perpetration by means, concentrating on the cases that it considered most relevant to international criminal law: the doctrine of *Organisationsherrschaft*.[61] These elements have been reiterated in subsequent Pre-Trial Chamber Confirmation of Charges decisions.[62]

The first element consists of the perpetrator's control over the organisation.[63] The *Katanga and Ngudjolo* Pre-Trial Chamber opined that Article 25(3)(a)'s provision for the commission of a crime through another culpable person would also encompass cases involving the principal's control over an organisation.[64] Several national jurisdictions employed this concept to hold leaders of organisations responsible as perpetrators rather than accessories,[65] on the basis that in cases of complex crimes, a person's degree of blameworthiness often increases in tandem with his rise in the hierarchy within an organisational structure.[66] The concept had also been recognised in the jurisprudence of international tribunals.[67]

The second element is the existence of an organised and hierarchical apparatus of power.[68] The organisation must be composed of superiors and a sufficient number of subordinates who are fungible, hence ensuring manifest compliance with orders. The leader must exercise authority through means such as his power to hire, train, discipline and provide resources to his subordinates. This control should be mobilised to secure compliance with orders that include the commission of crimes within the Court's jurisdiction.[69]

The interpretation of this element has posed some difficulties in the Kenya Confirmation of Charges decisions.[70] In particular, the manner in

---

[60] Ibid, paras 490–93; see also *Ruto, Kosgey and Sang*, above n 8, paras 287, 289 (stating that the concept of indirect co-perpetration was derived from merging the two modes of participation in Art 25(3)(a), which was a dynamic approach to interpretation in conformity with the Vienna Convention on the Law of Treaties); *Abu Garda*, above n 8, paras 156–57. See T Weigend, 'Perpetration through an Organization: The Unexpected Career of a German Legal Concept' (2011) 9 *Journal of International Criminal Justice* 91, 110 (stating that there is nothing novel about this mode of liability which is merely a combination of two accepted modes of perpetration).

[61] See *Katanga and Ngudjolo*, above n 24, paras 495–99.

[62] *Muthaura, Kenyatta and Ali*, above n 8, paras 407–10; *Ruto, Kosgey and Sang*, above n 8, paras 313–32.

[63] See *Katanga and Ngudjolo*, above n 24, paras 500–10; *Muthaura, Kenyatta and Ali*, above n 8, paras 407–10; *Ruto, Kosgey and Sang*, above n 8, paras 313–32.

[64] *Katanga and Ngudjolo*, above n 24, paras 501, 510.

[65] Ibid, paras 502–05 (citing the courts of Germany, Argentina, Peru, Spain and Chile).

[66] Ibid, para 503.

[67] Ibid, paras 506–09 (citing the jurisprudence of the ICTY, Nuremberg jurisprudence and a previous decision by Pre-Trial Chamber II of the ICC).

[68] Ibid, paras 511–14; *Muthaura, Kenyatta and Ali*, above n 8, para 408; *Ruto, Kosgey and Sang*, above n 8, paras 313–17.

[69] *Katanga and Ngudjolo*, above n 24, para 514.

[70] *Muthaura, Kenyatta and Ali*, above n 8, paras 408–09, 191–213; *Ruto, Kosgey and Sang*, above n 8, paras 315, 197, 315.

which it has been extended in the *Ruto, Kogsey and Sang* Confirmation Decision seems problematic. In this decision, the Pre-Trial Chamber upheld the prosecution's contention that William Ruto had control over and played a dominant role in an organisation called the 'Network',[71] which was used to carry out attacks against civilians who were perceived supporters of the Party of National Unity (PNU) in Kenya with a view to punishing and expelling them from the Rift Valley.[72] The members of this Network included 'aspiring members of Parliament, youth representatives, Kalenjin [members of an ethnic community] elders, farmers and businessmen'.[73] William Ruto was the designated leader of the Network, who co-ordinated all essential functions to secure its efficient functioning for the purposes of committing the attacks. The Network had a hierarchical structure: three generals were in charge of the attack in different areas of the Rift Valley, and four divisional commanders were responsible for its execution in the field. The generals and the commanders reported to William Ruto. Additional Network members co-ordinated more specific functions such as identification of targets during the attacks.[74]

In his Dissenting Opinion, Judge Kaul challenged this characterisation of the Network as an organisation. Though his dissent focused on whether the jurisdictional requirements of a crime against humanity are met if the crimes are not committed pursuant to the policy of a State or 'organisation',[75] his factual conclusions are also pertinent for assessing whether the Network would satisfy the objective element of *Organisationsherrschaft*. Judge Kaul's assessment of the evidence led him to conclude that the Network was an *ad hoc* 'ethnically based gathering of perpetrators' which was created for the sole purpose of assisting the ethnic community's political aspirations during Kenya's 2007 presidential elections. An 'amorphous alliance' of 'co-ordinating members of a tribe with a predisposition towards violence with fluctuating membership' was not transformed into an organisation merely by having planned and co-ordinated violence during a series of meetings.[76] This is a persuasive objection to the characterisation of the Network as an 'organisation', which would be equally valid in rejecting it as satisfying the second objective element for indirect perpetration.

---

[71] *Ruto, Kosgey and Sang*, above n 8, paras 307–09, 316–32.

[72] Ibid, paras 207, 216.

[73] Ibid, para 187.

[74] Ibid, paras 197, 315. The Chamber stressed these 'organisational' characteristics of the Network in the context of the elements required to establish a crime against humanity, but reiterated them for establishing the organisational element under indirect perpetration.

[75] Ibid, Dissenting Opinion by Judge Hans-Peter Kaul, paras 8–13.

[76] Ibid; see also *Prosecutor v Ruto, Kosgey and Sang*, No ICC-01/09-01/11-2, Dissenting Opinion by Judge Hans-Peter Kaul to Pre-Trial Chamber II's 'Decision on the Prosecutor's Application for Summons to Appear for William Samoei Ruto, Henry Kiprono Kosgey and Joshua Arap Sang', Pre-Trial Chamber II (15 March 2011) paras 18–49.

The third element is execution of the crimes through 'automatic' compliance with orders.[77] The organisational apparatus must be designed such that subordinates are mere cogs in the wheel and are easily replaceable. Thus, any single person's failure to follow orders cannot compromise the plan. In this fashion, the organisation develops a life of its own, which enables it to function independently of the identity of any single executor.[78] This automatic compliance, which is at the heart of the leader's liability as a principal, may not only be derived from the fungibility of the direct perpetrator, but can also be achieved through intensive and violent training regimens for subordinates.[79] Additional methods of securing automatic compliance with orders have been identified in the Kenya Confirmation of Charges decisions.[80] In *Muthaura, Kenyatta and Ali*, the Pre-Trial Chamber referred to the direct perpetrators being made to swear an oath of loyalty and obedience to the organisation in order to instil fear, and the use of disciplinary measures such as sanctions, killings and disappearances of disloyal members and defectors.[81] The *Ruto, Kogsey and Sang* Confirmation Decision determined that automatic compliance with orders was achieved through a combination of a payment mechanism, whereby members were paid salaries for motivation and rewarded upon the crime's commission, and a punishment mechanism, pursuant to which members of the community were forced to fight, and were sanctioned and even killed if they refused.[82]

The Pre-Trial Chamber has affirmed that a co-perpetrator can be held liable for the crimes committed by the culpable subordinates of his co-perpetrator on the basis of mutual attribution by combining the doctrines of *Organisationsherrschaft* and co-perpetration.[83] This is achieved by combining the objective and subjective elements of the two doctrines: the third subjective element of co-perpetration requiring awareness of the factual circumstances that establish joint control is discarded. It is replaced with the subjective element of the accused's awareness of the

---

[77] See *Katanga and Ngudjolo*, above n 24, paras 515–18; *Muthaura, Kenyatta and Ali*, above n 8, paras 409–10; *Ruto, Kosgey and Sang*, above n 8, paras 313–32.

[78] *Katanga and Ngudjolo*, above n 24, para 518.

[79] Ibid, para 518. This addition to the element of fungibility is not found in the original German doctrine: see Weigend, above n 60, 107 (critical of this position, stating that the Chamber may have found it necessary to adapt the doctrine to suit the exigencies of mass atrocity in Africa); for a more positive interpretation, see HG van der Wilt, 'The Continuous Quest for Proper Modes of Criminal Responsibility' (2009) 7 *Journal of International Criminal Justice* 307, 312 (arguing that this new element introduces flexibility in the doctrine).

[80] *Muthaura, Kenyatta and Ali*, above n 8, paras 408, 208–13; *Ruto, Kosgey and Sang*, above n 8, paras 317–31.

[81] *Muthaura, Kenyatta and Ali*, above n 8, paras 408, 208–13.

[82] *Ruto, Kosgey and Sang*, above n 8, paras 317–26.

[83] See *Katanga and Ngudjolo*, above n 24, paras 519–20; *Ruto, Kosgey and Sang*, above n 8, paras 287, 289; *Abu Garda*, above n 8, paras 156–57.

factual circumstances enabling him to exercise control over the crime through another person.[84]

B. Direct Contribution to the Crime

The above survey would suggest that the control theory has become fairly entrenched in the jurisprudence of the ICC, and that the Court will merely flesh out the details of the individual elements in subsequent cases. However, any complacency in this respect should immediately be discarded in light of the recent Concurring Opinion of Judge Wyngaert in the *Ngudjolo* case.[85] While Judge Wyngaert agreed with the majority that it was unnecessary for the determination of the case to rule on the mode of responsibility, she nevertheless set out her reasons for rejecting the control theory,[86] in particular the concept of indirect perpetration as a legitimate interpretation of Article 25(3)(a).[87] In her sophisticated Opinion, Judge Wyngaert challenged the approach to treaty interpretation that would be entailed by the application of the control theory, given that the theory was primarily derived from German legal doctrine. This would be contrary to the injunction of Article 31(1) of the Vienna Convention on the Law of Treaties, under which the Court should interpret treaty terms according to their 'ordinary meaning'.[88] Since terms denoting modes of responsibility such as 'committing' were terms of art and varied greatly from jurisdiction to jurisdiction, it was difficult to determine their 'ordinary meaning' by relying on national concepts.[89]

Article 25(3)(a), on the face of it, contained only 'basic' and 'traditional' forms of responsibility. The drafting history of the Article made it clear that the drafters had specifically chosen not to include other modes, such as planning and conspiracy, that would have targeted senior leaders. The desire to capture this class of offenders could not justify expanding treaty terms, especially given criminal law's insistence on the principles of strict construction and *in dubio pro reo* which were enshrined in Article 22(2) of the Rome Statute. This would be true even if the control theory could be regarded as a 'general principle of criminal law' under Article 21(1)(c), which was highly doubtful.[90]

---

[84] *Katanga and Ngudjolo*, above n 24, paras 533–37; *Muthaura, Kenyatta and Ali*, above n 8, para 410; *Ruto, Kosgey and Sang*, above n 8, para 292.

[85] *Prosecutor v Mathieu Ngudjolo Chui*, No ICC-01/04-02/12, Judgment Pursuant to Article 74 of the Statute, Concurring Opinion of Judge Christine Van den Wyngaert, Trial Chamber II (18 December 2012).

[86] See also *Lubanga Judgment*, above n 27, Separate Opinion of Judge Fulford, paras 10–12.

[87] *Ngudjolo*, above n 85, Concurring Opinion of Judge Wyngaert, paras 2–7.

[88] See also *Lubanga Judgment*, above n 27, Separate Opinion of Judge Fulford, paras 12, 13, 16 (adopting a plain reading of the Statute).

[89] *Ngudjolo*, above n 85, Concurring Opinion of Judge Wyngaert, paras 11–12, 17.

[90] Ibid, paras 14–20; see also *Lubanga Judgment*, above n 27, Separate Opinion of Judge Fulford, paras 10–12.

Judge Wyngaert also rejected the notion that there was an inherent difference in blameworthiness between principals and accessories, and asserted that nothing in the drafting history of Article 25(3) suggested this difference. The blameworthiness of the accused could not be tied to abstract legal categories but was dependent on his actual circumstances and role in the crime. The fact that the accused was in a leadership position could also be taken into account at the sentencing stage.[91] While Judge Wyngaert was sympathetic to the principle of 'fair labelling', whereby the accused's role in the crime should be reflected properly in the mode of criminal responsibility, she stressed that the Statute's drafters had deliberately chosen not to identify forms of responsibility that are aimed at leaders. Even if this was an oversight, the rules of treaty interpretation did not permit the judges to interpret Article 25(3)(a) to include this category within its ambit.[92]

Judge Wyngaert thus chose to interpret Article 25(3)(a) differently, and according to its 'ordinary meaning'. Under this analysis, 'joint perpetration' in Article 25(3)(a) only required a shared intent amongst the perpetrators to commit a crime. The perpetrators should work in a co-ordinated fashion and at the very least with the mutual awareness that these actions will result, in the ordinary course of events, in the commission of a crime.[93] The requirement of a 'common plan' as an objective element, as required by the jurisprudence of the Pre-Trial Chamber, was problematic because it focused on how the accused was connected to the common plan, rather than to the crime.[94]

Judge Wyngaert also did not find any support in the wording of Article 25(3)(a) for the second objective element for co-perpetration liability: the essential contribution of the accused. She was, however, equally reluctant to accept Judge Fulford's interpretation in *Lubanga*, whereby any causal contribution by the accused to the crime would suffice,[95] deeming it too elastic. Instead she suggested that the accused must make a 'direct' contribution to the realisation of the offence. Since to commit a crime was, in essence, to realise its material elements, the requirement of direct contribution was inherent in the concept of joint perpetration. A 'direct contribution' could not be defined in the abstract, but it would include acts that are 'an intrinsic part of the actual execution of the crime'.[96]

In a similar vein, Judge Wyngaert disagreed with the Pre-Trial Chamber's appropriation of the concept of *Organisationsherrschaft* to interpret Article 25(3)(a)'s requirement of commission 'through another person'. A 'person'

[91] *Ngudjolo*, above n 85, Concurring Opinion of Judge Wyngaert, paras 22–26; see also *Lubanga Judgment*, above n 27, Separate Opinion of Judge Fulford, paras 8–9.
[92] *Ngudjolo*, above n 85, Concurring Opinion of Judge Wyngaert, paras 28–29.
[93] Ibid, paras 31–32.
[94] Ibid, paras 34, 39.
[95] *Lubanga Judgment*, above n 27, Separate Opinion of Judge Fulford, paras 15–16.
[96] *Ngudjolo*, above n 85, Concurring Opinion of Judge Wyngaert, paras 43–48.

could not be interpreted to mean an 'organisation' without violating the principle of strict construction. Indeed, this organisational concept dehumanised the relationship between the indirect perpetrator and the physical perpetrator by shifting attention away from the actual control or influence that the former wielded over the latter.[97]

Lastly, Judge Wyngaert criticised the concept of 'indirect co-perpetration' as a novel, fourth form of perpetration which was not contemplated under Article 25(3)(a). The word 'or' signified that the commission must be either jointly with another person, or through another person, and ordinary language could not bear the strain of its being interpreted to mean both.[98]

One cannot but share some of Judge Wyngaert's concerns about the uncritical importation of national legal doctrines into international criminal law.[99] This is especially true given that, as we shall see in chapter seven, there is considerable debate about some aspects of the control theory, in particular the concept of *Organisationsherrschaft*, even in German academic circles. Nonetheless, it is worth reflecting on both the substance and the possible impact of Judge Wyngaert's Opinion. As a practical matter, it may not make a substantial difference to the path the ICC has chosen to tread. The Pre-Trial Chamber has embraced the control theory in every decision pertaining to Confirmation of Charges. Prosecution and defence strategies in all the cases currently before the ICC may be expected to be built around the use of the control theory. Moreover, as Judge Wyngaert herself notes, the determination on modes of responsibility was not necessary for deciding the case, so it is questionable if it will be authoritative for future judgments.

Substantively, while there is much to admire in the Opinion, Judge Wyngaert is perhaps too quick to move from principles of legality and strict construction as the correct approach to treaty interpretation, to a rejection of the control theory. For instance, as the following chapters will demonstrate, the control theory and the concepts of co-perpetration and

---

[97] Ibid, paras 52–54.

[98] Ibid, paras 60–63.

[99] There is some debate as to whether the control theory is a primarily German doctrine that has been imported by a few other domestic criminal law systems, or whether it has become sufficiently recognised in major national systems: cf Jessberger and Geneuss, above n 1, 868, with G Werle, 'Individual Criminal Responsibility in Article 25 ICC Statute' (2007) 5 *Journal of International Criminal Justice* 953, 963–64 (stating that while perpetration by means is recognised in major legal systems, it had not been regulated by international criminal law instruments or courts prior to the Rome Statute). See also KJ Heller, *The Nuremberg Military Tribunals and the Origins of International Criminal Law* (Oxford, Oxford University Press, 2011) 272 (arguing that in *United States v Ernst von Weizaecker, et al* ('*Ministries case*'), 4 Trials of War Criminals Before the Nuernberg Military Tribunals under Control Council Law No 10 (1949) the US military tribunal used a concept similar to perpetration by means); F Muñoz-Conde and H Olásolo, 'The Application of the Notion of Indirect Perpetration through Organized Structures of Power in Latin America and Spain' (2011) 9 *Journal of International Criminal Justice* 113 (analysing the application of the doctrine of indirect perpetration through an organisational power structure by courts in Latin America).

Organisationsherrschaft have been developed in much the same fashion in domestic German criminal law, notwithstanding its long tradition of adherence to the principle of legality. Indeed, Section 25 of the German Criminal Code (StGB) on perpetration uses almost exactly the same language as Article 25(3)(a). Of course, it does not follow naturally that the ICC can resort to the same interpretative techniques as the German courts – the prevalence of a *Dogmatik*, or a 'set of values and principles that provide the structure of a code of criminal law' as George Fletcher defines it, differentiates the German criminal law system from international criminal law which is still struggling to find its identity.[100] Thus, the same approach to interpretation may be far more controversial in international criminal law; it does not, however, make it automatically illegitimate.

Indeed, Fletcher has argued that this is precisely what the Pre-Trial Chamber did in the *Lubanga* and *Katanga and Ngudjolo* Confirmation Decisions, in attempting to develop a *Dogmatik* on principles of liability based on the jurisprudence of scholars. If the ICC were to follow this methodology consistently, it would involve a move away from strict adherence to the terms of the Statute towards interpreting it in light of a *Dogmatik* which evolves through the jurisprudence of the ICC and scholars.[101] The issue thus goes deeper than a challenge to the correct account of Article 25(3)(a); it goes to the very heart of the interpretative methodology to be used by the Court.[102]

One wonders though whether the Court can do anything other than adopt the *Dogmatik* approach, given the nascent state of international criminal justice. For instance, though Judge Wyngaert is at pains to emphasise the lack of support in the treaty for these novel concepts based on the control theory, the Opinion itself is not entirely free of the charge of going beyond strict textual interpretation. For instance, the Opinion's incursions into debates on whether the accused's blameworthiness must necessarily be reflected in a mode of participation, and whether perpetrators are indeed more blameworthy than accessories, themselves inject a *Dogmatik* whiff into what is ostensibly a strict construction of Article 25. This is also the problem with her requirement for a 'direct' contribution to the crime as an element of joint commission under Article 25(3)(a). The element of 'directness' itself does not appear to have much substantive content, especially if its establishment is left to the determination of judges on a case-by-case basis.[103] Moreover, as Judge Wyngaert herself acknowledges, terms such as 'commission' are terms of art and vary between

[100] GP Fletcher, 'New Court, Old Dogmatik' (2011) 9 *Journal of International Criminal Justice* 179.
[101] Ibid, 184.
[102] See Ambos, above n 31, 142 (making the same argument in the case of Judge Fulford's dissent in *Lubanga*).
[103] Ohlin et al, above n 10, 730.

national systems, and 'any causal contribution to the crime', which she rejects, would be an equally valid interpretation of 'joint commission' from a strict textualist perspective, and may well be how certain national systems choose to understand it.

One can certainly sympathise with the argument that ideally, the words of Article 25(3)(a) should clearly define the elements of joint commission and commission through another person. We are nonetheless left with the same fundamental problem: the lack of a coherent doctrine of perpetration in international criminal law that could be incorporated into the Statute, even if it were possible that the Statute could be amended to clarify the concept. Thus, we are left with little choice but to fall back on the attempt to develop a *Dogmatik*. The following chapters of this study are devoted to just such an effort.

III. CONCLUSION

For more than a decade of the operation of international criminal tribunals, JCE in its chameleon-like glory had been the darling of prosecutors and the favoured mode of liability for convictions. With the advent of the doctrines of co-perpetration and indirect perpetration at the ICC, it has been dethroned from its pre-eminent position as a form of principal liability for international crimes. International criminal law thus has two independent regimes governing the concept of perpetration that represent the collective nature of international crimes, and other forms of principal liability such as 'direct' participation are being introduced into the jurisprudence.

In this part of the study, I have attempted to show the loopholes and contradictions in the construction of these theories, and have also presented factual scenarios for which these theories have either no answers or only problematic ones. Underlying these surface (though vital, especially from the point of view of the accused who is charged under these modes of liability) problems, however, is the lack of a conceptual framework in international criminal law for delineating modes of responsibility. Attempt have been made to explain this theoretical poverty as caused by an under-theorised shift in principles of responsibility from public international law (which traditionally focused on States and collectives) to criminal law (which takes the individual as the central unit of attribution of responsibility).[104] To add to this deficit, the initial practice of international criminal law has been disproportionately driven by international

---

[104] GP Fletcher and JD Ohlin, 'Reclaiming Fundamental Principles of Criminal Law in the Darfur Case' (2005) 3 *Journal of International Criminal Justice* 539, 541.

lawyers working in human rights and humanitarian law, rather than in criminal law.[105]

The ensuing discussion will turn to domestic theories of parties to a crime, to derive analogies and lessons for the creation of a theoretical framework for forms of individual responsibility that cater to the collective dimension of international crimes. While the conceptual apparatus of domestic criminal law cannot be transposed, without more, to the international level, it can serve as an excellent starting point to ground and illuminate our understanding of the principles underpinning allocation of responsibility between parties to a crime. It is this terrain that we shall next explore.

---

[105] D Robinson, 'The Identity Crisis of International Criminal Law' (2008) 21 *Leiden Journal of International Law* 925, 928; J Wessel, 'Judicial Policy-Making at the International Criminal Court: An Institutional Guide to Analyzing International Adjudication' (2006) 44 *Columbia Journal of Transnational Law* 377, 449; M Damaska, 'The Shadow Side of Command Responsibility' (2001) 49 *American Journal of Comparative Law* 455, 495.

Part Two

The Principal in
International Criminal Law

6

The Principal in English Criminal Law Theory

I. CAUSATION AND THE CONCEPT OF THE PRINCIPAL

ENGLISH CRIMINAL LAW provides a seemingly straightforward definition of the principal party to a crime – it is the person who most directly and immediately fulfils the definitional elements of the offence.[1] There can be more than one principal party to an offence, for instance where P1 and P2 both separately meet all elements of the relevant offence, or where P1 and P2 are joint principals such that both have the requisite *mens rea* and their actions, in combination, fulfil the *actus reus* required for the offence.[2] In this situation P1 will personally not perform at least some part of the *actus reus* for the offence.[3]

The distinction between the principal and other parties to a crime is based on the notion of immediacy of the causal connection between the conduct of the offender and its consequences.[4] Generally speaking, the principal P's volitional actions are considered the cause of an act or omission if they constitute the ultimate human conduct before the result.[5] Thus, voluntary intervention by a third party, D, is regarded as having broken the chain of causation, resulting in D being held liable as the principal and P being considered only an accessory to the offence, provided he meets the relevant *actus reus* and *mens rea* requirements.[6] This view of what constitutes causation is grounded in Hart and Honoré's influential work distinguishing between occurrences in the realm of nature and those in the field of human relationships, based on the autonomy and agency of human actions. Thus, while it may be logical to talk about events in the natural world as having been 'caused' by other events or by a human

---

[1] KJM Smith, *A Modern Treatise on the Law of Criminal Complicity* (Oxford, Clarendon Press, 1991) 27–28.

[2] AP Simester and GR Sullivan, *Criminal Law: Theory and Doctrine*, 4th edn (Oxford, Hart Publishing, 2010) 207.

[3] Smith, above n 1, 28.

[4] Ibid, 80.

[5] A Ashworth, *Principles of Criminal Law*, 6th edn (Oxford, Oxford University Press, 2009) 105.

[6] Ibid, 106–11, discussing in detail the exceptions to this principle.

agent, the conduct of a voluntary human actor cannot be 'caused' by any other human being – the latter can at best give 'reasons for action' to the former.[7] This is because every human being, in Kadish's inimitable style, is ultimately a 'wild card' who is, in the final analysis, free to make any decision he likes or to change his mind.[8]

The only exception that Hart and Honoré recognise to this view of human actions is when the conduct of the primary actor P is involuntary or not wholly voluntary. They cite instances of when an accused D intends P to perform a particular action and P's action is not fully voluntary in that it is induced by coercion, deceit or the exercise of authority. In these situations, D may still be considered the principal party.[9] The exact scope of 'not fully voluntary actions' in their thesis is unclear. They suggest that these are not limited to cases where P would be exempt from criminal liability.[10] Thus, the scope of non-voluntary actions appears broader than situations where P is excused or justified in his conduct. Elsewhere, they also list a number of non- exhaustive factors that may take away from the voluntariness of P's conduct, including lack of muscular control or consciousness, duress and predicaments created by D for P where P cannot be said to have a fair choice.[11] They do not elaborate further on these circumstances, however, or on the limits of their operation.

The traditional formulation of the accessory's liability in English law conceives of it as derivative in nature, that is, it arises from and is dependent upon D's contribution to, or participation in, the offence committed by the primary party P.[12] As we shall see in Part Three on accessorial liability, this is now a matter of considerable dispute, and prominent commentators argue that the derivative theory has been superseded by alternative theories which attach more importance to D's independent conduct. This is particularly true after the introduction of Part II of the Serious Crime Act 2007, which introduces a new range of auxiliary offences of complicity of 'encouraging or assisting crime'.[13] Nonetheless, the debates surrounding the derivative doctrine are important for understanding the limits of prin-

---

[7] HLA Hart and AM Honoré, *Causation in the Law* (Oxford, Clarendon Press, 1959) 48–54. For a critical look at this thesis, see JH Mansfield, 'Hart and Honoré, Causation in the Law – A Comment' (1963) 17 *Vanderbilt Law Review* 487, 510–14. This view of causation has been subjected to persuasive criticism in the literature on the metaphysics of causation. See, eg, MS Moore, *Causation and Responsibility* (Oxford, Oxford University Press, 2009) 254–79. The positive law nonetheless continues to adhere to this conception of causation, and this study will proceed on the positive law's treatment of the causation requirement.

[8] SH Kadish, 'Complicity, Cause and Blame: A Study in the Interpretation of Doctrine' (1985) 73 *California Law Review* 323, 360.

[9] Hart and Honoré, above n 7, 323–24.

[10] Ibid, 340.

[11] Ibid, 70.

[12] Kadish, above n 8, 337. Other prominent common law countries such as the United States also adhere to the derivative approach. See J Dressler, *Understanding Criminal Law* (Newark, NJ, LexisNexis, 2009) 466.

[13] See Ashworth, above n 5, 426–27.

cipal responsibility in English law. For instance, does D's liability result from his participation in the *crime* perpetrated by P, or does it flow from his participation in the *wrongful act* carried out by P?[14] If the latter is true, D could possibly incur criminal responsibility even when P is excused (for example on grounds of duress), but not when P is justified in committing the act.[15] Secondly, must the nature of D's participation be causal in some way, that is, should it have made a difference to the outcome of the ultimate offence by P?[16] Alternatively, is it sufficient that D intentionally contributed to P's conduct while possessing the *mens rea* required for the offence committed by P and intending that P performs the actions that ultimately resulted in P's liability?[17] As we shall see in the following sections, these questions have a bearing on our notion of principalship.

II. THE PROBLEM OF THE ACCESSORY'S GREATER LIABILITY

Since on the traditional account the accessory's liability is derivative in nature, the orthodox view was that the accessory D's liability could not exceed that of the principal P. In the frequently cited case of *R v Richards*,[18] the defendant hired two men with the intention that they grievously hurt her husband, but the men inflicted only minor injuries. The issue was whether the defendant could be charged as an accessory for the more serious offence of unlawful and malicious wounding with intent to do grievous bodily harm, when the principal was convicted only of unlawfully and maliciously wounding another person. The Court answered the question in the negative, holding that since only one offence of unlawful

---

[14] On the implications of this distinction, see GP Fletcher, *Rethinking Criminal Law* (Oxford, Oxford University Press, 2000) 641–45. Several commentators have advocated basing the responsibility of the accessory on the wrongful act of the principal, rather than on the offence. See Kadish, above n 8, 379–82; P Alldridge, 'The Doctrine of Innocent Agency' (1990) 2 *Criminal Law Forum* 45, 46–47.

[15] Fletcher, above n 14, 641–43.

[16] Smith, above n 1, 6–7, 245–46.

[17] Kadish, above n 8, 346–50. English law seems to have followed Kadish in not requiring that the accessory's contribution have any causal potency. See CMV Clarkson, HM Keating and SR Cunningham, *Clarkson and Keating's Criminal Law: Text and Materials*, 7th edn (London, Sweet & Maxwell, 2010) 509; G Williams, 'Complicity, Purpose and the Draft Code – I' [1990] *Crim LR* 4, 6. Dennis remarks that the accessory's causal connection with the offence may be immaterial. See IH Dennis, 'The Mental Element for Accessories' in P Smith (ed), *Criminal Law: Essays in Honour of JC Smith* (London, Butterworths, 1987) 40, 41. The position is somewhat similar in the United States: WR LaFave, *Criminal Law* (St Paul, MN, West Academic Publishing, 2010) 711–12. There have, however, been calls for taking the causation element in accomplice liability more seriously: J Dressler, 'Reassessing the Theoretical Underpinnings of Accomplice Liability: New Solutions to an Old Problem' (1985) 37 *Hastings Law Journal* 91; J Dressler, 'Reforming Complicity Law: Trivial Assistance as a Lesser Offense?' (2008) 5 *Ohio State Journal of Criminal Law* 427.

[18] *R v Richards* [1974] 1 QB 776 (CA). The case has been the subject of much debate. See Fletcher, above n 14, 672–73; Clarkson et al, above n 17, 542.

wounding had been committed, it was not possible to hold an accessory liable for an offence greater than the one that had actually been committed. This position was overturned by the decision of the House of Lords in *R v Howe*,[19] where their Lordships affirmed that a secondary party may be convicted of murder, despite the principal's conviction for manslaughter. However, their reasoning for this proposition was quite cursory, and it did not address the theoretical implications of taking this position.[20] Lord Mackay simply stated that where D intends the offence that has occurred, the fact that P may be convicted only of a lesser offence *for some reason special to him* would not necessarily work to reduce the offence for which D is held responsible.[21] The ambiguity in this statement is disappointing, for it could encompass an entire range of excuses as well as justifications. If P were indeed convicted of a lesser offence on the ground that his conduct is justified, it is difficult to see how D could ever be convicted of the higher offence on a theory of derivative accessorial liability. Indeed, the decision in *Howe* has been interpreted by some commentators to constitute a partial abandonment of the derivative theory, since D's liability can hardly be said to derive from the more serious offence of murder which was never committed. It is instead based on his own personal culpability stemming from what he intended or contemplated.[22]

The problem of accessorial liability that potentially exceeds that of the principal may perhaps be dismissed as a minor anomaly in the theory of derivative liability. Most situations that we encounter in our lives, and those that come before courts, would involve principals that our intuitions would consider more culpable than their accessorial counterparts. However, examples abound of situations where convicting the secondary party D of a lesser offence would seem to understate the degree of his culpability versus the primary party P. Commentators frequently take inspiration from *Othello* in indicating that even though Othello, the principal, is clearly guilty in murdering Desdemona, the greater culpability lies with Iago, who masterminds and engineers the ultimate killing by exploiting Othello's weakness of character and manipulating everyone else into

---

[19] *R v Howe* [1987] 1 AC 417.

[20] Smith, above n 1, 130; Clarkson et al, above n 17, 543.

[21] *R v Howe*, above n 19, 458 (emphasis added). Criminal law in the US follows a similar rationale in the case of homicide: once it is established that a crime has occurred, the guilt of each party to the crime is assessed according to his own *mens rea*; thus, the secondary party may be convicted of a greater offence than the primary party: Dressler, above n 12, 490.

[22] Ashworth, above n 5, 427; Simester and Sullivan dispute this interpretation, arguing that murder and manslaughter should not be considered as independent offences since the core of the wrong is identical in both cases. See Simester and Sullivan, above n 2, 249–50. Dressler follows a similar line of argument in the context of US law, where he says that 'criminal homicide' may justifiably be regarded as a single offence which involves multiple degrees of culpability. However, if the greater harm intended by the secondary party never came to pass, he cannot be convicted of a greater offence than that ultimately committed by the principal: Dressler, above n 12, 491–92.

falling in line with his schemes.[23] Prosecutions for international crimes are in fact rarely concerned with the Othellos as perpetrators. An international crime such as genocide may be the result of a highly organised bureaucratic apparatus with clearly identified chains of responsibility, or it could be consequent upon a more diffused and seemingly spontaneous outbreak of mass atrocities. In either event, the actual physical perpetrator of an offence is usually too minor a participant in the mass crime composed of thousands of similar offences to be subject to the jurisdiction of an international tribunal.

English criminal law theory has devised three main ways in which greater liability may be attributed to the 'secondary' party in the crime.[24] The first relies on a broader conceptualisation of the derivative nature of accessorial liability, whereas the other two depend on an expansion of the concept of principalship. While the latter two hold greater interest for our purpose, the first merits a brief examination here.

III. A BROADER CONCEPTION OF DERIVATIVE LIABILITY

The broader conception of accessorial liability rests the liability of the accessory D not on the crime committed by the principal P, but on the objectively harmful wrong perpetrated by P.[25] It has been recommended as a sound basis for derivative accessorial liability by academics drawing upon German criminal law theory,[26] and has also been proposed by the Law Commission's Report, *Participating in Crime*.[27] The argument is that while wrongfulness is a feature of the act objectively considered, culpability is always personal in nature.[28] P's culpability cannot therefore be imputed to D, and D's culpability must be judged in terms of his own mental state with respect to the objectively wrongful act.[29]

At first glance, the theory appears especially promising for attributing liability for international crimes.[30] As we saw earlier, imputation of liability for international crimes is a very different enterprise from that for

---

[23] See, eg, the discussion by Kadish, above n 8, 385–88.

[24] I do not discuss the offences of 'encouraging or assisting crime' here, which introduce a wholly new category of parties to a crime by holding persons responsible for the inchoate offences of encouragement or assistance under the Serious Crime Act 2007, ss 44–46.

[25] Smith, above n 1, 130.

[26] Kadish, above n 8, 390; Fletcher, above n 14, 641–44.

[27] Law Commission, *Participating in Crime* (Law Com No 305, 2007) paras 4.14, 4.15.

[28] Fletcher defines culpability as a form of accountability, which is distinct from it in that it is limited to wrongful acts (and not those that are justified) and that it is linked to the degree of wrongdoing: Fletcher, *Rethinking*, above n 14, 459.

[29] Ibid, 642.

[30] Ashworth's objection to the *Howe* holding, on the ground that the higher crime for which the accessory is convicted never took place, would be inapplicable in this context. See Ashworth, above n 5, 427.

domestic crimes. Thus, while in factual scenarios like *Richards* and *Howe*, it is possible (though not ideal) for the court to be able simply to reduce P's liability on a vague basis such as 'some reason special to him', this reasoning does not carry much weight in international crimes. Unlike a reduction of liability from murder to manslaughter that P may incur due to some excuse, in a prosecution for an international crime such as genocide, P is culpable for an entirely different crime such as murder. P's objectively wrongful act appears a much stronger basis for assessing D's liability. So long as D possesses the requisite mental state for the crime of genocide, while intending P to commit the single crime of murder, D's liability would still be derivative of P's act. This is of course only a partial explanation of D's liability, as one murder by itself does not constitute an international crime. D's liability would ultimately be derivative of thousands of wrongful acts carried out by principals such as P, with D possessing the *mens rea* for genocide, and regardless of whether P and the other physical perpetrators conceived of their actions as amounting to genocide.[31]

Whichever doctrine of accomplice liability one chooses to follow, the problem still persists that holding D responsible only as an accessory misstates his actual role and participation in the offence. While language can possibly bear the strain of an accessory being held liable for murder while the principal is convicted only of manslaughter, it is more difficult to assign the label of an 'accessory' to a *génocidaire* where the principal is guilty only of murder or rape, as the case may be. It also goes against the notion of the principal as the dominant party in the chain of events leading up to the wrongful act.[32] Is it possible, then, to conceive of D as the principal while remaining true to English law's account of complicity and participation in crime? This is what we shall next examine.

IV. INNOCENT AND SEMI-INNOCENT AGENCY

The principal as a party to the crime is not particularly widely discussed in English criminal law. English legal practice (as well as theory) lavishes most of its attention on the accessory, and on the *mens rea* and *actus reus* requirements for accessorial liability. This is in contrast to legal systems such as that of Germany, where the principal is the primary focus of dis-

---

[31] It is worth noting that if one accepts recent commentary that the derivative theory has been partially eclipsed by doctrines that view the accomplice's culpability separately from that of the principal, and based on what the accomplice intended or contemplated will happen, this objection loses much of its force. See ibid, 426–27.

[32] On the principal as the actor who occupies centre-stage in a criminal scheme, see Fletcher, above n 14, 656.

cussion and the accessory is defined negatively by first identifying the potential scope of principal conduct.[33]

This problem becomes apparent when one considers situations in which English criminal law departs from its basic premise that P's voluntary conduct is the cause of an offence if it is the final human conduct before the result, and expands the scope of principals to include parties whose conduct in relation to an offence is interrupted by the act of an intervening third party.[34] The most striking instance of this is found in the doctrine of 'innocent agency', where the innocent agent is a person whose actions are not deemed free, informed and voluntary due to some personal factors such as insanity, ignorance or minority, and for this reason are considered to be caused by the words or conduct of another person (for instance through coercion or deception).[35] Some of the more controversial applications of the innocent agency doctrine by English courts have been in situations where the agent was acting under duress, or out of necessity. In *Pagett*,[36] the defendant fired shots at the police pursuing him, while using his girlfriend as a shield. The police fired back at the defendant, resulting in the killing of the girlfriend. The court convicted the defendant of manslaughter on the ground that the police officer's shooting back at the defendant was an involuntary action that arose out the necessity of self-preservation, and was in the course of his duty to prevent crime and to arrest the defendant. As Ashworth suggests, a better rationale for the decision would perhaps have been a test of 'alternative danger', that is, when D places a person in a situation of having to choose between the possibility of harming himself or harming another, the causal connection is better traced through D who compels this choice, rather than the person who is forced to make it.[37] This test echoes Hart and Honoré's examples of circumstances where P's actions are not considered wholly voluntary if they are induced by an emergency engineered by D, thus robbing P of a fair choice.[38]

The typical case in international criminal law merits a slightly different approach: the range of actions that would be considered excused or

---

[33] Smith, above n 1, 80–81. Indeed, the subject of parties to a crime as a whole, including complicity, has commanded even less attention in common law countries with otherwise rich and influential academic scholarship in the criminal law, such as the US. See Dressler, 'Reforming Complicity Law', above n 17, 429; R Weisberg, 'Reappraising Complicity' (2000) 4 *Buffalo Criminal Law Review* 217, 222.

[34] Ashworth, above n 5, 106–11. Ashworth mentions three such situations – non-voluntary conduct of third parties; conduct of doctors; and conduct of the victim.

[35] G Williams, 'Innocent Agency and Causation' (1992) 3 *Criminal Law Forum* 289, 294. In the US, the Model Penal Code as well as several state statutes recognise the doctrine of innocent agency: see JF Decker, 'The Mental State Requirement for Accomplice Liability in American Criminal Law' (2008) 60 *South Carolina Law Review* 237, 255–56. On the doctrine generally, see Dressler, above n 12, 468–69.

[36] *R v Pagett* (1983) 76 Cr App R 279 (CA).

[37] Ashworth, above n 5, 107.

[38] Hart and Honoré, above n 7, 70.

justified in domestic crimes, and therefore labelled involuntary, is far broader than similar conduct in international crimes. International criminal law permits the defences of duress and superior orders to the physical perpetrator of the crime only in very limited circumstances.[39] Moreover, there is something intuitively false in speaking of the actions of a person who commits a murder or a rape as innocent, even if his conduct stems from the permissibility of such acts in a climate of mass atrocity.

The better approach is to consider his responsibility under the doctrine of 'semi-innocent' agency. As described by the Law Commission, the notion of semi-innocent agency applies when the perpetrator, P, satisfies the fault element of a less serious offence, but is innocent because he lacks the fault element for the more serious offence intended by the secondary party D, and which shares the same *actus reus*.[40] The basis for D's liability is not the derivative doctrine of complicity but the doctrine of causation. P's actions are considered less than wholly voluntary, but not to such an extent so as to absolve him of criminal responsibility in full.[41] They may be characterised as having been caused, to the extent that he does not possess complete knowledge with respect to the nature or circumstances of his conduct.[42] This certainly seems a logical extension of the doctrine of innocent agency. As Williams puts it, if D can act through a completely innocent agent P1, there is no reason why he cannot do so through a semi-innocent agent P2. It would be unreasonable for the partial guilt of P2 to operate as a defence for D.[43] P2 would be treated as an innocent agent in respect of part of the responsibility of D.[44]

This doctrine would perhaps capture quite well the relationship and consequent liability between a senior leader or a person in a position of authority who intends to commit genocide, and the individual physical perpetrator of an offence such as murder. Two issues that would need to be fleshed out in greater detail are, first, to what extent the *actus reus* of the two offences may be considered 'shared', given that the *actus reus* of murder (by P2) will usually form a tiny part of the *actus reus* of genocide (by D), and whether there are conceptual problems with aggregating the *actus reus* of several offences in order to form that of the larger offence perpetrated by D. The second is the extent to which P2 can strictly be called an 'agent' of D in a situation of mass conflict, where P2 and D may not form part of a vertical chain of command and where P2 may in fact be unaware of D's existence and machinations.

---

[39] See, eg Rome Statute of the International Criminal Court, 17 July 1998, UN Doc A/Conf 183/9*, 2187 UNTS 90 (entered into force 1 July 2002) ('Rome Statute of the ICC') Arts 31, 33.

[40] Law Commission, above n 27, paras 4.14, 4.15. See also Smith, above n 1, 130.

[41] Kadish, above n 8, 388 citing Hart and Honoré, above n 7, 296–304.

[42] Smith, above n 1, 130.

[43] G Williams, *Textbook of Criminal Law*, 2nd edn (London, Stevens & Sons, 1983) 374.

[44] G Williams, *Criminal Law: The General Part*, 2nd edn (London, Stevens & Sons, 1961) 391.

It is also useful to consider whether the traditional limits to the doctrine of innocent agency recognised in English law would make the doctrine inapplicable in the context of international crimes. The applicability of the doctrine of innocent agency is controversial in at least two cases:[45] the first is where the offence cannot be committed except through the agency of a defined class of persons, and the second is where the nature or definition of the offence renders anything except personal physical perpetration conceptually impossible.[46] Gardner, following Kadish,[47] calls the latter offences 'nonproxyable'[48] and asserts that where nonproxyable actions are wrongs by themselves, or necessary ingredients of more complex wrongs, a secondary party cannot be a principal to these wrongs by making a causal contribution through another person. Kadish rests this distinction on linguistic considerations that guide our understanding of certain actions – such as being drunk, or being married, or having sexual intercourse – as conduct that can be performed only through one's own person.[49] Gardner's reason for differentiating between nonproxyable wrongs and other wrongs is embedded in the structure of rational agency: human beings have a different relationship to their own actions as compared to their relationships with the actions of others. While they are directly responsible for the former, their responsibility for the latter arises only to the extent they contribute to them.[50]

The case of *Cogan and Leak*[51] demonstrates the potential problems with applying the innocent agency doctrine to nonproxyable crimes such as rape. Leak forced his wife to have sexual intercourse with Cogan, who believed that she had consented. Cogan was acquitted on the ground of his mistaken belief in her consent (which then operated as a defence), while Leak was convicted as a principal to the crime of rape on the basis that he used Cogan simply as a 'means to procure a criminal purpose'.[52] The decision has been criticised for convicting D as a principal by way of acting through an innocent agent, when conviction would have been impossible had he physically perpetrated the rape (at that time a husband could not be held guilty of raping his wife). If the logic of the decision is

---

[45] Ibid, 350–51. However, as Simester and Sullivan note, the proposals in the Law Commission's Report, *Participating in Crime*, would serve to eliminate both these limitations. See Simester and Sullivan, above n 2, 209, referring to the Law Commission, above n 27, para 4.9.

[46] Williams, above n 43, 369–72; Kadish, above n 8, 374.

[47] Kadish, above n 8, 373.

[48] Gardner has a wider definition of these wrongs than Kadish. While Kadish would limit these wrongs to those that do not consist in making a causal contribution to anything, such as drinking or having sex, Gardner would include actions that require a causal contribution of a refined sort, such as in killing or coercing or lying. J Gardner, 'Complicity and Causality' (2007) 1 *Criminal Law & Philosophy* 127, 135–36.

[49] Kadish, above n 8, 373–74.

[50] Gardner, above n 48, 135–36.

[51] *R v Cogan and Leak* [1975] 1 QB 217 (CA).

[52] Ibid, 223.

taken to its extreme, even a woman may be guilty as a principal for the crime of rape, even though the offence is defined such that it can be committed only by a man.[53]

Several responses may be made to these claims. As Moore argues, if killing is considered a nonproxyable wrong, and the difference between someone who kills and another person who causes the killing is simply a linguistic one, the solution to the problem of a limited class of principals is simply to redefine the offence using non-causative verbs (homicide as 'causing death' rather than 'killing' for instance).[54] On the other hand, if the difference between causing death and killing is moral in nature, then the moral difference turns on the degree of causal contribution rather than on the semantic nature of certain verbs in a language.[55] There are of course still certain actions that may be considered nonproxyable, depending on the evil sought to be prohibited by the criminal provision. For instance, if the evil of rape consists in the violation of a person's body, rather than its violation by the perpetrator's own body, situations like that in *Cogan* may easily be accommodated within its definition. However, this may not be true of offences such as bigamy, because it is not an offence to cause someone else to get married while being married, only to cause oneself to do so.[56]

Regardless of the merits of the arguments surrounding the limitation of innocent agency to offences that are not nonproxyable in nature, they should not pose a serious barrier in the case of attribution of liability for international crimes. On the contrary, they would only support the secondary party D, who acts through the semi-innocent physical perpetrator P2, being held responsible as the principal. International crimes certainly fall within the range of wrongs that Gardner identifies as complex wrongs that may contain certain nonproxyable wrongs. For instance, crimes against humanity as defined in the Rome Statute of the ICC comprise a number of acts that warrant this label when 'committed as part of a widespread or systematic attack directed against any civilian population, with knowledge of the attack'. These acts include murder, enslavement, forcible transfer of population, torture, rape and other forms of sexual violence.[57] The Elements

---

[53] Williams, above n 43, 371; Kadish, above n 8, 377.

[54] MS Moore, 'Causing, Aiding, and the Superfluity of Accomplice Liability' (2007–08) 156 *University of Pennsylvania Law Review* 395, 416. Ashworth would agree that the problems with definition are primarily linguistic, rather than embedded in moral or social distinctions. Ashworth, above n 5, 430.

[55] Moore, above n 54, 417–18. Simester and Sullivan put forward a third option: the gist of the crime relates to the particular behaviour or *conduct* of the individual, and not to the bringing about of some *consequence*. They acknowledge, however, that it is not always clear what type of conduct requires P's direct involvement. Simester and Sullivan, above n 2, 208.

[56] Moore, above n 54, 419–20.

[57] Rome Statute of the ICC, above n 39, Art 7.

of Crimes[58] that assist the ICC in interpreting and applying the Statute further specify the elements of different offences. The first element in the definition of murder as a crime against humanity is that the perpetrator killed one or more persons.[59] 'Killed' is further defined as interchangeable with the term 'caused death'. This definition applies to all elements which use either of these concepts.[60] The Elements of Crimes have similar provisions in respect of several other crimes.[61] Therefore, the requirement of personal perpetration through the body of the perpetrator does not seem to feature very strongly in the understanding of these crimes. Moreover, there may be situations where it is linguistically inappropriate to describe the physical perpetrator P2 as belonging to the class of persons who legitimately can commit a crime against humanity. Given the definitional element of a widespread attack directed against civilian population, with knowledge of the attack, it may not always be the case that P2 personally perpetrates enough acts with the requisite knowledge to qualify as the principal of such a crime. There is a strong case that the logical principal for meeting these qualifications is D, who either plans or masterminds the attacks, or who is in a position of authority to order the individual attacks that make up the crime against humanity.

V. OUTCOME RESPONSIBILITY AND PRINCIPALSHIP

The final alternative that has been put forward by Sullivan for attributing liability to D as a principal rather than an accessory, in a situation where D is not the direct physical perpetrator of the offence, is where D by his own conduct bears 'outcome responsibility' for the wrong perpetrated and possesses the *mens rea* commensurate with the gravity of the crime.[62] This doctrine rests on the premise that P's conduct may be characterised as having been caused by D in a *de minimis* sense in certain circumstances, even if D's action does not take the form of deception or coercion.[63] Sullivan argues that the proposition that we can cause persons to do things while still considering their actions in general to be freely chosen is deeply embedded in social life. Indeed, it would be difficult to maintain

---

[58] Report of the Preparatory Commission for the International Criminal Court, Elements of Crimes, UN Doc PCNICC/2000/1/Add.2 (2 November 2000).

[59] Ibid, Art 7(1)(a)1.

[60] Ibid, fn 7.

[61] See, eg, ibid, fn 17, which recognises that given the complexity of the crime of sexual slavery, its commission could involve several perpetrators.

[62] R Sullivan, 'Principals and Accomplices – a Necessary and Useful Division' in A Duff and C Wong (eds), *Foundational Issues in the Philosophy of Criminal Law*, Special Workshop at the 23rd IVR Congress, 1–6 August 2007, Kraków, Poland, 151, 158, 163, available at <www.cracow.nordstraff.net/omnes_02.pdf> accessed 12 December 2010.

[63] Ibid, 158–61.

social order unless there were some degree of certainty that should D perform *x*, it is more likely than not that P would perform *y*.[64]

Sullivan borrows the phrase 'outcome responsibility' from Honoré, who uses it in the sense of unmediated causal responsibility for an outcome.[65] Sullivan extends the concept, however, to include situations where there is some material relationship between the act or omission of the agent and the instantiation of the wrong.[66] Thus, D may be held responsible as a principal in the event that his conduct has more than a minor causal impact on the instantiation of the wrong perpetrated by P, or if he has agreed with P that the wrong be committed, even if the actual *actus reus* of the wrong is carried out by P.[67] In the latter case, D would have outcome responsibility regardless of whether the agreement between P and D has a causal effect, and on the basis that he is party to the agreement which renders P's actions assignable to him.[68]

It is difficult to accept the extension of principal liability to D, who may not perform any part of the *actus reus*, to the extent advocated by Sullivan. Attributing principal liability on the mere fact of an agreement would make D liable for an offence based on his status (as a party to the agreement) rather than his conduct towards the offence. It is not clear that simple identification with a plan to commit an offence can do enough work to take the place of the requirement for a causal contribution for liability as a principal. Unless this is coupled with the condition that D makes some material difference through his participation in the offence (which reintroduces causation into the picture), this would be an unacceptable expansion of the class of potential principals to an offence.

In any event, it is not a particularly useful basis for attributing liability for international crimes. If D is to be held liable as a principal on the basis of his status as a party to an agreement which he has reached with P and other perpetrators of the offence, and in the absence of any causal contribution, fairness in labelling would demand that the agreement be fairly concrete, between a defined class of individuals, and proof of it be readily forthcoming. This would be extremely difficult to prove in a situation of armed conflict where there is no easily discernible chain of command

[64] Ibid, 160. Sullivan suggests the English courts have in fact indirectly recognised this proposition in cases such as *Environment Agency v Empress Car Co (Abertillery)* [1999] 2 AC 22 (HL), where the House of Lords held that the company had caused riverine pollution by storing oil close to the river, despite the fact that the immediate cause of pollution was the voluntary trespass of a third party. For criticism of this decision, see Ashworth, above n 5, 107.

[65] T Honoré, *Responsibility and Fault* (Oxford, Hart Publishing, 1999) 7–40.

[66] Sullivan, above n 62, 155, fn 24. See also R Sullivan, 'First Degree Murder and Complicity – Conditions for Parity of Culpability between Principal and Accomplice' (2007) 1 *Criminal Law & Philosophy* 271, 276.

[67] Sullivan, above n 62, 165–66.

[68] Ibid, 165.

between D, who is in a position of authority, and P, the ordinary civilian who simply imitates his compatriots in the commission of offences.

VI. CONCLUSION

As the analysis in the preceding sections shows, some of the concerns with using modes of principal liability in English criminal law to attribute responsibility for international crimes stem from the group or collective nature of these crimes. The reason for this limitation is partly that this collective dimension has been accounted for through accessorial modes of responsibility. The doctrine of joint enterprise, which will be discussed in Part III, provides for the possibility of secondary liability for crimes that are committed as part of a collective.

Despite this paucity, there is some potential for adapting the existing conceptual basis for principal liability in English criminal law to the case of responsibility for international crimes. While this involves an important reconceptualisation of the concept of causation in English legal doctrine, it does not constitute too radical a departure from the notion of innocent agency already widely recognised in English law. Before we explore the feasibility of this option in greater detail, it is pertinent to explore what a very different and equally influential legal system has to say about the concept of principalship in criminal law – the German system.

7

The Principal in German Criminal Law Theory

I. FORMS OF PARTICIPATION IN GERMAN CRIMINAL LAW

GERMAN CRIMINAL LAW presents a complicated and minutely theorised account of the principal party to a crime, especially as compared to English criminal law. This is partly on account of the fact that a party to a crime can be classified as an accessory only once it has been established that he cannot be considered a principal.[1] The German Criminal Code (StGB)[2] regulates the following categories of participation in a crime:

Section 25 Principals

(1) Any person who commits the offence himself or through another shall be liable as a principal.
(2) If more than one person commit the offence jointly, each shall be liable as a principal (joint principals).

Section 26 Instigation

Any person who intentionally induces another to intentionally commit an unlawful act (abettor) shall be liable to be sentenced as if he were a principal.

Section 27 Aiding

(1) Any person who intentionally assists another in the intentional commission of an unlawful act shall be convicted and sentenced as an aider.
(2) The sentence for the aider shall be based on the penalty for a principal. It shall be mitigated pursuant to section 49(1).

---

[1] KJM Smith, *A Modern Treatise on the Law of Criminal Complicity* (Oxford, Clarendon Press, 1991) 80–81.

[2] Criminal Code (*Strafgesetzbuch*, StGB) promulgated on 13 November 1998 (*Federal Law Gazette* I, 345, 3322). I have relied on the English translation by Michael Bohlander authorised by the Federal Ministry of Justice, available at <www.gesetze-im-internet.de/englisch_stgb/index.html>. The only variation I have introduced is in the translation of the term *Anstiftung* as 'Instigation' rather than the original 'Abetting' as I believe it more appropriately reflects the understanding of the term in English law. I am grateful to Claus Kress and Rebecca Williams for helping me arrive at an accurate translation.

Thus, a principal or perpetrator is one who commits the offence himself (*unmittelbare Täter* or direct perpetrator) or through another person (*mittelbare Täter* or indirect perpetrator), or jointly with another principal (*Mittäter* or co-perpetrator). In addition, commentators recognise the category of *Nebentäterschaft*, or independent multiple principals acting alongside each other towards the commission of an offence.[3] An accessory is one who intentionally induces another person intentionally to commit an unlawful act (*Anstifter*, or abettor or instigator), or who intentionally renders aid to another in the latter's intentional commission of an unlawful act (*Gehilfe*, or aider).[4]

The distinction between principals and accessories rests on the basis that perpetration is direct, indirect or joint *personal* commission of an offence, whereas accessorial responsibility arises from specific kinds of contribution to the *act of another*.[5] This basic differentiation permits an assessment of the weight and quality of one's contribution to an act (constituting an offence). If A's contribution is of such weight and quality that the act may be described as his own then A is liable as a principal. He can thus be attributed with the act of a joint principal (in the context of co-perpetration) or the act of a secondary party used by him as a tool (in the context of indirect perpetration). On the other hand, if A's contribution to the act is only of such secondary weight that it is best described as a contribution to the act of some other individual then A is liable as an accessory. In this case, A's criminal responsibility is derivative in nature, that is, it exists only when the act of the main perpetrator can be described as an unlawful offence.[6]

The StGB is silent on the criterion for distinguishing between principals and accessories, and different theories have been developed by courts and commentators to justify the classification.

II. THEORIES ON PARTIES TO A CRIME

A. Objective Theories

According to the most notable of the objective theories, the Formal-Objective theory, the perpetrator is the person who realises the elements

---

[3] J Wessels and W Beulke, *Strafrecht, allgemeiner Teil: Die Straftat und ihr Aufbau (Schwerpunkte)* (Heidelberg, CF Müller Verlag, 2012) 191; M Bohlander, *Principles of German Criminal Law: Studies in International and Comparative Criminal Law* (Oxford, Hart Publishing, 2009) 153.

[4] Wessels and Beulke, above n 3, 191; Bohlander, above n 3, 153.

[5] Wessels and Beulke, above n 3, 191.

[6] U Sieber and M Engelhart, *Strafbare Mitwirkung von Führungspersonen in Straftätergruppen und Netzwerken in Deutschland* (Max-Planck-Institut für ausländisches und internationales Strafrecht, unpublished report, Freiburg im Breisgau, 2009) ('MPICC Report') 12–13.

of an offence, either in full or in part, himself; all other contributors to the offence are accessories. This theory is now acknowledged as too narrow – it cannot, for example, account for the StGB's category of indirect perpetration – and is seldom advanced today. Other examples of objective theories are the Necessity Theory, according to which a perpetrator is a person who contributes to an essential part of the act, without which the offence could not have been accomplished, and the Contemporaneity Theory, under which all parties working jointly during the realisation of the offence are perpetrators.[7]

B. Subjective Theories

The subjective theories differentiate between parties to a crime based on the will and inner attitude of the participant.[8] Two prominent representatives of the subjective theories are the *Dolus* Theory and the Interest Theory. According to the *Dolus* Theory, the accessory subordinates his will to another and surrenders to him the decision of whether an act will be committed. The principal, in contrast, does not recognise the controlling will of another. The Interest Theory makes the degree of one's interest in the result of the (criminal) act the main criterion for distinguishing between the parties to a crime. The accessory has no, or very little, personal interest in the result of the act; the perpetrator brings about the result due to his personal interest.[9]

The courts have been inconsistent in their application of the subjective theories. Some decisions have rejected them outright, whereas others have convicted the accused as an accessory even when he personally fulfilled all the elements of an offence[10] (this is unlikely to be possible any longer given the definition of principals in Section 25 of the StGB). For instance, in the *Badewannenfall* ('Bath Tub Case'), the sister of the mother of an illegitimate newborn child had drowned the baby in a bathtub on the mother's urging. The court convicted the mother as the principal and the sister only as an accessory, on the ground that the latter had acted without the will of a perpetrator and solely in the interests of the mother.[11] In contrast, in the *Kameradenmordfall* ('Case of the Murder of the Fellow Soldier'), the BGH held that a person who kills another with his own hands would be considered the principal notwithstanding his having acted in the presence, under the influence, or for the sake of another person.[12] The BGH reversed its posi-

---

[7] HW Laufhütte et al (eds), *Strafgesetzbuch Leipziger Kommentar (Großkommentar): Band 1* (Berlin, de Gruyter Recht, 2006) 1848; MPICC Report, above n 6, 16.

[8] MPICC Report, above n 6, 16; Wessels and Beulke, above n 3, 194.

[9] *Leipziger Kommentar*, above n 7, 1846–47.

[10] See Bohlander, above n 3, 162–63.

[11] Entscheidungen des Reichgerichts in Strafsachen (RGSt) 74, 84.

[12] Entscheidungen des Bundesgerichtshof in Strafsachen (BGHSt) 8, 393.

tion in the *Staschynskij* case. Here, a KGB assassin who had murdered two persons on the direct orders of the head of the KGB was convicted only as an aider, while the head of the KGB was considered the principal, on the ground that Staschynskij had acted without the will of a perpetrator.[13]

Academic commentary mostly rejects the subjective theories for being too unclear and arbitrary. The assessment of whether a person has the will of the perpetrator has little to do with psychological reality, which gives rise to unjustified judicial discretion.[14] The extreme version of the subjective theories also ignores the participant's objective contribution to the realisation of the elements of an offence. This leads to an improper isolation of the will of the perpetrator from its relationship with the elements of the offence.[15] While the later jurisprudence of the BGH continues to adhere to a subjectively orientated demarcation criterion, it is overlaid by considerable objective elements in its assessment of this subjective criterion. The will of the participant is determined through the use of objective criteria: the extent of the contribution and control over the act, the will to control the act, and the degree of personal interest in the result of the act.[16]

C. Act Domination or Control Theory

The theory most widely endorsed by prominent commentators on German criminal law is the theory of 'Act Domination or Control' (*Tatherrschaftslehre*), which represents a synthesis of the objective and subjective theories. On this account, the decisive criterion for establishing the boundary between principals and accessories is control over the act: the perpetrator dominates or controls the commission of the act, and the accessory participates in its occurrence without domination. To have control over the act means to hold in one's hands the elements constituting the offence (with the requisite intent).[17] This control can take different forms: direct domination over the act in the case of direct perpetration (*Handlungsherrschaft*); control over the will of the direct perpetrator, or domination arising out of the superior knowledge of the indirect perpetrator in the case of indirect perpetration (*Willensherrschaft*); functional domination of the participating joint actor in the case of co-perpetration (*funktionalle Tatherrschaft*).[18] The perpetrator is the person who, as the key figure (*Zentralgestalt*) in the events, exercises this control through his ability to mastermind strategically the commission of the act (in indirect perpetration) or through his joint hegemony over the act

[13] BGHSt 18, 87.
[14] *Leipziger Kommentar*, above n 7, 1859.
[15] Wessels and Beulke, above n 3, 195.
[16] Wessels and Beulke above n 3, 194; MPICC Report, above n 6, 17.
[17] Ibid, 193; ibid, 17.
[18] Wessels and Beulke, above n 3, 193.

(in co-perpetration). He can thereby execute or obstruct the commission of the offence according to his will. In contrast, the accessory is the marginal figure in the course of events and merely advances the commission of the criminal act.[19]

The Control Theory is more multi-faceted and persuasive than the objective and subjective theories, both theoretically as well as pragmatically. It brings together several modes of conduct (act domination, will domination, functional domination) under the umbrella term of 'control', and thus provides the possibility of a more nuanced concept of perpetration. Unlike the subjective theories, the Control Theory recognises that the perpetrator is the subject of the offence, and that his conviction is tied to the unlawfulness of the elements of the offence rather than the blameworthiness of his internal attitude.[20] It also transcends the narrowness of the objective theories in dispensing with the requirement of personal fulfilment of all the elements of the offence and acknowledging that they can be realised with the help of a coerced human instrument, or in co-operation with another person.[21]

The Control Theory was first systematised by German scholar Claus Roxin, and is now endorsed by the majority of commentators, though in varying forms. Furthermore, even though the courts continue to adhere to the subjective theory, the current jurisprudence comes quite close to the Control Theory in its use of objective criteria for the identification of the will of the perpetrator.[22] For instance, in the *Katzenkönigfall* ('Cat King Case'),[23] H and P induced R, a psychologically dependent man, to believe in a demon called the Cat King as the supreme power in the universe. H wanted to get rid of N, and together with P convinced R that if he did not kill N as a human sacrifice, the Cat King would instead massacre a million people. R was persuaded to act on this belief and stabbed N three times. H, P and R were all convicted of attempted murder. One of the main questions considered by the court was whether H and P should be held liable as perpetrators or only as accessories to the attempted murder. The court stated that the issue of whether H and P might be classified as indirect perpetrators would depend on their objective control measured by the criterion of the will of the perpetrator. The indirect perpetrator is the person who induces and manipulates the conduct he intends through deliberately causing a mistake of law, such that the person labouring under the mistake can still be regarded as his (culpable) tool. H and P deluded R and then consciously manipulated him into carrying out the act of murder intended by them. They also determined substantially the mode of its execution – for example, P handed R the murder weapon and instructed him

---

[19] Ibid, 193; MPICC Report, above n 6, 17.
[20] *Leipziger Kommentar*, above n 7, 1860.
[21] Ibid, 1860.
[22] Ibid, 1848, 1856–57.
[23] BGHSt 35, 347. For a summary of the case, see *Leipziger Kommentar*, above n 7, 1895–96.

how to use it. R was in a dependent relationship with H and P, which they used to control him, and from which he could extricate himself only with great difficulty. Thus, H and P could induce R to commit the crime, and could control the execution of the act through the strength of their influence and their superior knowledge of the circumstances of the case.

The following section will catalogue the various categories of perpetration based on the Control Theory, given its predominant position in German criminal law.

III. CATEGORIES OF PERPETRATION

A. Direct Perpetration (*Die unmittelbare Täterschaft*)

According to Section 25 of the StGB, an individual who personally commits the criminal act, that is, who fulfils or realises the constituent elements of the offence himself, is the direct perpetrator. This commission may be by way of an act or an omission, though culpability for the latter presupposes that the omission arises from a specific duty, the successful performance of which is obligated (Section 13 StGB).[24]

The dominant view is that Section 25 no longer permits a person who fulfils all the elements of the offence himself to be held liable as an accessory simply because he lacks the will of a perpetrator.[25] As Roxin states, direct act domination is the prototype of perpetration: it is not possible for a person to control an act more definitively than by doing it himself.[26] This is the case even when he acts under a situation of duress (Section 35 StGB) – he would still be a perpetrator, albeit an excused one.[27]

B. Indirect Perpetration (*Die mittelbare Täterschaft*)

Section 25 states that a person who commits a crime *through* another is an indirect perpetrator. The word 'through' signifies that the indirect perpetrator (*Hintermann*) controls the direct perpetrator (*Vordermann*) of the criminal act in such a manner that he uses or manipulates him as a human tool or instrument. Due to this 'tool' function, the *Vordermann* normally possesses some deficit (for instance, he lacks the requisite intent for the offence), which the *Hintermann* exploits in order to control or dominate him.[28] While the *Vordermann* still possesses *Handlungsherrschaft* (act hegemony), this is

---

[24] MPICC Report, above n 6, 18.
[25] Ibid, 18–19; *Leipziger Kommentar*, above n 7, 1874–75.
[26] C Roxin, *Täterschaft und Tatherrschaft* (Berlin, de Gruyter Recht, 2006) 127.
[27] *Leipziger Kommentar*, above n 7, 1876.
[28] MPICC Report, above n 6, 19; Wessels and Beulke, above n 3, 202.

overlaid by the *Willensherrschaft* (or domination over the will of the *Vordermann*) of the *Hintermann*.[29] This hegemony of the *Hintermann* presupposes an active contribution on his part, though most commentators recognise the concept of domination through omissions.[30] The *Hintermann* must be shown to possess a double intent – he must have intent with respect to the elements of the offence, as well as intent in relation to the elements that constitute the act of indirect perpetration (for instance, the circumstances that establish his indirect perpetration). In both cases, intent to the degree of *dolus eventualis* is sufficient – that is, he must be aware of the possibility of the result of the act and accept it.[31]

There are two main categories of indirect perpetration. The first category comprises cases where the *Hintermann* dominates and exploits a human tool who acts without culpability or who is excused, thus absolving him of criminal responsibility.[32] This includes situations where the *Vordermann* acts under duress,[33] or where the *Hintermann* possesses superior knowledge and utilises the *Vordermann's* ignorance of circumstances to make the latter act as he intends in committing the offence.[34] The second category is the case of the 'perpetrator behind the perpetrator', where the *Vordermann* is responsible alongside the *Hintermann* despite the latter's hegemony.[35] In the *Katzenkönigfall* ('Cat King Case'),[36] for instance, in addition to convicting the direct perpetrator, R, the BGH held H and P responsible as indirect perpetrators on the basis of their hegemony resulting from the intensity of their effect on R, and their inducement and exploitation of his mistake of law about the permissibility of killing one person in order to save a million other lives.[37] A controversial application of the 'perpetrator behind the perpetrator' is in the form of the doctrine of *Organisationsherrschaft*. Since this theory is the most relevant form of indirect perpetration in the context of international crimes, it will be discussed in detail in sections IV to VI below.

C. Co-perpetration (*Mittäterschaft*)

Co-perpetration is the joint commission of a criminal act[38] through a knowing and willing working together of the individual participants.[39]

---

[29] Roxin, above n 26, 143.
[30] MPICC Report, above n 6, 26.
[31] Ibid, 27.
[32] Ibid, 20–22.
[33] *Leipziger Kommentar*, above n 7, 1885.
[34] MPICC Report, above n 6, 20–22; Roxin, above n 26, 242.
[35] MPICC Report, above n 6, 20.
[36] BHGSt 35, 347.
[37] MPICC Report, above n 6, 22–23.
[38] § 25, StGB.
[39] MPICC Report, above n 6, 29; Wessels and Beulke, above n 3, 197.

Co-perpetration is based on the functional act domination of each co-perpetrator, which arises from the principle of division of labour and functional role allocation.[40] This allocation ensures that the success of the criminal act is possible only through the co-operation of all co-perpetrators, so that the plan succeeds or fails depending on the functional contribution of each perpetrator. The act domination of the co-perpetrator is based on the fact that through his part of the act, he simultaneously controls the total act; his failure to perform his part of the act also results in a failure of the entire plan for all the other participants.[41] If two bank robbers, A and B, rob a bank together, where A threatens the employees with a gun while B removes the cash from the tills, each participant acts an equal partner – he participates in a common agreement or plan and a joint commission of the criminal act. The act contributions complement each other in such a manner that they collectively make the criminal act a joint venture, and the joint result is fully attributable to each co-worker.[42] There are mainly two requirements for co-perpetration: an objective requirement of collective act execution for the realisation of the elements of the offence, and a subjective requirement of a common act plan.[43]

The co-perpetrators must work together jointly, based on a division of labour, towards the result of the elements of the offence. The act contribution of each co-perpetrator must therefore be of sufficient weight and importance such that it grounds the necessary co-domination over the act.[44] As a general rule, the contribution must consist of an act by the perpetrator, though the jurisprudence of the courts and part of the literature endorses co-perpetration through omissions.[45] Thus, if A and B, two prison officers, agree to enable the escape of a prisoner such that A hands him the prison key (act) while B leaves the outer prison gates unlocked in violation of his duty (omission), they will be co-perpetrators of the offence of facilitating the escape of prisoners.[46] If the conditions for co-perpetration are present, the objective act contributions of the participants are mutually attributed as if they had realised all the elements themselves. However, an attribution is not possible when the elements of the offence have special requirements for the perpetrator and call for personal commission by the perpetrator. Also, it is not possible to attribute subjective characteristics such as special intent requirements. [47]

There is a good deal of controversy over whether act contributions in the preparation stage suffice for co-perpetration. According to the BGH,

---

[40] *Leipziger Kommentar*, above n 7, 1931.
[41] Ibid, 1931–32.
[42] MPICC Report, above n 6, 29; *Leipziger Kommentar*, above n 7, 1931–32.
[43] MPICC Report, above n 6, 30.
[44] Ibid.
[45] Ibid.
[46] § 120, StGB; *Leipziger Kommentar*, above n 7, 1935.
[47] MPICC Report, above n 6, 32; Wessels and Beulke, above n 3, 200.

even a small degree of co-operation in the preparation stage may lead to liability as a co-perpetrator if it is carried out with the will of a perpetrator,[48] but commentators are divided on this requirement. The typical example given is that of a gang leader who conceives of the criminal scheme and decides on its mode of commission, but who leaves its execution entirely to the other gang members.[49] One strand of opinion insists that the co-perpetrator must take part in some manner in the execution of the crime.[50] Others argue that unlike an accessory, an individual, such as a gang leader, who does not take part in the execution does not participate in the act of another; instead, the result follows from his willing collective participation in a joint act.[51]

There is, however, merit in the argument that since perpetration is tied to the realisation of the elements of the offence, co-perpetration must consist of joint domination of these elements.[52] Thus, only co-operation in the execution stage would justify responsibility as a co-perpetrator. This execution stage is not limited to the core elements of the offence but encompasses the entire phase between the beginning of the attempt and the formal completion of the act, and covers actions that would form an inseparable part of the complex action chain.[53]

As the functional act domination based on co-operation presupposes an overall plan, co-perpetration requires that the contributors to the criminal act reach an agreement to commit the act as equal partners.[54] There must be mutual consent over the joint realisation of the act at the time of, or even before the beginning of, the act; this agreement need not take place explicitly but may also take place by implication.[55] This would exclude situations where a joint accord is missing, such as a coincidental simultaneous exploitation of a situation by persons working side by side but without a mutual understanding.[56] Co-perpetration is also possible if the individual participants do not know each other, as long as each person is conscious that there are other participants who are likewise working towards a common goal, and these other participants have the same knowledge.[57]

From the necessity for a common act plan, it follows that the act of one of the contributors that goes beyond the plan, the so-called 'excess', cannot be attributed to the others.[58] This is because the other contributors do

[48] *Leipziger Kommentar*, above n 7, 1942, and cases cited therein.
[49] Wessels and Beulke, above n 3, 199; Roxin, above n 26, 298–300.
[50] Roxin, above n 26, 298–300.
[51] Wessels and Beulke, above n 3, 199.
[52] *Leipziger Kommentar*, above n 7, 1943.
[53] Ibid, 1943–44.
[54] MPICC Report, above n 6, 31; *Leipziger Kommentar*, above n 7, 1938.
[55] Ibid, 31; ibid, 1938.
[56] Ibid, 31; ibid, 1938.
[57] Ibid, 31; ibid, 1939.
[58] Ibid, 32; ibid, 1940.

not have hegemony over the act or the requisite intention regarding the deviation.[59] Thus, if several persons plan a robbery and one of them gets carried away and commits a murder during the robbery, he alone will be responsible for the killing.[60] There are some exceptions to this rule, as it is not necessary that the common plan covers each and every detail of the execution; each co-perpetrator may be given some leeway to act as the situation demands, as long as this helps accomplish the common goal. Therefore, deviations from the common plan that are within the range of the relevant acts one would normally foresee do not count as an excess. The main test is the foreseeability of the deviant course of action.[61] A deviation from the original plan during the joint executing action may also be introduced into the agreement by a mutual understanding, which again negates excess.[62]

IV. ORGANISATIONSHERRSCHAFT

A. Roxin's Formulation of *Organisationsherrschaft*

The doctrine of *Organisationsherrschaft*, developed by German scholar Claus Roxin,[63] refers to cases where the *Hintermann* has an organised power apparatus at his disposal through which he can accomplish the offences at which he aims, without having to leave their realisation contingent on an independent decision by the *Vordermann*.

Organisationsherrschaft is a form of indirect perpetration which transfers control over the course of events to the *Hintermann* despite a fully criminally responsible intermediary.[64] Roxin differentiated these cases from other forms of domination by will by referring to real-life examples. He relied on the cases of Eichmann and Staschynskij.[65] Eichmann was a member of the SS (*Schutzstaffel*) in the Nazi regime, who was charged with the task of facilitating and managing the mass deportation of Jews to extermination camps in Eastern Europe. Staschynskij was a KGB (*Komitet gosudarstvennoy bezopasnosti*) agent who assassinated two exiled politicians on behalf of the Secret Service. Roxin argued that in such cases, it would be difficult to argue that either person was excused due to domination of will through coercion or mistake. For instance, documentary material on the Nazi regime showed that no one would have been shot, or

---

[59] MPICC Report, above n 6, 32.
[60] RGSt 44, 321, 324; BGH NJW 1973 377.
[61] MPICC Report, above n 6, 32; *Leipziger Kommentar*, above n 7, 1940.
[62] Wessels and Beulke, above n 3, 201.
[63] C Roxin, 'Straftaten im Rahmen organisatorischer Machtapparate' (1963) *Goltdammer's Archiv für Strafrecht* 193.
[64] Roxin, above n 26, 242–43.
[65] Roxin, above n 63, 201–03.

even threatened with a death sentence, on account of his refusal to follow orders to kill. Similarly, while it was not impossible that the killer of a defenceless human being did not see the material injustice of his act under the grip of an ideological infatuation, the more convincing explanation was that the offender simply suppressed the voice of his conscience by thinking of the greater responsibility of the instruction giver. Thus, in these cases, direct perpetrators would not be excused due to coercion or mistake.[66]

However, Roxin argued, no one could fail to realise that the head of the Secret Service, or a highly placed official responsible for the organisation of mass deportation of the Jews, controlled the execution of the offences in a way that was different from the normal accessory.[67] The special position of the *Hintermann* in these cases resulted from the specific mode of action within the framework of the organisational apparatus. Such an organisation develops a life that is independent of the changing existence of its members, and of the decisions of the individual act executors; it functions, as it were, automatically. The *Hintermann* sits at the operational centre of the organisational structure, and if he presses a button to order a killing, he can expect it to be fulfilled without his even knowing who executes the action.[68] This expectation of fulfilment does not arise from any deception or duress on the part of the *Hintermann*. Instead, it is based on the fungibility of the executing organs, such that if one organ refuses to participate, another immediately steps into its place, and the execution of the total plan continues unhindered. Each executing organ is therefore an anonymous and arbitrarily exchangeable figure, much like a simple cog in the machine-like organisation, which places the *Hintermann* in the central position of the occurrence and lends him domination over the act.[69]

It is irrelevant for *Organisationsherrschaft* whether the *Hintermann* acts on his own initiative or on the instructions of more highly placed superiors. All that is required is that he can direct or steer the part of the organisation which is subordinate to him, without having to rely on the resolution of his subordinates for the commission of the offence.[70]

---

[66] Ibid, 99; Roxin, above n 26, 243–44.

[67] Ibid, 200; ibid, 244–45.

[68] Ibid, 200; ibid, 245.

[69] Ibid, 200–01; ibid, 245. The criterion of fungibility has invited much criticism, as we shall examine in section V, on doctrinal and empirical grounds.

[70] Ibid, 203–04; ibid, 248. This aspect of *Organisationsherrschaft* has been criticised by Ambos. See K Ambos, 'The Fujimori Judgment: A President's Responsibility for Crimes Against Humanity as Indirect Perpetrator by Virtue of an Organized Power Apparatus' (2011) 9 *Journal of International Criminal Justice* 137, 152–53.

B. Alternative Versions of *Organisationsherrschaft*

In 1965, German scholar Friedrick-Christian Schroeder gave a different account of the concept of a perpetrator behind a fully responsible perpetrator.[71] Instead of the fungibility of the act intermediaries, Schroeder grounded the responsibility of the *Hintermann* on his use of a *Vordermann* who is already determined to carry out the criminal act. In this case too, the *Hintermann* may rely on the almost automatic regular implementation of his criminal goal, based not on the replaceability of the intermediary, but on his already complete, though conditional, readiness to commit the offence.[72] The culpability of the *Hintermann* arises from the fact that he consciously provides the igniting spark for the explosive material and avails himself of a pliable tool for a criminal result in his own direct interest.[73]

Schroeder argued that the criterion of replaceability used by Roxin cannot be decisive for criminal responsibility, because organisations often have functionally qualified and trained individuals, such as poisonous gas specialists, who are not easily substitutable. However, their irreplaceability does not impact the responsibility of the other participants. It is more important that the executor who is already resolved to commit the criminal act is ready for the *Hintermann*'s instruction at any time.[74] Unlike the instigator who cannot be sure of the certainty of the criminal result because the *Vordermann* may still be susceptible to contrary reasons, the *Hintermann* acts in knowledge of the *Vordermann*'s certain act resolution.[75]

Schroeder's position has been effectively criticised in literature.[76] Even if, as Schroeder argues, there is a high degree of certainty attached to the criminal result due to the determined executor, this still does not mean that the *Hintermann* has control over the occurrence;[77] the *Vordermann*

---

[71] F-C Schroeder, *Der Täter hinter dem Täter: Ein Beitrag zur Lehre von der mittelbaren Täterschaft* (Berlin, Duncker & Humblot, 1965).

[72] T Rotsch, 'Tatherrschaft kraft Organisationsherrschaft?' (2001) 112 *Zeitschrift für die gesamte Strafrechtswissenschaft* 518, 524. By 'conditional', Schroeder meant only that the act resolution of the intermediary was still pending activation. See F-C Schroeder, 'Der Sprung des Täters hinter dem Täter aus der Theorie in die Praxis' (1995) *Juristische Rundschau* 177, 179.

[73] Schroeder, above n 71, 158.

[74] Schroeder, above n 72, 178. Roxin himself has recently stated that in the case of a specialist who is not easily replaceable, the head of the organisation will not qualify as a perpetrator. See C Roxin, 'Organisationsherrschaft und Tatentschlossenheit' (2006) 7 *Zeitschrift für Internationale Strafrechtsdogmatik* 293, 297.

[75] Schroeder, above n 72, 178.

[76] Recently, however, Roxin himself has suggested that the direct perpetrator's readiness to commit the act could have a symbolic value and be considered a characteristic, rather than an independent criterion, of *Organisationsherrschaft*. See C Roxin, 'Organisationsherrschaft und Tatentschlossenheit' in A Hoyer et al (eds), *Festschrift für Friedrich-Christian Schroeder zum 70. Geburtstag* (Munich, CF Müller, 2006) 387, 397–98; C Roxin, 'Bemerkungen zum Fujimori-Urteil des Obersten Gerichtshofs in Peru' (2009) 4 *Zeitschrift für Internationale Strafrechtsdogmatik* 565, 567.

[77] H Otto, 'Täterschaft kraft organisatorischen Machtapparates' (2001) *Jura* 753, 757–58.

may yet, if he suddenly develops scruples, refrain from the criminal act – this situation is hardly different from instigation.[78] On the other hand, if the *Vordermann* is really so determined that the result is practically guaranteed, it is difficult to understand why the provocation by the *Hintermann*, which moreover occurred before the time of the commission of the act, would grant him sufficient control over the act so as to justify his punishment as an indirect author.[79] Further, Schroeder's factual scenario is difficult to support empirically; the absolute readiness of the *Vordermann* to commit the criminal act is the exception rather than the rule. Cases such as those of the German guards at the wall between East and West Germany show that many of the act executors actually tried to avoid the criminal tasks, or performed them only to avoid a substantial personal disadvantage.[80]

Schroeder and Roxin's versions both find their way into the BGH's decision in the German border guards case.[81] In this case, the BGH combined Roxin's account of *Organisationsherrschaft* with Schroeder's criterion of the intermediary's (absolute) readiness to realise the criminal act.[82] It held that a *Hintermann* has domination over an act, despite a fully responsible *Vordermann*, if he uses the basic framework conditions of an organisational structure within which his act contribution gives rise to a regular operational sequence. Such framework conditions may exist in command hierarchies as well as in State, business or business-like organisational structures. If the *Hintermann* acts in the knowledge of these circumstances, if he in particular uses the absolute readiness of the executing organ to fulfil the elements of the offence, and if he wants his action to culminate in the result of the element of the offence, he will be the indirect perpetrator.[83] The BGH went beyond Roxin, however, in introducing the possibility of using *Organisationsherrschaft* in the case of economic and business-like enterprises,[84] whereas Roxin limits the application of his theory to crimes committed by the State authorities and to crimes committed by organisations such as underground movements, secret organisations, criminal organisations and similar unions that function as a 'state within the state'.[85]

---

[78] Rotsch, above n 72, 525.

[79] Ibid, 525.

[80] C Roxin, 'Anmerkung' (1995) *Juristen-Zeitung* 49, 51; K Ambos, 'Tatherrschaft durch Willensherrschaft kraft organisatorischer Machtapparate' (1998) *Goltdammer's Archiv für Strafrecht* 226, 230.

[81] BGHSt 40, 218–40.

[82] Roxin, above n 74, 293–94.

[83] See BGHSt 40, 218–40.

[84] On this extension of *Organisationsherrschaft*, see MPICC Report, above n 6, 23–24; T Weigend, 'Perpetration through an Organization: The Unexpected Career of a German Legal Concept' (2011) 9 *Journal of International Criminal Justice* 91, 99.

[85] Roxin, above n 63, 205; Roxin, above n 26, 250.

To assess the merit of these different approaches, it is now important to consider each of the elements in the original doctrine of *Organisationsherrschaft* put forward by Roxin.

V. ELEMENTS OF ORGANISATIONSHERRSCHAFT

There are three main elements in Roxin's theory of *Organisationsherrschaft:*

(a) the existence of a vertical hierarchically structured power apparatus;
(b) the direct executor's fungibility within the apparatus; and
(c) the apparatus's detachedness from the law.[86]

A. Taut Hierarchical Organisational Structure

Roxin's elucidation of *Organisationsherrschaft* requires an organisational structure which functions such that the instructions of the *Hintermann* lead to an automatic implementation of the elements of the offence. Roxin also talks of an organisation that is independent of its individual members, who act as functional parts of a larger machine-like structure; this is the basis on which he excludes a group of asocial elements who simply unite to commit common criminal offences.[87] This presupposes a fairly tightly organised hierarchical structure.[88]

Roxin ties this structure to the existence of a large number of fungible act intermediaries. It is a little difficult, however, to reconcile these two elements: the larger the number of act intermediaries, the more difficult it would be to control the system so that the *Hintermann's* instructions are implemented smoothly.[89] This is even more so if these intermediaries are arbitrarily replaceable. Roxin could be taken as referring to a functionally differentiated large enterprise, where the actors often do not know of each other's exact roles and perform their tasks more or less independently. It is, however, more difficult to ensure a 'regular operational sequence' within such a structure,[90] and the arbitrary replaceability of the intermediaries becomes far more limited.

---

[86] H Radtke, 'Mittelbare Täterschaft kraft Organisationsherrschaft im nationalen und internationalen Strafrecht' (2006) *Goltdammer's Archiv für Strafrecht* 350, 354. In his article on the *Fujimori* judgment rendered by the Peruvian Supreme Court, Ambos refers to two additional criteria cited by the Court: a responsible command of the indirect perpetrator, and the direct perpetrator's readiness to commit the criminal act (Ambos, above n 70, 149–50).

[87] Roxin, above n 63, 206; Roxin, above n 26, 251.

[88] Ambos, above n 80, 240–41.

[89] Rotsch, above n 72, 557.

[90] RD Herzberg, 'Mittelbare Täterschaft und Anstiftung in formalen Organisationen' in K Amelung (ed), *Individuelle Verantwortung und Beteiligungsverhältnisse bei Straftaten in bürokratischen Organisationen des Staates, der Wirtschaft und der Gesellschaft* (Sinzheim, Pro Universitate Verlag, 2000) 33, 36.

Moreover, as far as international crimes are concerned, Roxin's organisational structure, though conceded by him to be an ideal type,[91] does not reflect the reality of the majority of situations of mass conflict.[92] Crimes committed by the direct perpetrators in these situations are often spontaneous, or crimes of opportunity. The direct executor can hardly be said to be part of any power structure, and even less a tightly organised and controlled one, especially given that the crimes are spatially and temporally dispersed.

B. Fungibility of the Act İntermediaries

Commentators have been highly critical of the criterion of fungibility, which forms a central part of Roxin's theory. It is argued that the expectation of automatic execution of the crime by the intermediaries contradicts holding them criminally responsible as direct perpetrators.[93] The assumption of soulless humans is also contested; even in the most tightly controlled organisational structure, the fundamental unpredictability of freely acting humans cannot be done away with. *Organisationsherrschaft* presents us with a crooked picture of humans who are merged into an organisational structure and become one with the machine. Just because some or all of the individuals are replaceable, however, does not make the enterprise any less a union of human beings, or lessen the imponderability of the result that follows from this basis. If the picture of the soulless power apparatus is taken seriously, it is hard to see why this does not at the same time justify relieving the act executors of criminal responsibility.[94]

These internal contradictions of a criminally responsible yet machine-like direct executor may be partially resolved if one distinguishes more clearly between individual unlawfulness and collective unlawfulness – that is, unlawfulness that arises in organisational settings.[95] Unlike in the normal case of indirect perpetration, where the responsibility of the *Hintermann* is based on his control over the direct perpetrator, in cases of macro-criminality the *Hintermann* controls the intermediary only indirectly through the mechanism of the organisational apparatus.[96] The direct

[91]   Roxin, above n 63, 207; Roxin, above n 26, 252.

[92]   Ambos relies on few cases decided by the Peruvian courts and the ICC to argue that the criterion can be applied even to less formal non-State groups, but does not cite any independent arguments to support his conclusion: Ambos, above n 70, 150. *Cf* S Manacorda and C Meloni, 'Indirect Perpetration versus Joint Criminal Enterprise: Concurring Approaches in the Practice of International Criminal Law?' (2011) 9 *Journal of International Criminal Justice* 159, 171.

[93]   Otto, above n 77, 755.

[94]   U Murmann, 'Tatherrschaft durch Weisungsmacht' (1996) *Goltdammer's Archiv für Strafrecht* 269, 273–74.

[95]   Ambos, above n 80, 234; Ambos, above n 70, 148.

[96]   Ibid, 234; ibid, 148.

perpetrator is, on the one hand, responsible for his own criminal acts; on the other hand, his actions are part of the acts of the organisation as a whole. This organisational aspect does not relieve him as an individual for the individual unlawfulness. However, the only person who can be held responsible for this organisational unlawfulness is the person who has control over the organisation – the *Hintermann*.[97] This response is particularly relevant in the context of international crimes. It signals that principles of attribution may be different in cases of individual and collective criminality. It nevertheless fails to address the troubling aspect of viewing the direct perpetrator as a soulless tool of the *Hintermann*.

This objection is connected to the second set of arguments against fungibility: in the context of the concrete act, there are usually only a limited number of act intermediaries. One cannot therefore refer to an unlimited number of exchangeable act executors. For instance, in the case of the border guards posted between East and West Germany, in the context of the specific act of preventing the escape of refugees, only a few soldiers were present.[98] At best, then, the soldiers were not instantly but only successively replaceable. This does not differ in any material way from other forms of co-perpetration, or guarantee automatic implementation of the elements of the concrete offence.[99]

One response to this objection is to consider that control over the 'act' has a different meaning in the context of *Organisationsherrschaft*. In the usual case of indirect perpetration, the 'act' represents the direct criminal act committed by the *Vordermann*. In *Organisationsherrschaft*, the 'act' may be taken to refer to the entire expiration of events leading to the fulfilment of the result of the elements of the offence. The *Hintermann* would thus have the central position if he controls the sequence of events till the implementation of the crime.[100] However, this would result in a decoupling of the domination over the act from the elements of the offence. If Roxin were to accept this solution, it would contradict his stance that the perpetrator must have the key position in the execution action constituting the elements of the offence.[101]

This objection may not apply with the same strength, however, in the case of international crimes. International offences have an inbuilt collective element in their definition – a crime against humanity is not an individual act of murder or rape; such individual acts reach the level of an

[97] See R Bloy, 'Grenzen der Täterschaft bei fremdhändiger Tatausführung' (1996) *Goltdammer's Archiv für Strafrecht* 424, 441.

[98] Murmann, above n 94, 273.

[99] Ambos, above n 80, 232.

[100] T Rotsch, 'Neues zur Organisationsherrschaft' (2005) *Neue Zeitschrift für Strafrecht* 13, 15–16. Other authors have suggested that Roxin's theory in fact does not explain domination over any particular act at all, but only over the end result. See Weigend, above n 84, 100, and references therein.

[101] Rotsch, above n 100, 15–16.

international crime only if they are part of a widespread or systematic practice. The *Hintermann* can thus only be someone who occupies the central position in this entire sequence of events, including the collective element of the crime. To decouple his involvement from each individual micro-crime that comprises this group crime would still not result in a complete detachment from the elements of the offence.

C. Detachedness from the Legal Order

Roxin limits the operation of *Organisationsherrschaft* to organisations that are detached from the legal order, for it is only in these organisations that the administration and execution organs of the power apparatus are not bound to laws that have a higher ranking. The latter would normally exclude the automatic implementation of the *Hintermann's* illegal instructions. This criterion is challenged primarily by Ambos, who argues that if the organisation forms part of the legal order, the *Hintermann's* domination over the act is even greater.[102] For instance, non-State power apparatuses which have a symbiotic relationship with the State, such as the Sicilian mafia or Colombian drug cartels, are not detached from the law but integrated into it in order to achieve a common interest. This does not change anything in the effective domination of the top management of the apparatus over the act and direct executors.[103] Ambos is guilty here of eliding the distinction between the *government* and the *State* – a symbiotic relationship between the former and the organisation cannot be equated with an integration of the organisation within the positive legal order which may still be committed to fighting the organisation's criminal acts.

Ambos is more careful of this distinction when discussing State-organised power apparatuses, where the legal order forms the basis of State-sanctioned crime, such as in the military dictatorships of Argentina and Chile, and crimes are perpetrated in the name of the law, by the authority of the executive and through the instrumentality of the courts. Here, there is no element of detachedness from the law; instead, with the concentration of unlawfulness and the authority of the law in the hands of the same national power apparatus, the automatic implementation of the illegal instructions by the act intermediary is even more assured than in a case of law detachedness.[104]

Ambos admits that 'law' in Roxin's sense can also refer to natural rather than positive law; the State apparatus may act in violation of the natural law even if it is in conformity with the positive law. He rejects this inter-

---

[102] Ambos, above n 80, 242.
[103] Ibid, 242–43.
[104] Ibid, 244.

pretation, though, on the ground that it is too abstract and that such unwritten supra-legal principles cannot be readily understood by the act executor. Thus, they cannot form a normative barrier to the execution of the *Hintermann*'s orders.[105]

Ambos's criticism of law detachedness is convincing if Roxin indeed takes law to mean positive law. It is not clear, however, in what sense Roxin uses the term. In a later article,[106] Roxin attempts to dispel two mistaken interpretations of this element: first, he claims that the organisation need not operate outside the law in every case but merely in those areas where the crimes are committed; secondly, the criterion must be assessed not from the point of view of the law in operation in the criminal systems, but from that of the current law. Using this reasoning, he concludes that even if some of the measures undertaken by the GDR regime were in accordance with the law, shooting to prevent flights across the border between East and West Germany was clearly detached from the law.[107] This is not a particularly convincing explication of the criterion. It is difficult to see why the law currently in force should be the guiding feature for assessing the organisation's previous activities, and even if it is, whether that should be limited to the domestic law of the State where the crimes are committed, or if it also includes international law. Moreover, the certitude with which Roxin is able to state that the shootings at the border were undisputed instances of this law detachedness, and to do so without reference to any positive law, seems to point more in the direction of some notion of 'natural law'. Roxin's earlier references to a 'higher ranking' of this law[108] and to the rarity of such an organisation existing in a constitutionally stable legal order,[109] also support this interpretation.

This may in fact be one of the major strengths rather than weaknesses of Roxin's theory when applied to international crimes. It is exactly because an act executor who operates under the ideological glare that surrounds mass atrocity cannot immediately comprehend such unwritten higher laws, that they do not present a barrier to him for executing the *Hintermann*'s illegal instructions. Roxin's criterion of law detachedness would then perform two very important functions in clarifying the basis for international criminal responsibility: it would capture the social context in which mass crimes are committed; at the same time, it would provide a moral compass for the behaviour expected of the executor when surrounded by a climate that sanctions horrific acts of brutality.

---

[105] Ibid, 244–45.
[106] Roxin, above n 74.
[107] Ibid, 98.
[108] Roxin, above n 63, 204; Roxin, above n 26, 249.
[109] Ibid, 207; ibid, 252.

VI. ALTERNATIVES TO *ORGANISATIONSHERRSCHAFT*

A. Instigation

Several commentators favour characterising the *Hintermann* in *Organisationsherrschaft* as an instigator rather than an indirect perpetrator. The first set of arguments focuses on the fully responsible direct perpetrator. Individuals such as Hitler, Himmler and Honecker, who instructed the commission of killings, should be punished not as indirect perpetrators but only as instigators, because of the intervention of a deliberate and personally criminally responsible third person between the instructions and the criminal result.[110] This concern has already been addressed in the context of our discussion in section V.B. that the attribution of responsibility in cases of macro-criminality may be based on principles different from those applicable to normal crimes.

Another set of objections emphasises that there is little difference between instigation and *Organisationsherrschaft* with respect to the uncertainty of the criminal result. Murmann gives the example of a professional thief who is instigated by X to procure a certain article for him for a reasonable price. In this case, X can be as certain of achieving his criminal result as the *Hintermann* in Roxin's example.[111] This example is not an apt comparison, however, since *Organisationsherrschaft* by its very nature is not meant to regulate the relationship between two determinate individuals. A more relevant example is put forward by Rotsch, of a politician (P) who promises, in a demonstration comprised of 500 fanatical supporters, to award a million dollars to anyone who kills his unpopular competitor, X. Rotsch argues that P can be as sure or unsure that the criminal result he wants will be carried out as can the *Hintermann* in Roxin's case, even though Roxin would accept only instigation here due to the lack of an organisational structure. This is because there are diverse reasons capable of motivating a large number of humans to commit a criminal offence.[112] Rotsch is undoubtedly correct in his conclusion, but his objection does not fully address *Organisationsherrschaft*'s focus on the element of control exercised by the *Hintermann* by virtue of the organisational structure. In Rotsch's example, while there is a very high empirical probability of P's criminal desires being carried out, his instigation of his motley crowd of supporters still does not give him any control over their actions – whether or not they decide to kill X for a monetary reward depends entirely on their own motivations.

The third objection relates to Roxin's argument that characterising individuals such as the accused in the German border guards case severely

[110] Herzberg, above n 90, 48.
[111] Murmann, above n 94, 274.
[112] Rotsch, above n 100, 14.

underestimates the extent of their contribution to the crime by disguising the fact that they were the true decision makers in the illegal enterprise.[113] Herzberg counters this reasoning by suggesting that with respect to the nature of the injury caused to the protected legal interest, there is no difference between instigation and perpetration. The demarcation between the forms of participation does not depend on the degree of unlawfulness (which is a matter for sentencing) but only on whether the crime is committed personally or by a criminally responsible third person.[114] He also refutes Roxin's assertion that due to their tremendous destructive potential, individuals such as Hitler and Himmler cannot be equated with normal instigators.[115] Undoubtedly, various kinds of instigators abound, but in order to characterise them differently, the distinctions between them must co-relate with the criteria for differentiating between modes of responsibility. For instance, even the head of a mafia who extorts funds in the name of protection, or a KGB functionary who occasionally orders a killing, would be considered perpetrators under *Organisationsherrschaft*, even though their potential for destruction cannot be compared to that of Hitler.[116]

While these are certainly powerful objections, they paint a misleading picture of the *Organisationsherrschaft*. The doctrine does not demand that a certain degree of destructive potential must be reached before X can be labelled a perpetrator. Different perpetrators within *Organisationsherrschaft* may enjoy different degrees of power and authority, and operate at different levels within the organisational structure. Roxin acknowledges this by categorising Eichmann as a perpetrator, even though he functioned under the instructions of the Nazi regime.[117] To say that a KGB agent is not as dangerous as Hitler, and therefore not a perpetrator, is thus a fairly meaningless comparison.

Moreover, all the objections outlined above miss some crucial points of difference between instigation and indirect perpetration. The portrayal of Hitler or Himmler as instigators who would have left the decision on whether their criminal aims were implemented to the discretion of their subordinates, does not sit too well with historical and social reality; the criminal acts committed were not the acts of third parties but very much intended as their own plans and work.[118] The relationship of the *Hintermann* and the act intermediary is also very different from that of the instigator and the direct executor; the instigator must normally establish contact with the act executor and convince or persuade him to commit the offence. None

---

[113] Roxin, above n 80, 49.

[114] Herzberg, above n 90, 49.

[115] C Roxin, 'Anmerkungen zum Vortrag von Prof Dr Herzberg' in Amelung (ed), above n 90, 55, 56.

[116] RD Herzberg, 'Antwort auf die Anmerkungen von Prof Dr Roxin' in Amelung (ed), above n 90, 57.

[117] Roxin, above n 63, 202, 203; see also Ambos, above n 80, 234.

[118] See *Leipziger Kommentar*, above n 7, 1915.

of this applies to the *Hintermann* in *Organisationsherrschaft*, who can ensure the implementation of his orders on account of his control over the power apparatus.[119]

B. Co-perpetration

Organisationsherrschaft is also considered a superfluous doctrine on the ground that the situations it addresses are better categorised as co-perpetration. Even though the *Hintermann*'s contributions in an organisation may be limited to the planning and preparation stage, there is no reason why their remoteness from the execution stage cannot be overcome by their importance and the *Hintermann*'s position within the apparatus. Thus, the *Hintermann* is more appropriately classified as a co-perpetrator.[120]

This is a persuasive position. In the context of *Organisationsherrschaft*, it may not be too problematic to include preparatory acts within the common act execution. The *Hintermann* here fulfils the requirement that the co-perpetrator occupies a key position within the course of events. The concern that an individual who participates only in the preparatory stage has mere influence, but no control, over the criminal result does not apply with as much force in *Organisationsherrschaft*. The control of the *Hintermann* arises from his position within the power apparatus and its specific mode of functioning that ensures the implementation of his instructions regardless of the will of the direct actors.

The more serious challenge with using co-perpetration as an alternative to *Organisationsherrschaft* arises due to the absence of a common plan. It is argued that a common act plan or resolution does exist in situations to which *Organisationsherrschaft* applies. This common resolution is engendered through a common consciousness between the instructors and the act executors that certain criminal acts are to be committed in accordance with the instructions of the leadership level. Whether the direct executors have any say in this division of labour is quite irrelevant; indeed this negotiation is rare in even normal large-scale enterprises. It suffices that the act execution is done in consciousness of the common resolution.[121] Some commentators go even further and argue that the common knowledge of the criminal acts is tied to the participant's readiness to become a member of the organisation. The joint resolution of the executors arises from the identification with the common organisational objective.[122]

---

[119]   Roxin, above n 115, 55.
[120]   Otto, above n 77, 759.
[121]   G Jakobs, 'Mittelbare Täterschaft der Mitglieder des Nationalen Verteidigungsrats' (1995) *Neue Zeitschrift für Strafrecht* 26, 27.
[122]   Otto, above n 77, 758–59.

This interpretation of a common plan, however, transforms the collective act resolution into mere acquiescence.[123] It loses sight of the element of mutuality that is the foundation of a common plan. It also does not reflect the reality of the position and authority of direct executors involved in mass crimes. These individuals will often have very little agency or voice in the formulation of the criminal goal or plan, or in deciding on its method of execution.

Lastly, a hierarchically structured power apparatus presupposes a vertical structure that is characteristic of indirect perpetration (a top to bottom operational sequence flowing from the instruction giver to the direct executor) rather than the horizontal structure typical of co-perpetration (a mutual co-operation based on division of labour).[124] It is contended that since the direct executor is held fully criminally responsible in *Organisationsherrschaft*, legally, the *Hintermann* does not have a superior position in relation to the *Vordermann* – both are liable as perpetrators.[125] However, this assertion ignores the structurally subordinate relationship of the *Vordermann* in the power apparatus; while each executor may refuse to perform his part of the plan, there are always other executors that can replace him (the criterion of fungibility). Hence, the *Vordermann* does not possess the ability to obstruct the implementation of the criminal plan.[126] Moreoever, the fact that both the *Vordermann* and the *Hintermann* are criminally responsible does not make them equal partners. Their responsibility is based on different factors – while the *Vordermann* is responsible for the individual act of unlawfulness, the *Hintermann* is responsible for the organisational unlawfulness.

The preceding analysis reveals that Roxin's theory of *Organisationsherrschaft* represents a potential model for a theory of perpetration for international crimes. This is especially true of his criterion of detachedness from the law, which captures the social climate in which international crimes take place while being able to isolate the attribution of responsibility to individuals rather than collectives. It also highlights some of the challenges in adapting the theory in the context of international criminal law, prominent amongst which is the requirement of a tightly organised power apparatus.

Now that we have examined some of the promising aspects of English and German criminal law theories of perpetration as concerns their application to international criminal law, we can turn to how they may be restructured and moulded to address the challenges peculiar to international crimes.

---

[123] *Leipziger Kommentar*, above n 7, 1915; G Küpper, 'Zur Abgrenzung der Täterschaftsformen' (1998) *Goltdammer's Archiv für Strafrecht* 519, 524.
[124] *Leipziger Kommentar*, above n 7, 1915; Bloy, above n 97, 440; Küpper, above n 123, 524.
[125] Jakobs, above n 121, 27; Otto, above n 77, 759.
[126] *Leipziger Kommentar*, above n 7, 1915–16.

8

A Theory of Perpetration for International Crimes

I. LESSONS FROM DOMESTIC CRIMINAL LAW

AT FIRST GLANCE, English criminal law does not appear to offer much scope for an expansive concept of principalship that would encompass the liability of several perpetrators for a collective crime. The basic assumption for perpetrator liability is that the perpetrator directly and immediately fulfils the definitional elements of the offence,[1] and as outlined in previous chapters, it is not easy to establish this condition for international crimes. English law also makes it difficult to trace the chain of causation from the immediate physical perpetrator to the mastermind behind the crime, such that the latter can be held responsible as a principal despite and in addition to the criminal responsibility of the former.[2] It does provide for exceptions to these premises in the form of the doctrine of innocent agency, where the conduct of the physical perpetrator is not wholly free, informed and voluntary.[3] Further, the concept of a semi-innocent agent, where the primary party's actions cannot be considered fully voluntary, but still do not result in complete absolution from criminal responsibility, holds out the possibility of two parties being held liable as principals for the same conduct to different degrees (for example murder and manslaughter). In these cases, the secondary party is deemed to 'cause' the actions of the immediate perpetrator.[4] English law does not, however, address a situation of mass criminality, where there may be several thousand immediate perpetrators and where tracing liability back to the policy-level perpetrator using a simple one-to-one causation analysis (leader D 'caused' the actions of immediate perpetrators A, B, C, D . . .) will be very difficult. Moreover, it does not appear to contemplate situations where this high-level perpetrator may not know of the exact identity of his so-called agent, and indeed have no contact with him. Neither does it capture the distinctive aspects of mass criminality: its collective nature

---

[1] See ch 6, text to nn 1–3.
[2] See ch 6, text to nn 4–8.
[3] See ch 6, text to nn 35–38.
[4] See ch 6, text to nn 40–44.

and the climate of moral permissiveness that encourages or endorses this conduct. The reason for this paucity is partly the much greater emphasis given to the doctrine of JCE, which accounts for collective action but is an accessorial form of responsibility.

German criminal law theory on perpetration, on the other hand, attempts to accommodate these aspects of international crimes. The emphasis on the concept of 'control' rather than causation, and on the perpetrator as the *Zentralgestalt* based either on his functional control over the act (co-perpetration) or on his control over the will of the direct perpetrator (indirect perpetration),[5] opens up the possibility of holding several individuals simultaneously responsible as principals. While English law also recognises the concept of joint principals, because of its exacting conditions for causation and the requirement that the perpetrator must personally fulfil at least some part of the *actus reus*,[6] the scope for perpetrator responsibility is much narrower.

German criminal law also recognises the concept of the 'perpetrator behind the perpetrator' in ways that are pertinent for international crimes. For instance, in the 'Cat King Case' (see chapter seven), the *Hintermann*'s domination over the act was grounded on the intensity of his effect on the *Vordermann* and in his inducement and exploitation of the latter's mistake of law.[7] This could prima facie apply to the relationship between the high-level and immediate physical participants in mass atrocity, where the leader induces and exploits the physical perpetrators' belief that the crime is necessary and permissible. We would still need to establish, however, how this influence and effect might occur if the parties were never in contact.

Even more significant than these concepts is the category of *Organisationsherrschaft*, which recognises that individuals in leadership positions may be held responsible as perpetrators of crimes that are committed by a very large number of anonymous and exchangeable physical perpetrators.[8] Roxin's criterion of detachedness from the law is also sensitive to the perversion of norms that makes these crimes possible.[9] The doctrine's shortcomings lie in its treatment of the physical perpetrator as a soulless automaton. It also simplifies, to the point of caricature, the conditions under which mass atrocity occurs: a vertical, tautly structured hierarchical organisation that gives rise to an automatic implementation of commands is simply non-existent in most cases of international crimes.

---

[5] See ch 7, text to nn 17–19.
[6] See ch 6, text to nn 1–3.
[7] *Katzenkönigfall*, BGHSt 35, 347; U Sieber and M Engelhart, *Strafbare Mitwirkung von Führungspersonen in Straftätergruppen und Netzwerken in Deutschland* (Max-Planck-Institut für ausländisches und internationales Strafrecht, unpublished report, Freiburg im Breisgau, 2009) ('MPICC Report') 22–23.
[8] See ch 7, text to nn 68–69.
[9] See ch 7, text to nn 102, 108–09.

Despite these reservations, *Organisationsherrschaft* addresses several of our intuitions about mass atrocity and provides a promising template around which one can construct a theory of perpetration for international crimes. This is, for instance, true of Schroeder's observation that the *Hintermann* should be liable as a perpetrator because he deliberately inflames the dormant passions of the intermediary and uses him as a tool to achieve criminal results.[10] This is certainly one part of the reality of how high-level perpetrators can harness ordinary people to commit the crimes which they have planned and set in motion. The BGH's version of *Organisationsherrschaft* also emphasises the carefully planned, culpable actions of the *Hintermann*: his liability hinges on the conscious creation and utilisation of the basic framework conditions of an organisational structure that result in the realisation of an offence.[11] In both cases, the focus is, as Roxin states (though not quite for the same argument), on the *Hintermann*'s ability to unleash destruction on a scale that far exceeds that of an ordinary instigator.[12] Though the language of the law can scarcely accommodate an element as vague as 'destructive potential' in its lexicon, it is an important insight to be kept in mind while constructing an alternative account of perpetration.

The other important insight of *Organisationsherrschaft* is the distinction between individual and collective unlawfulness. The *Hintermann*'s criminal responsibility is derived from organisational unlawfulness rather than the act of any single perpetrator.[13] This obviates the problem of having to trace the chain of causation from each physical perpetrator's individual act of murder or rape, to the overall genocidal enterprise in which the *Hintermann* occupies a leadership position. It also circumvents the contradiction in holding the *Hintermann* liable despite a criminally responsible intermediary. It offers the closest domestic analogue to the uniquely collective dimension of international crimes.

The ICC, as discussed in chapter five, has already attempted to combine *Organisationsherrschaft* with the concept of co-perpetration for attributing responsibility to high- and mid-level perpetrators. It would be useful to consider whether some promising aspects of *Organisationsherrschaft* can indeed be taken together with certain aspects of co-perpetration to develop a doctrine of principal responsibility for situations of mass atrocity.

---

[10] See ch 7, text to nn 72–73.

[11] See ch 7, text to nn 82–83.

[12] C Roxin, 'Anmerkungen zum Vortrag von Prof Dr Herzberg' in K Amelung (ed), *Individuelle Verantwortung und Beteiligungsverhältnisse bei Straftaten in bürokratischen Organisationen des Staates, der Wirtschaft und der Gesellschaft* (Sinzheim, Pro Universitate Verlag, 2000) 55, 56.

[13] See ch 7, text to nn 95–97.

II. A THEORY OF PERPETRATION FOR INTERNATIONAL CRIMES

A. Rationale and Framework

The conception of the perpetrator of a crime as the *Zentralgestalt* in the course of events constituting the offence, is a powerful starting point for a theory of perpetrator responsibility: it accords with our intuitions to assign perpetrator responsibility to an individual whose contribution to the offence pushes him to the very centre of its occurrence. We then need to fill this concept of the *Zentralgestalt* with content, to discover what conditions would qualify for holding someone responsible as a perpetrator.

In order to ascertain these conditions, we must look at the roles played by the participants in the collective endeavour that is an international crime. The immediate physical participant plays a significant role in the commission of the individual crime which constitutes an essential part of the collective offence. Indeed, it is difficult to imagine a person more in the centre of an act than someone who physically commits it.[14] However, this applies only to the individual offence, such as torture or killing, which may by itself form a tiny part of the widespread and systematic planned attacks that characterise international crimes. It is the person who occupies the central position in this collective part of the offence who is most of interest to us, rather than the one who controls the individual micro offence.

Mass atrocity cannot, strictly speaking, be 'controlled' by any one individual: the spontaneity, initiative and arbitrariness displayed by mid- and low-level participants, some of which is deliberately harnessed by the policy-level participant, are characteristic of mass atrocity[15] and preclude a scenario where any one individual, or even set of individuals, has the last and final say on whether the international crimes will occur. Instead, we must shift the focus to control over what is truly central to their commission –control over the unleashing of a destructive potential that can lead to the commission of mass atrocity, and is intended to do so. Osiel's metaphor of the culpable village watchmaker who constructs a clock, attaches a bomb to it and then walks away so that detonation occurs much later,[16] is over-simplified, but it is nonetheless instructive here in identifying some important features of where the crux of the action lies in mass atrocity. As Osiel notes, in this situation, assuming the non-intervention of a third party, by assembling and winding up the clock, the watchmaker sets into motion a process which results in the explosion and the harm

---

[14] C Roxin, *Täterschaft und Tatherrschaft* (Berlin, de Gruyter Recht, 2006) 127.
[15] MJ Osiel, *Making Sense of Mass Atrocity* (Cambridge, Cambridge University Press, 2009) 98–104.
[16] Ibid, 105.

arising from it. He will thus be responsible for it, even if he does not know the exact identity of the potential victims, or the manner in which they will be harmed.[17] This approach transfers the temporal focus from the scene of the crime, to the place and time of the construction and winding up of the clock. Osiel likens this to the Argentinean courts' account of the military juntas, where the juntas established an elaborate administrative system to carry out political repression at the very beginning of the military rule. Subsequently, individual members of the juntas did not need to intervene directly in the functioning of this system to achieve the crimes they intended.[18]

For cases of mass atrocity, Osiel's metaphor helps us look for the central figure in their occurrence away from the time and place of the concrete crime, and to the scene where they were orchestrated and the machinery for their operationalisation was set up. The *Zentralgestalt* in an international crime is the person who sets this entire machinery in motion and utilises it in order to achieve the criminal results he intends, or knows will occur. The significance of this position has been acknowledged, albeit in a different context, by most analysts of genocide and ethnic cleansing,[19] and lies at the heart of what commentators such as Schroeder and Roxin are concerned about: the potential for destruction possessed by the *Hintermann*.[20] This potential can exist by virtue of his leadership position, charisma or de facto authority over a large number of biddable individuals, and through his conscious creation and manipulation of a situation[21] that results in tremendous harm. It also echoes the BGH's recognition of the rationale behind the responsibility of the perpetrator behind the perpetrator: the *Hintermann*'s superior knowledge of the circumstances of the conduct as compared to the *Vordermann*, and his deliberate inducement or exploitation of this fact to manipulate the latter.[22]

B. Objective/*Actus Reus* Elements

The objective elements for perpetration responsibility outlined here may be accommodated within the definition of perpetration under Article 25(3)(a) of the Rome Statute (see chapter five). They borrow in some respects from the concept of *Organisationsherrschaft*, but with substantial modifications to suit the specific circumstances of mass atrocity. As discussed above, the

---

[17] Ibid.

[18] Ibid.

[19] See, eg, ibid.

[20] See, eg MA Drumbl, *Atrocity, Punishment, and International Law* (Cambridge, Cambridge University Press, 2007) 25–26 and references therein.

[21] See text to nn 10, 12.

[22] See ch 7, text to nn 82–83.

Zentralgestalt in an international crime is the person who creates and sets into motion or utilises the process which results in the commission of mass atrocity. Following this rationale, the first objective element is identified as the perpetrator's 'control over the act' by virtue of his conscious creation, operationalisation, or utilisation of the framework conditions of the process that results in the realisation of the international crime.[23] Thus, the *actus reus* consists of the accused's creation or manipulation of the apparatus that results in the realisation of the elements of a crime within the jurisdiction of the court. This may encompass a series of activities ranging from formulating a plan, deciding on the mode of its execution, setting up a framework to achieve the intended outcome and ordering subordinates to ensure its implementation.

Several clarifications are in order here. First, instead of the direct individual criminal act committed by the physical perpetrator, hegemony over the 'act' here must be taken to mean control over the sequence of events leading to the result of the elements of the offence. The perpetrator would thus have the central position if he controls the sequence of events till the implementation of the international crime.[24] Secondly, this 'control' of the perpetrator is not based on the law's absolution of the physical perpetrator from criminal liability. Neither does it reflect that he has the 'last and final say' over whether the crime will occur. Instead, we must shift the temporal focus of the control from the conduct that immediately precedes the commission of the crime, to the conduct which results in the events leading to the mass crime.

The 'control' is based on the perpetrator's creation or manipulation of the apparatus that results in mass atrocity. This does not imply that the apparatus he sets up or exploits must and can only result in the commission of an international crime. Rather, there must be a high degree of certainty, greater than that present in ordinary cases of instigation, that the crime intended will occur.[25] The perpetrator's control stems from the intensity of the effect of his conduct[26] over the destructive machinery of violence. Quite often, this will be based on his occupying a position of authority within the apparatus that initiates or fuels mass atrocity.[27]

---

[23] This is a modified version of the BGH's definition of the elements of *Organisationsherrschaft*. See ch 7, text to nn 82–83.

[24] See ch 7, text to nn 100–01 and text following n 101.

[25] See ch 7, text to nn 111–12. In this sense, the modified version of *Organisationsherrschaft* acknowledges that there is an element of uncertainty attached to the element of 'domination', which is better regarded as a mixed factual-normative concept. See the objection levelled to the concept of domination by T Weigend, 'Perpetration through an Organization: The Unexpected Career of a German Legal Concept' (2011) 9 *Journal of International Criminal Justice* 91, 100–01.

[26] See ch 7, text to n 37; above n 7.

[27] This is similar to the criterion used in by the ICC Pre-Trial Chamber in *Prosecutor v Germain Katanga and Mathieu Ngudjolo Chui*, No ICC-01/04-01/07, Pre-Trial Decision on the Confirmation of Charges (30 September 2008) paras 511–14.

Secondly, there must exist an operational framework or apparatus which the perpetrator either establishes or uses, through which he can set in motion the events that result in the commission of the crime. The perpetrator must occupy a position within, or in relation to, this apparatus, which enables him to harness its potential to achieve the criminal result. However, this apparatus need not be vertically structured or rigidly hierarchical. Informal networks of power with weak links may sometimes prove more useful or efficient for the commission of international crimes than tautly structured apparatuses.[28] Neither is it necessary that each individual physical perpetrator is part of the apparatus. However, the individual micro crimes committed by the direct perpetrators must be related, in more than a *de minimis* way, to the activities of this operational framework. For instance, consider a situation where X, belonging to ethnic group A, kills his neighbor Y, who is a member of ethnic group B, because he covets his property. This crime is nevertheless committed within a context where the public radio, owned by the government comprised of members of group A, exhorts all members of group A to eliminate all members of group B. Militia members supported by the government distribute weapons in X's village, print pamphlets with incendiary messages targeting group B and make public lists of all the residents of the village belonging to group B. X is also conscious that members of group B are being routinely killed with the approval of, or at least without fear of sanction by, the government. In this situation, the operational framework or apparatus will consist of the network of militia, media and governmental entities that members of group A utilise to encourage and perpetrate violence against members of group B. The killing of Y will be related in more than a *de minimis* sense to the network of militia and State policy that sanctions the elimination of group B.

The third objective element is the existence of circumstances such that the individual crime conforms to the prevailing social norm. This element admittedly goes beyond a simple assessment of the responsibility of the individual defendant before the court, and involves the court in ascertaining the veracity of complicated historical, social and political facts. It is this element, however, that makes international crimes distinct from their domestic counterparts. Moreover, it is this perversion of norms that lends the high-level perpetrator his destructive potential. It makes the commission of the individual crimes by ordinary people far more likely than in a situation where these acts are condemned by the moral and social climate, and where the individual must overcome his scruples in acting against them. This does not mean that the positive legal order in the State where these crimes are committed must endorse them. There can be a formal commitment to fighting crime in a State despite the crimes being encour-

---

[28] Osiel, above n 15, 115.

aged, ordered or tolerated by the government in practice. Neither does it imply that the sanction for the crimes must come only from the government or the State. There can be a 'para-State', or a state within a State, that is based on achieving these criminal aims. This could even be constituted by rebel groups that enjoy a great deal of authority or power over significant portions of the population in the State where these crimes are committed. In this situation, even though there may be the possibility of individuals who engage in these crimes being punished by the government, the probability of this is remote either because the government is in a state of collapse, or because the rebel group enjoys sufficient popular support to put it outside the bounds of the government's ability to sanction individuals.

C. Subjective/*Mens Rea* Elements

The subjective elements for perpetrator liability are quite close to those required for indirect perpetration in German criminal law and elaborated by the ICC in its adoption of *Organisationsherrschaft*.[29] The perpetrator must have a 'double intent' – that is, he must have intent with respect to the elements of the offence in question, as well as in relation to the elements that enable him to establish his control over the act. Thus, he must fulfil the *mens rea* elements for each individual crime with which he is charged. This includes the specific intent required for the crime of genocide. This part of the mental element might be included within the definition of the crime (as is the case with the definition of 'genocide' in all international instruments), or it might be included within a separate provision that applies to all the crimes which fall within the jurisdiction of the international tribunal in question (as in Article 30 of the Rome Statute of the ICC). In addition, the perpetrator must be aware of the circumstances that enable him to create and utilise the framework conditions within an organisational apparatus which result in the commission of the crimes. For instance, he must have knowledge of his position or authority that allows him to harness this apparatus for the ends he desires, and the atmosphere of moral permissibility for the crimes he wants. In keeping with Article 30 of the Rome Statute, *dolus eventualis* will not reach the level of knowledge required of the accused.

---

[29] *Katanga and Ngudjolo*, above n 27, paras 527–32.

III. *ORGANISATIONSHERRSCHAFT* AND OTHER
MODES OF PARTICIPATION

A. *Organisationsherrschaft* Distinguished from Instigation

Unlike the perpetrator in the modified version of *Organisationsherrschaft* proposed in section II, the instigator is not the *Zentralgestalt* in the course of events constituting the crime. The quality and weight of his contribution to this sequence of events is sufficient only to make him a marginal figure in its occurrence, and his conduct is in the form of a contribution to the act of another, rather than his own act.

In terms of the objective and subjective elements for responsibility, the instigator lacks 'control' over the apparatus; he does not possess the authority or capacity to create and manipulate its operational framework to achieve the criminal result he desires. Imagine a scenario where A is one of the leaders of a militia aimed at cleansing a region of all members of ethnic group X. Together with the other leaders, he devises an elaborate plan to achieve this purpose. Under this plan, the militia is organised into smaller units which patrol the region, holding rallies inciting hatred against X, threatening members of X and distributing weapons amongst the local population so that they may attack X. On a day determined by the militia leaders, members of the units start directly attacking members of X. In the ensuing violence, ordinary people not belonging to the militia are caught up in the climate of atrocity, and also commit killings and acts of torture and rape against members of X. A month later, almost all members of X have been killed, or have been grievously injured or have fled to neighbouring parts. A has not directly committed any of these acts. Neither has he involved himself with the operation of ethnic cleansing after the elaboration of the scheme and the setting up of the machinery to achieve this. Nonetheless, he will be responsible as a perpetrator under our theory of control, provided he acts – that is, he devises the plan and organises the militia in which he holds a leadership position in order to accomplish the aims of the plan – with the requisite *mens rea*. The same factual scenario also includes journalist B, who whole-heartedly supports A's plan, and who writes incendiary articles in newspapers and pens fiery speeches echoing the leadership policy of ethnic cleansing. These materials are used by the militia to exhort people to violence. B will certainly qualify as an instigator if he acts with the *mens rea* for the crime of ethnic cleansing. However, he will not incur perpetrator liability if he does not possess any authority over the administrative and military framework such that he can use it to achieve the goal of ethnic cleansing.

The second major difference lies in the subjective element for liability. In contrast with the perpetrator, the instigator does not need to fulfil the *mens rea* required for each individual crime, especially the special intent for the crime of genocide. The difference in *mens rea* requirements will be dealt with in greater detail in Part Three on accessorial responsibility.

B. *Organisationsherrschaft* Combined with Co-perpetration

Mass atrocity often involves several individuals in leadership positions acting together to achieve the criminal results they desire. The participants can work together at the leadership/policy level in various ways. They may all be part of a centralised committee which decides collectively on each aspect of the policy and its mode of implementation (for instance, the Khmer Rouge party leadership in Cambodia was organised along these lines),[30] or there may be distinct areas of policy and operational control at the leadership level. In both cases, however, the issue becomes relevant of whether the conduct of the other high-level perpetrators can be mutually attributed so that they are all equally and jointly responsible for all the crimes committed by each one of them. The ICC recognised this possibility in its Confirmation of Charges decisions, by combining the doctrine of co-perpetration with the doctrine of *Organisationsherrschaft* in order to achieve this mutual attribution.[31] The modified concept of *Organisationsherrschaft* may also be combined with the doctrine of co-perpetration to come to the same result. However, the elements of this co-perpetration must be spelt out with greater clarity than the ICC's formulation in *Lubanga*.

In *Lubanga*, the ICC outlined the objective and subjective elements for co-perpetration liability as follows:

(a) A common plan between two or more persons. This plan may be implicit and should include an element of criminality, even though it need not be directed specifically at the commission of a crime.
(b) A co-ordinated essential contribution by each perpetrator, resulting in the realisation of the objective elements of the crime. This contribution may be at any stage of the crime.
(c) The perpetrator's intention to fulfil the elements of the crime, or his awareness that by implementing the common plan they will be realised in the ordinary course of events.

---

[30] *Judgment, Kaing Guek Eav, alias Duch*, No 001/18-07-2007-ECCC/TC, Trial Chamber (26 July 2010) paras 84–91.
[31] See *Katanga and Ngudjolo*, above n 27, paras 519–20; *Prosecutor v Ruto, Kosgey and Sang*, No ICC-01/09-01/11, Decision of the Confirmation of Charges Pursuant to Article 61(7)(a) and (b) of the Rome Statute, Pre-Trial Chamber II (23 January 2012) paras 287, 289; *Prosecutor v Abu Garda*, No ICC-02/05-02/09, Corrigendum of the Decision on the Confirmation of Charges, Pre-Trial Chamber I (8 February 2010) paras 156–57.

(d) The perpetrator's awareness that he provides an essential contribution to the plan's implementation.[32]

The subjective elements are relatively accurate and do not require any modification. The objective elements may be clarified further:

(a) The element of a common plan requires mutual consent over the joint realisation of the act, including acceptance or approval of an already formed plan. The co-perpetrators must work together jointly, based on a division of labour towards the implementation of the plan, with the (subjective) awareness of the risk that this will result in the commission of the crime. The plan cannot be predominantly non-criminal, and it must include the commission of a concrete crime.

(b) The act contribution of each co-perpetrator must be of sufficient weight and importance that it grounds the necessary co-domination over the act. This essential contribution must then exist for each individual international crime with which the accused is charged (the crime of recruitment of child soldiers in the *Lubanga* decision), rather than simply for the common plan (broadening the base of the army). Similar to the ICC's position, this contribution may even be at the preparation stage. What is essential is that it is of sufficient importance so that the lack of act immediacy is compensated for by the weight of the contribution, and the importance of the position of the co-perpetrator within the criminal plan is such that he can ensure its success or failure. Further, as affirmed in German jurisprudence,[33] it is not necessary that the accused had been part of the criminal plan from its very inception. Even if he participates in the execution of the plan after it has already begun, based on a mutual understanding and with the necessary act domination through his essential functional contribution, he will be responsible as a co-perpetrator. This is particularly relevant in the context of international crimes which may be spread over several years and involve several changes in personnel, including at the very top levels of policy making and co-ordination.

C. Scope for the Application of JCE

At first glance, there seems to be little in common between JCE and the modified doctrine of *Organisationsherrschaft* developed in section II. The most striking difference between the two doctrines is the structural framework for imputing liability to high-level perpetrators. While JCE does not

---

[32] *Prosecutor v Thomas Lubanga Dyilo*, No ICC-01/04-01/06, Trial Chamber I Judgment (14 March 2012) paras 980–1018.

[33] HW Laufhütte et al (eds), *Strafgesetzbuch Leipziger Kommentar (Großkommentar): Band 1* (Berlin, de Gruyter Recht, 2006) 1950.

appear to require any particular structural framework for its application – its adaptability to the particular circumstances of the case is indeed considered one of its strengths – the requirement of a common plan or agreement is central to JCE liability. This implies at least a minimum degree of mutual understanding and concerted action. In contrast, the modified account of *Organisationsherrschaft* requires no such mutual understanding or agreement between the participants. The operational framework created and utilised by the perpetrator in order to achieve his criminal ends may be rigid or flexible, horizontal or vertical, tightly organised or loosely structured. The physical perpetrator may desire to contribute to the macro- crime, or he may simply act for personal motives, and without awareness of the broader criminal objective. This situation captures, far better than JCE, the relationship between the contributors to mass atrocity, their different motivations and the operational framework which makes crime on such an endemic scale possible. Since the focus is on the person who is the *Zentralgestalt* in the course of events leading up to the crimes, and his liability is derived from his use of the framework conditions of a process or organisational structure, identifying the direct executors of the crimes becomes less important. Instead, it is vital to understand and articulate the operational framework correctly.

The second major difference lies in the extent of the contribution required by the accused. As mentioned in chapter three, there is some confusion as to whether JCE requires a substantial contribution to the crime or to the common plan, or whether it is sufficient that the accused performs an act that is *in some way directed to the furtherance of the common plan or purpose*.[34] In contrast, the modified account of *Organisationsherrschaft* uses both objective and subjective criteria to distinguish between parties to a crime. Thus, if the accused does not occupy the central position in the course of events and have a major role in its occurrence, he will not qualify as a perpetrator. This is a more convincing basis for holding him liable as a perpetrator than the one provided by JCE.

Lastly, the mental element for liability under *Organisationsherrschaft* is different from the *mens rea* required for responsibility under the various categories of JCE. For *Organisationsherrschaft*, the perpetrator must fulfil the *mens rea* requirements for each individual offence with which he is charged, including the specific intent for the crime of genocide. While JCE I also requires the perpetrator to 'share' the intent to commit the crime with other JCE participants, JCE II and JCE III have lower *mens rea* requirements. For JCE II, except in the case of special intent crimes, the accused does not need to possess the intent to commit the specific crime with which he is charged, only the intent to further the system of ill-treatment.[35]

[34] See ch 3, text to nn 64–71.
[35] *Prosecutor v Krnojelac*, No IT-97-25-A, Appeals Chamber Judgment (17 September 2003) paras 89, 94, 96; G Boas, JL Bischoff and NL Reid, *International Criminal Law Practitioner*

JCE III goes even further by holding a JCE member responsible for the crimes of other participants that were not agreed upon or intended but only foreseeable.[36] This is not possible under the modified version of *Organisationsherrschaft*, which demands that the accused fulfil the mental elements for the specific crime with which he is charged.

There is nonetheless some place for the application of JCE I in combination with the modified version of *Organisationsherrschaft*, in so far as it approximates the elements of co-perpetration stated above. The objective elements for JCE I and co-perpetration overlap to some extent, in that both require a plurality of persons and a common plan based on mutual understanding. However, the contribution of the co-perpetrator needs to be of sufficient weight and importance such that it grounds the necessary co-domination over the act.[37] Co-perpetration and JCE I also have similar subjective requirements. In each case, the accused must possess the *mens rea* required for the specific offence in question. The 'sharing' of this intent in JCE I may be likened to *Lubanga*'s criterion that the co-perpetrators must be mutually aware of and accept that the execution of the common plan may result in the realisation of the objective elements of the crime. Co-perpetration additionally requires the accused to be aware of the circumstances that enable him to co-dominate the crime.[38]

IV. CONCLUSION

The modified version of *Organisationherrschaft* that we have constructed here is an attempt to restructure and combine divergent theoretical perspectives on perpetration responsibility in order to develop a suitable account of the criminal responsibility of senior and mid-level participants in mass atrocity. This mode of responsibility engages with domestic criminal law principles and theory, while simultaneously capturing the unique features of international crimes. Though the specific elements of this form of *Organisationsherrschaft* undoubtedly constitute a departure from settled principles of perpetration responsibility in both German and English criminal law (and by extension criminal law doctrine in other countries that are based on these systems), they remain true to the fundamental

---

Library Vol I: Forms of Responsibility in International Criminal Law (Cambridge, Cambridge University Press, 2007) 59–63, citing and interpreting *Prosecutor v Tadić*, No IT-94-1-A, Appeals Chamber Judgment (15 July 1999) para 228; *Prosecutor v Brdanin and Talić*, No IT-99-36-PT, Trial Chamber II Pre-Trial Decision on Form of Further Amended Indictment and Prosecution Application to Amend (26 June 2001) para 27; *Prosecutor v Krnojelac*, No IT-97-25-T, Trial Chamber Judgment (15 March 2002) para 78.

[36] See ch 3, text to nn 104–16.

[37] See H Olásolo, *The Criminal Responsibility of Senior Political and Military Leaders as Principals to International Crimes* (Oxford, Hart Publishing, 2009) 277.

[38] As Olásolo notes, JCE liability does not have this element: ibid, 284.

concerns that guide the allocation of criminal responsibility in both jurisdictions. In addition, they highlight the distinctive features of international crimes as compared to their domestic counterparts – their inherently collective nature, the climate of moral permissiveness which characterises their occurrence, and the nature and motivations of the various participants in their commission. When combined with JCE I (to the extent it corresponds to co-perpetration as outlined above), this version of *Organisationsherrschaft* presents a more accurate picture of the role and function of high-level participants in international crimes, and situates them in the political context of mass atrocity perpetuated through the acts of several thousands of anonymous individuals. It is also capable of adoption as a theory of responsibility under Article 25(3)(a) of the Rome Statute of the ICC to hold an accused responsible for the commission of an international crime, 'whether as an individual, jointly with another or through another person, regardless of whether that other person is criminally responsible'.

This account of *Organisationsherrschaft* nevertheless rules out the possibility of employing JCE II and JCE III as modes of commission responsibility. The next part of this study will turn to examining whether either of these forms of responsibility may be accommodated within accessorial responsibility for international crimes. As with perpetration responsibility, the analysis will be based on theories of accessorial responsibility in English and German criminal law, and adapted to the unique circumstances of mass atrocity.

Part Three

The Limits of
Accessorial Responsibility for
International Crimes

9

The Accessory in English Criminal Law Theory

I. PARTICIPATION IN CRIME, COMPLICITY AND CAUSALITY

AFTER THE CHANGES to English criminal law introduced by the Serious Crime Act 2007, a person may become a party to a crime in one of three ways:

(a) as a principal (who most directly and immediately fulfils the definitional elements of the offence);
(b) as a secondary party (who aids, abets, counsels or procures the commission of an offence, or who is liable as a participant in a joint unlawful enterprise); and
(c) as someone who incurs responsibility for the inchoate offences of encouragement or assistance under sections 44 to 46 of the Serious Crime Act 2007.[1]

While there is some area of overlap between (b) and (c), our concern here is mainly with the secondary party.

Accomplice liability in English law is governed by section 8 of the Accessories and Abettors Act 1861:

> Whosoever shall aid, abet, counsel, or procure the commission of any indictable offence . . . shall be liable to be tried, indicted, and punished as a principal offender.

Section 8 does not create any substantive offence or provide a definition of accomplice liability as such; it was intended mainly as a procedural rule specifying that accessories could be convicted and sentenced as principals.[2] In 1975, the Court of Appeal held that the words 'aid, abet, counsel, or procure' should be given their ordinary meaning.[3] It is now widely conceded that there is no real critical distinction to be drawn between the

---

[1] A Ashworth, *Principles of Criminal Law*, 6th edn (Oxford, Oxford University Press, 2009) 404; AP Simester and GR Sullivan, *Criminal Law: Theory and Doctrine*, 4th edn (Oxford, Hart Publishing, 2010) 205–06.
[2] Ashworth, above n 1, 407; D Ormerod, *Smith and Hogan's Criminal Law: Cases and Materials*, 10th edn (Oxford, Oxford University Press, 2009) 291.
[3] *Attorney General's Reference (No 1 of 1975)* [1975] 1 QB 773 (CA), 779.

terms and that all four may be used as a catch-all phrase in an indictment.[4]

Although the principal and the accomplice are treated identically for the purposes of punishment in that they are both guilty of the full offence, the distinction between the two still has some limited significance. Most importantly, the status of an accomplice is in part contingent upon the existence of a principal who commits an offence.[5] There are also practical differences. In contrast with the principal, strict liability offences require *mens rea* on the part of the accessory. There is also no vicarious liability for the act of an accomplice. Further, the definitions of certain offences allow for the possibility of their commission (as a principal) only by a defined class of persons.[6]

The conventional account of secondary responsibility rests on the doctrine of derivative liability: the liability of the accomplice D arises from and is dependent upon D's participation in the offence committed by the primary party P.[7] However, as was noted in Part Two, commentators have challenged whether this doctrinal basis is truly representative of current English law, and have argued that there is a shift towards viewing the culpability of the accomplice separately from that of the principal and based on what the accomplice intended or contemplated would happen.[8] Nonetheless, the traditional importance of derivative liability as a fundamental principle underlying secondary responsibility has given rise to a spirited debate concerning the nature of the link between the accessory's conduct and that of the harm brought about by the principal.[9] This link has been explained using one of three rationales: causal, risk and agency.[10]

The causal explanation has some prominent supporters in English law, who argue that both the principal and the accessory make a causal contribution to the offence; the difference lies in the nature of their contribution. As Smith notes, 'it has always been implied in the concept of complicity that an accessory's involvement . . . did make some difference to the outcome'.[11] The difference between the causal contribution of the principal and that of the accomplice is based on the immediacy or directness of the cause – while the principal's act is the most immediate cause of the *actus reus*, the accessory's causal contribution is through encouragement

---

[4] CMV Clarkson, HM Keating and SR Cunningham, *Clarkson and Keating's Criminal Law: Text and Materials*, 7th edn (London, Sweet & Maxwell, 2010) 547; Simester and Sullivan, above n 1, 210.

[5] Ormerod, above n 2, 291–92; Simester and Sullivan, above n 1, 206.

[6] Ibid, 295; ibid, 206.

[7] SH Kadish, 'Complicity, Cause and Blame: A Study in the Interpretation of Doctrine' (1985) 73 *California Law Review* 323, 337.

[8] See Ashworth, above n 1, 426–27.

[9] KJM Smith, *A Modern Treatise on the Law of Criminal Complicity* (Oxford, Clarendon Press, 1991) 73–74.

[10] Ibid, 73–79.

[11] Ibid, 246.

or assistance of the perpetrator.[12] Gardner observes that both categories of participants in the crime make a difference in the world. The accessory, however, makes the difference through the principal, or 'by making a difference to the difference principals make'.[13] Kadish suggests a diluted form of 'potential causation', where the accomplice's liability is based on the potential difference his assistance could have made to whether the offence was committed, that is, it is unclear whether the offence could have been committed in its absence.[14]

English law has nonetheless chosen to follow the orthodox formulation of causation put forward by Hart and Honoré, which treats the voluntary and willed actions of a human agent (the principal) as breaking the causal chain.[15] No causal link is required to be proved for accomplice liability. For instance, in *Giannetto*, the Court held that the mere utterance of 'oh goody' by a husband to a plan already in existence to kill his wife would suffice for secondary liability.[16] An exception is made in the case of procuring, which has been defined to mean to produce by endeavour, and thus requires a causal link between the conduct of the accessory and the commission of the offence.[17] The non-essential nature of the causal link combined with the partial abandonment of derivative liability signals a shift in focus in the basis for secondary responsibility. The liability of the accessory no longer flows from his contribution to the offence committed by the primary party but is contingent on his own conduct towards the offence he intended or contemplated. This suggests a move towards a risk or endangerment rationale for accessorial responsibility. It is not possible, however, to reconcile all the case law with this approach. For instance, liability based on 'encouragement' requires both encouragement in fact as well as an intention to encourage on the part of the accessory, which is closer to a causal explanation.[18]

The third rationale based on ratification or agency also commands limited support in doctrine and decisions. This approach relies on consensus to ground responsibility: the principal assents to the agent's actions, and the agent consents to be the agent of the principal.[19] In so acting, the agent identifies herself with the actions of the principal and forfeits her right to be treated as an individual. The principal's actions may thus be imputed

---

[12] Ibid, 80.

[13] J Gardner, 'Complicity and Causality' (2007) 1 *Criminal Law & Philosophy* 128. *Cf* Simester and Sullivan, who argue that though causation need not be present, accomplice liability presupposes that there is a sufficient degree of connection between D's conduct and P's commission of the offence. See Simester and Sullivan, above n 1, 214–15.

[14] SH Kadish, *Blame and Punishment: Essays in the Criminal Law* (New York, Macmillan, 1987) 162.

[15] See ch 6, text to nn 7–11.

[16] *R v Giannetto* [1997] 1 Cr App R 1 (CA).

[17] *A G's Reference (No 1 of 1975)*, above n 3.

[18] Clarkson et al, above n 4, 351–52.

[19] Smith, above n 9, 74, discussing and ultimately rejecting this approach.

to her to hold her responsible.[20] Robert Sullivan's concept of the outcome responsibility of the accessory based on the agreement to commit a crime mirrors this position.[21] The agency rationale has also been alluded to in earlier English cases concerning joint enterprise. In *Anderson and Morris*, Lord Parker CJ concluded for the Court that the unauthorised actions of a co-adventurer in breach of what had been tacitly agreed to as part of the common purpose, would not incriminate his fellow adventurers.[22] In the subsequent Privy Council case of *Chan Wing-Siu*, Sir Robin Cooke stated that the case depends

> on the wider principle whereby a secondary party is criminally liable for acts by the primary offender of a type which the former foresees but does not necessarily intend. That there is such a principle is not in doubt. It turns on contemplation or, putting the same idea in other words, *authorisation*, which may be express but is more usually implied. It meets the case of a crime foreseen as a possible incident of the common unlawful enterprise. The criminal culpability lies in participating in the venture with that foresight.[23] (emphasis added)

While Sir Robin Cooke's interchangeable use of the concepts of contemplation (risk rationale) and authorisation (agency doctrine) is unfortunate,[24] his statement nevertheless relies on agency as an underlying principle justifying accessorial responsibility. Subsequent English case law has abandoned this basis, however, and now relies on (subjective) foresight alone.[25] Moreover, the structure of agency responsibility differs significantly from accomplice liability in criminal law. While the agent's liability is derived from the principal's initial acts of authorisation, this situation is reversed in criminal complicity. Also, unlike in criminal law, agency responsibility mainly focuses on the inactive party in the relationship.[26]

Different aspects of secondary responsibility in English law thus appear to be based on different rationales, and there is no apparent attempt to find a single coherent justification. As will be demonstrated in section II though, agency occupies a limited place in the current law of accomplice liability – mainly in the case of encouragement. The risk/endangerment rationale, on the other hand, seems more influential in the law, especially in the retention of liability arising from participation in a joint unlawful enterprise and in the creation of auxiliary offences of complicity under the Serious Crime Act 2007.

---

[20] J Dressler, 'Reassessing the Theoretical Underpinnings of Accomplice Liability: New Solutions to an Old Problem' (1985–86) 37 *Hastings Law Journal* 91, 111.

[21] R Sullivan, 'Principals and Accomplices – A Necessary and Useful Division' in A Duff and C Wong (eds), *Foundational Issues in the Philosophy of Criminal Law*, Special Workshop at the 23rd IVR Congress, 1–6 August 2007, Kraków, Poland, 165.

[22] *R v Anderson and Morris* [1966] 2 QB 110 (CCA), 118–19.

[23] *R v Chan Wing-Siu* [1985] AC 168 (PC), 175.

[24] See Smith, above n 9, 220.

[25] See text to nn 79–84 and nn 94–95 below.

[26] Smith, above n 9, 75.

II. DISTINCT MODES OF SECONDARY LIABILITY

The main forms of secondary liability are aiding, abetting, counseling and procuring. Participation in a joint enterprise also gives rise to accomplice liability, but it has a somewhat unique status in English criminal law and we shall examine it separately (see section IV below).

A. Aiding

A secondary party (D) aids a primary party (P) through any form of assistance, for example supplying a weapon or acting as a lookout, before or at the time of the offence.[27] While there must be *actual* assistance, it need not be substantial.[28] For instance, if D supplies a weapon to P for use during a bank robbery, which P ultimately does not use, D would still be liable as an aider. D's act is important because it helped or might have helped P in some way in the commission of the offence, even if it was not a cause of the offence.[29]

There is some controversy over whether P must be aware of the fact of assistance if she is in fact assisted. In the American case of *State v Tally*, Judge Tally, who knew that his brothers-in-law intended to kill V, prevented a third party from warning V and V was ultimately killed. Tally was held guilty as an aider and abettor, notwithstanding that his brothers-in-law were unaware of his assistance.[30] Some commentators favour this conclusion on the ground that aiding does not require any consensus between D and P,[31] but others argue that there is no meeting of minds in this situation.[32] While *Tally* certainly extends the boundaries of complicity liability, it may be justified on the basis that the diluted form of causation (D's conduct might have helped P) combined with the *mens rea* required of D still serves to limit its operation.

B. Abetting and Counselling

The natural meaning of 'abet' is to 'incite, instigate, or encourage', and abetting is typically identified in terms of some form of encouragement of

---

[27] Ormerod, above n 2, 309; Ashworth, above n 1, 407.
[28] Simester and Sullivan, above n 1, 210–11.
[29] Ashworth, above n 1, 407.
[30] *State v Tally* 102 Ala 25, 15 So 772 (1894).
[31] Ormerod, above n 2, 309; see also Simester and Sullivan, above n 1, 211 who do not, however, put forward any justification for this conclusion.
[32] Ashworth, above n 1, 408.

the principal to commit the offence.[33] This encouragement may be by way of words or conduct. Even mere presence (for instance at the scene of an illegal prize fight)[34] may constitute abetment if the presence in fact encourages P to commit the offence and is intended to do so.[35] The requirement of an encouragement in fact necessitates that D's encouragement must be communicated to P, that is P must be aware of the encouragement even if he is ultimately not influenced by it.[36]

Counselling covers conduct such as advising on an offence or supplying the information required for its commission.[37] In *Attorney General's Reference (No 1 of 1975)*, it was suggested that both abetting and counselling might require a meeting of minds between D and P.[38] This would certainly accord with the position that there must be encouragement in fact to constitute abetment.[39]

C. Procuring

In contrast with aiding, abetting and counselling, procuring requires a much stronger connection between the secondary party and the offence: D must deliberately induce or influence P to commit the offence,[40] and there must be a causal connection between D's conduct and the commission of the offence, even if it does not form a *sine qua non* for the commission.[41] Procuring does not require a meeting of minds between D and P, and P may be quite ignorant of D's persuasion or inducement.[42] In *Attorney General's Reference (No 1 of 1975)*,[43] D added alcohol to P's drink without his knowledge, and an unaware P subsequently drove home. D was convicted of procuring P's strict liability offence of drink-driving, since he knew that P intended to drive and that the added alcohol would bring his blood/alcohol concentration above the prescribed limit.[44]

---

[33] Ormerod, above n 2, 310–11; Simester and Sullivan, above n 1, 212.
[34] *Queen v Coney* (1882) 8 QBD 534.
[35] *R v Clarkson* [1971] 1 WLR 1402; Simester and Sullivan, above n 1, 212.
[36] Ormerod, above n 2, 311–12; Simester and Sullivan, above n 1, 213.
[37] Ashworth, above n 1, 414.
[38] *AG's Reference (No 1 of 1975)*, above n 3.
[39] Ormerod, above n 2, 310–11.
[40] Simester and Sullivan, above n 1, 214.
[41] Ormerod, above n 2, 314–15; Simester and Sullivan, above n 1, 214.
[42] Ibid, 314–15; ibid, 214.
[43] *AG's Reference (No 1 of 1975)*, above n 3.
[44] Ormerod, above n 2, 306–08; Ashworth, above n 1, 414.

III. THE MENTAL ELEMENT FOR COMPLICITY

The *mens rea* for secondary participation is twofold: the accessory (D) must possess the necessary fault elements with respect to his own acts, as well as with respect to the acts of the principal (P):[45]

(a) D must intend his own acts of contribution (ie to aid, abet, counsel or procure P) and be aware of their ability to assist or encourage P.
(b) D must appreciate the nature of P's actions: D must know or foresee the 'essential matters' relating to P's actions which make these actions an offence. These 'essential matters' include the facts, circumstances and other matters which constitute the *actus reus* of the offence.[46]

A. Requirement of Purpose

The first prong of the fault element for accessorial liability requires a voluntary act performed by D with the awareness that it will assist or encourage P in the commission of an offence. There is controversy over whether D must possess a mental attitude with respect to the offence going beyond mere awareness and actually intend the offence to occur. In other words, is it sufficient that D acts in a manner which he knows will facilitate the offence intended by P, or should he act *in order* to assist its commission, even if he ultimately did not desire that the offence be committed?[47]

The bulk of English authorities support the conclusion that D's knowledge that his act will assist is sufficient.[48] The main decision in this respect is *NCB v Gamble*,[49] where a weighbridge operator issued a ticket to a lorry driver certifying the lorry's weight, thus allowing the driver to take his overweight lorry onto a public road. The operator was convicted of aiding and abetting the offence on the basis that it was sufficient that he was aware that the lorry was overweight and that it was about to be driven on a public road. It was irrelevant that he might have been indifferent to its commission.[50] Indeed, in *DPP for Northern Ireland v Lynch*, it was held that

---

[45] Ashworth, above n 1, 415; Clarkson et al, above n 4, 559.
[46] Ashworth, above n 1, 415–16; Ormerod, above n 2, 320; Simester and Sullivan, above n 1, 220–21.
[47] See RA Duff, '"Can I Help You?" Accessorial Liability and the Intention to Assist' (1990) 10 *Legal Studies* 165, 165–66; Smith, above n 9, 141.
[48] An exception is carved out for procurement, which requires a causal contribution by D that induces P to commit the offence. This implies that D must intend to facilitate the commission of the crime by P, and not merely to intend the act of facilitation. See Simester and Sullivan, above n 1, 220, fn 107, 221.
[49] *NBC v Gamble* [1959] 1 QB 11 (QBD).
[50] See Ashworth, above n 1, 417.

an accessory acting with knowledge in pursuance of a murderous plan would be liable even if he was horrified by it.[51]

The only clear contradictory authority which requires the accessory to have a purposive attitude is the decision in *Fretwell*, where D, who had reluctantly given an abortifacient to a woman who used it and died, was not held liable as an accomplice because he had been unwilling for the woman to take it.[52] The case of *Gillick* is also adduced as evidence of the requirement of a purposive intention.[53] Here, a doctor who supplied contraceptive advice and treatment for girls aged under 16 was not held guilty as an accomplice to the offence of unlawful sexual intercourse since he intended only to act in the best interests of the girl by protecting her from the risk of pregnancy or disease.[54] However, since their Lordships based their opinions on differing considerations and did not fully examine the earlier authorities in reaching their decisions, *Gillick* is not conclusive of the matter.[55] Indeed, some authors argue that *Gillick* and even *Fretwell* are better regarded as being implicitly based on the defences of duress or necessity on the part of the accessory.[56] In both cases, while D may have hoped that P would not commit the offence, it is incorrect to say that he did not intend the act of facilitation, regardless of whether he undertook the act for benevolent purposes or with reluctance.[57] Another approach is to view *Fretwell* as evidence for the proposition that clear disapproval of, or non-consent to, the principal's criminal act may negative the mental element required for accomplice liability.[58]

The purposive intent requirement favours a narrower reach of complicity responsibility by excluding cases of D's peripheral involvement in the conduct of P, where D and P lack any community of purpose.[59] It rejects penalising D when he is simply going about his ordinary course of business, such as selling certain commodities with the awareness that they may assist the commission of an offence by P.[60] This approach favours free trade and individual freedom,[61] and shifts the emphasis from the actual conduct of D, from what he actually did to his mental attitude for acting

[51]   *DPP for Northern Ireland v Lynch* [1975] AC 653 (HL), 678.
[52]   *R v Fretwell* (1862) Le & Ca 161.
[53]   See I Dennis, 'Intention and Complicity: A Reply' [1988] *Crim LR* 649, 655.
[54]   *Gillick v West Norfolk and Wisbech AHA* [1984] 1 QB 581 (QBD).
[55]   Smith, above n 9, 147–49; Ashworth, above n 1, 417.
[56]   Simester and Sullivan, above n 1, 221–22.
[57]   Ibid, 221.
[58]   IH Dennis, 'The Mental Element for Accessories' in P Smith (ed), *Criminal Law: Essays in Honour of JC Smith* (London, Butterworths, 1987) 52; Smith, above n 9, 149.
[59]   GR Sullivan, 'Intent, Purpose and Complicity' [1988] *Crim LR* 641.
[60]   Smith, above n 9, 150–51.
[61]   Ibid, 153; Ashworth, above n 1, 412.

thus.[62] It is consonant with the philosophy that men should not, in general, act as their brothers' keepers.[63]

However, the intent based on knowledge approach is not as grave an intrusion into personal liberty as the purposive stance would have us think. On this account, D's liability is based on a voluntary and knowing association with P's criminal behaviour.[64] D does not have to supervise P's actions, enquire after her purpose or take any steps to prevent P from acting. D must simply desist from voluntarily assisting P when he is aware that P intends to commit an offence.[65] The intrusion into D's freedom, in so far as it exists, may be justified in the interests of protecting the rights of victims not to be attacked, burgled or subject to any other criminal activities.[66]

Nonetheless, there is perhaps good reason to incorporate a purpose requirement into the fault element for secondary liability. Doing so would ensure that the link between D's conduct and the offence committed by P is not so attenuated as to make the parity of culpability between D and P a mockery. At the same time, concerns that this requirement would unduly restrict the scope of the criminal law in protecting rights of potential victims should to some extent be alleviated by the introduction of section 45 of the Serious Crime Act 2007, which provides for the offence of encouraging or assisting an offence believing that it will be committed.[67] While D would not be accountable as an accessory in the same manner and to the same extent under this provision , it would still provide for the possibility of his culpability in a situation where he acts with the knowledge that his conduct will assist the commission of an offence by P.

B. Knowledge/Foresight of Essential Matters

The classic statement on the accomplice's mental state with respect to the offence committed by the principal is found in the decision of *Johnson v Youden*: the accessory must know the 'essential matters' that constitute the offence.[68] This implies:[69]

(a) D must know the conduct element of P's offence;
(b) D must know the consequences and circumstances of P's conduct; and
(c) D must know the fact of P's *mens rea*.

---

[62] Sullivan, above n 59, 641.
[63] Duff, above n 47, 180; Smith, above n 9, 153; Ashworth, above n 1, 412.
[64] Duff, above n 47, 171 setting out the position.
[65] Simester and Sullivan, above n 1, 225.
[66] Ibid.
[67] See Ashworth, above n 1, 412–13.
[68] *Johnson v Youden* [1950] 1 KB 544 (DC), 546.
[69] Smith, above n 9, 178, 180; Ormerod, above n 2, 328–30.

Questions arise as to the degree of specificity of knowledge required on the part of D: must D have actual knowledge, or is it sufficient that he was reckless? What are the 'essential matters' of the offence?

On the latter question, two main principles have evolved. D must know either:

(a) the type of offence intended (and eventually committed) by P; or
(b) that P would commit any one of a number of offences (and P eventually commits one of them).[70]

The former test was adopted by the Court of Criminal Appeal in *Bainbridge*, where the court held that D must not merely suspect but actually know that P intends to commit a crime of the *type* actually committed.[71] The content of the term 'type' was left unresolved.[72] The latter test was propounded by the House of Lords in *DPP for Northern Ireland v Maxwell*,[73] where Maxwell drove a group of terrorists to a public house knowing that it would form the target of an attack of violence, but being unaware of what exactly was planned. He was held liable as an accessory on the basis that even though he did not know the particular crime intended, he knew or contemplated the crime eventually committed as having been on the principal's 'shopping list' of offences.[74] In other words, it was sufficient that the crime committed by P was within the range of possible offences contemplated by D.[75] The relationship between the *Bainbridge* and *Maxwell* tests is not quite clear.[76] For instance, under *Maxwell*, D may not be liable for a crime which was not within the range of offences he contemplated P might commit, even if it is of the same type as one of these offences.[77] In any event, section 46 of the Serious Crime Act 2007 brings within its ambit the situation represented by *Maxwell* by providing for the offence of encouraging or assisting offences believing that one or more will be committed.[78]

The principle in *Maxwell* also highlights the issue of the requirement for the accomplice's *knowledge* of the offence as contrasted with simple *foresight*. The earlier position was that mere recklessness or a belief that an offence is likely to be committed is not enough; there must be actual

---

[70] Dennis, above n 58, 45; Ormerod, above n 2, 341–42 (Ormerod also mention a third test concerning joint enterprise cases which we shall consider in section IV. below); Simester and Sullivan, above n 1, 230.

[71] *R v Bainbridge* [1960] 1 QB 129 (CCA).

[72] Smith, above n 9, 164: Ormerod, above n 2, 336–37.

[73] *DPP for Northern Ireland v Maxwell* [1978] WLR 1350.

[74] See Dennis, above n 58, 45.

[75] Ibid.

[76] Smith, above n 9, 166.

[77] Ormerod, above n 2, 203.

[78] See Ashworth, above n 1, 420.

knowledge.[79] However, the current law supports a test of recklessness as sufficient.[80] *Maxwell* itself points to that conclusion, for if it is only required that D must know that one of a certain range of offences will be committed then, with respect to the particular offence which is eventually committed, D need only believe that it is likely to be committed.[81] Other decisions have also clearly articulated the test of foresight.[82] For instance, in *Carter v Richardson*, D was convicted as an accessory for the offence of drink driving since he was aware that P had consumed so much alcohol that it was 'probable that his blood alcohol content was over the limit'.[83] Similarly, in *Bryce*, the court considered it sufficient that at the time D aided P (by transporting him to the scene of the crime), he contemplated a 'real possibility' that P would commit the type of offence he eventually did.[84]

Simester challenges this dilution of the knowledge standard by arguing that the holdings in the cases supporting this standard are either obiter, or elide the distinction between the fault elements for aiding and abetting on the one hand and for joint enterprise liability on the other.[85] He opposes the lowering of the *mens rea* standard on the basis that any less stringent requirement would not sufficiently involve D in P's conduct so as to justify her conviction as an accessory.[86] It is only when D acts either with the purpose or with the awareness of facilitating P's crime that her otherwise lawful conduct becomes a wrong, and establishes a link between her culpability and the ultimate harm.[87] The knowledge standard also entails fewer sacrifices on the part of the citizen and is more conducive to individual freedom.[88] Simester's arguments are persuasive, particularly after the enactment of the provisions of Serious Crime Act 2007, which would still operate to cover situations such as *Maxwell* and prevent the net of criminal liability from being cast too narrowly. However, they are difficult to accept in light of the weight of the case law which supports the test of recklessness, unless one can make a convincing case that joint enterprise liability (with which most of the cases upholding this standard were concerned) is a distinct species of accessorial responsibility from aiding and abetting.

---

[79] AP Simester, 'The Mental Element in Complicity' (2006) 122 *LQR* 578, 583; Simester and Sullivan, above n 1, 226–27.

[80] Simester and Sullivan, above n 1, 227, 228 and references therein.

[81] Ashworth, above n 1, 419. See also Smith, above n 9, 169.

[82] See, eg *Rook* [1993] 1 WLR 1005; *Reardon* [1999] Crim LR 392.

[83] *Carter v Richardson* [1974] RTR 314 (QBD). For criticism of the reasoning in *Carter*, see Simester and Sullivan, above n 1, 227.

[84] *Bryce* [2004] EWCA Crim 1231, [2004] 2 Cr App R 35 (CA).

[85] Simester, above n 79, 585.

[86] Ibid, 589.

[87] Ibid, 589–90.

[88] Ibid, 592; Simester and Sullivan, above n 1, 228.

IV. JOINT ENTERPRISE LIABILITY

A. Elements and Structure of Joint Enterprise Liability

Under current English law, secondary responsibility also includes the concept of joint venture, though the precise elements required for its establishment are quite controversial.[89] Joint enterprise liability may take one of two forms. The first or 'basic' form is when D and P agree or act in concert to commit crime X (say burglary). D will be party to the joint venture if he intended that the burglary be committed, or if he foresaw that P or any other party to the agreement might commit the burglary.[90] The second and more controversial form, which Smith labels 'parasitic accessory liability',[91] arises when in the course of committing crime X, P goes on to commit a further crime Y (say, murder). In this situation, D will be liable on the basis of joint enterprise liability if:[92]

(a) D and P embark on a joint venture for the commission of crime X;
(b) D had foreseen that in the course of committing crime X, there was a real risk that P might commit a further crime; and
(c) crime Y committed by P occurred as an incident of the joint enterprise and did not fundamentally differ from the crime anticipated by D.

The leading case on joint enterprise liability is the Privy Council decision in *Chan Wing Siu*, where in the course of a joint enterprise to commit a robbery, one of the parties to the venture killed one of the victims with a knife. The defendants argued that the knives they carried were meant only to frighten the victims and not to cause any injury. In upholding the conviction of the defendants for the killing, Sir Robin Cooke used the language of

> contemplation, or putting the same idea in other words, authorisation, which may be express but is more usually implied. It meets the case of a crime foreseen as a possible incident of the common unlawful enterprise. The criminal culpability lies in participating in the venture with that foresight.[93]

As was noted in section I. above, the rationale of authorisation or agreement has now given way to the test of subjective foresight of a substantial

---

[89] Ashworth, above n 1, 420; Ormerod, above n 2, 182, who state that, unlike in Australian law, participants in a JCE are not principals but secondary parties.
[90] JC Smith, 'Criminal Liability of Accessories: Law and Law Reform' (1997) 113 *LQR* 453, 454; R Sullivan, 'First Degree Murder and Complicity – Conditions for Parity of Culpability between Principal and Accomplice' (2007) 1 *Criminal Law & Philosophy* 271, 274.
[91] Smith, above n 90, 454–55.
[92] Ibid, 455; Sullivan, above n 90, 275; Ashworth, above n 1, 420; Ormerod, above n 2, 341–42.
[93] *Chan Wing-Siu* [1985] AC 168, 175.

risk that the collateral crime might be committed.[94] Thus, if D and P plan a robbery, and D foresees that P may possibly use force while committing the robbery, he will be held liable for the harm resulting from the contingent use of force by P, regardless of whether he intended the harm to occur and even if he dreaded its possibility.[95]

B. Scope of the Common Purpose and Fundamentally Different Act

The issue of the accessory's foresight or contemplation is central to the determination of responsibility arising out of participation in a joint criminal venture. The very scope of the joint enterprise depends on 'what was contemplated by parties sharing that purpose'.[96] Thus, D will not be liable for a crime Y committed by P in the course of committing crime X, if the act done by P was 'fundamentally different' from what D contemplated.[97]

The scope of the joint venture becomes controversial in cases of spontaneous violence that are alleged to be in pursuance of a joint enterprise. For instance, *O'Flaherty*[98] and *Mitchell*[99] both concerned cases of spontaneous violence where the idea of a prior plan or agreement to commit certain acts could not be applied to the conduct of the defendants. In both instances, the issue was whether the ultimate offence with which D had been charged was committed in the course of an evolving joint enterprise of which D had continued to be a part, or whether there were two discrete joint enterprises, and D had been involved in only one of them and had withdrawn from the other which led to the crime. In *O'Flaherty*, R and T had participated in the initial attack on V at place A, but then refrained from accompanying the group to place B where V was further assaulted, suffered stab wounds and a head injury, and died. F did follow the attackers to B, armed with a cricket bat, and was present when the attack at B occurred, though he did not participate in it. The Court held that in such cases of spontaneous violence, the scope of the joint enterprise must be inferred 'from the knowledge and actions of individual participants'. Since there was no evidence to support that the pursuit was part of a joint enterprise by R and T, their appeals against the murder conviction were permitted. On the other hand, since F had continued in the pursuit armed with a weapon, he was still within the joint enterprise and could be

---

[94] Smith, above n 90, 457; Ashworth, above n 1, 422.

[95] See Simester and Sullivan, above n 1, 234.

[96] *R v Powell and English* [1999] 1 AC 1, citing with approval *McAuliffe v Queen* (1995) 183 CLR 108 (HCA), 30, and *Hui Chi-ming v Queen* [1992] 1 AC 34. See Clarkson et al, above n 4, 557.

[97] Ormerod, above n 2, 347.

[98] *R v O'Flaherty* [2004] EWCA Crim 526, [2004] 2 Cr App R 20 (CA (Crim Div)).

[99] *R v Mitchell* [2008] EWCA Crim 2552, [2009] 1 Cr App R 31 (CA (Crim Div)).

considered to have provided encouragement, or at least be ready to lend support to the attackers. His appeal was therefore dismissed. The distinction made by the Court between R, T and F does not seem to depend so much on what each party had contemplated – indeed, all three might very well have foreseen that V might be killed in the violence. However, through their *actions*, R and T were considered to have withdrawn from the enterprise. This was not true of F, whose conduct still potentially contributed (through his act of encouragement) to the commission of the fatal offence. The distinction between R and T on the one hand and F on the other thus appears to be based on the causal contribution to the principal's conduct by the accessory in a joint enterprise.

The question of what makes P's act 'fundamentally different' from that contemplated by D has also caused some confusion, that is, whether it relates to the difference in weapons used by P, P's actions or intentions, or the consequences of P's acts.[100] For instance in *English*, during an attack by D and P using wooden stakes, P killed the victim with a knife. Lord Hutton held that the use of the knife in this case was fundamentally different from that of a wooden post and thus fell outside the scope of the enterprise as contemplated by D.[101] This principle was reiterated by the House of Lords in *Rahman*, where D, along with a group of people armed with a variety of blunt instruments, engaged in a gang fight during the course of which the victim was stabbed, resulting in his death. D argued that he did not know that any of the members possessed a knife, nor that they would act with the intent to kill. The House of Lords held that P's intent to kill was not fundamentally different from the real risk of death or grievous bodily harm being caused intentionally that had been foreseen by D.[102] The test of fundamental difference applied to the nature of P's acts or his actual conduct rather than to his intent.[103]

Simester and Sullivan interpret the concept of fundamental difference in *English* and *Rahman* to be most closely related to the degree of dangerousness, that is, if the weapon used by P was different from the weapon which D contemplated he might use but equally dangerous, D will still be liable under joint enterprise liability.[104] The degree of dangerousness is not evaluated solely according to the weapon used, however, but also by taking into account the context and other evidence.[105] This test of dangerous-

---

[100] Ormerod, above n 2, 347–49.

[101] *Giannetto* [1997] 1 Cr App R 1 (CA); Simester and Sullivan, above n 1, 237.

[102] *R v Rahman* [2008] UKHL 45, [2009] 1 AC 129 (HL). See Ashworth, above n 1, 423, 425.

[103] Ashworth, above n 1, 425; Simester and Sullivan, above n 1, 238. As has recently been emphasised, this holding does not imply that D need not foresee that P might act with intent. D must foresee not only that P may commit the *actus reus* of crime Y, but that he may do so with the requisite *mens rea* for crime Y. See *R v A* [2010] EWCA Crim 1622, [2011] QB 841(CA (Crim Div)); D Ormerod, 'Case Comment: R v A' [2011] *Crim LR* 61, 63–64.

[104] Simester and Sullivan, above n 1, 238–39. They also cite the decision of the Court of Appeal in *R v Uddin* [1999] QB 431 (CA), 441, as supporting this reasoning.

[105] Simester and Sullivan, above n 1, 239.

ness appears to be endorsed by the Court of Appeal's decision in *R v Mendez*.[106] There, V was chased and attacked by a group of partygoers, resulting in injuries that were not particularly serious. However, he died as a result of three stab wounds that were inflicted on his chest. The defendants were both convicted of murder as secondary parties. One of the issues before the Court was whether the first defendant was guilty of murder, since it had not been suggested that he knew that anyone in the group possessed a knife. The Court held that it would be unjust for D to be held guilty of V's murder by P, if its direct cause was a deliberate act by P which was of a different kind and significantly more life-threatening than the kinds of acts D intended or foresaw.[107]

However, the Court also appeared to reintroduce the notion of causation into the test of fundamental difference by framing it thus:[108] 'Conduct by P which involves a total and substantial variation from that encouraged by D could not properly be regarded as the "fruit" of D's encouragement, nor with propriety be said to have been committed under D's influence.'[109] This is not an accurate summation of the test, as joint enterprise liability does not rest on whether D's act is causally connected to the eventual crime committed by P but on whether D contemplated that P might commit it with the requisite *mens rea*.[110]

In any event, the interpretation of fundamental difference based on dangerousness seems too narrow, as it concerns primarily cases of differences in weapons and does not yield a broader principle that would apply to other deviations. A more useful approach is to look at whether P acted so as to bring about the consequence which D contemplated. Whether P chooses to use a knife or a gun, the victim is equally dead in either case. The method by which he accomplished this result should be irrelevant.[111] Conversely, even if D knew that P had a knife, if he contemplated only that P would use it to frighten the victim, he should not be held responsible if P stabbed the victim instead causing his death.[112] The test of foresight or contemplation thus seems mostly closely related to the expected outcome of P's conduct.[113] Smith's example of D and P who jointly act to administer drug X to the victim, where P knows that X will kill the victim whereas D believes that it will only make him ill, illustrates this point. The administration of a fatal drug is fundamentally different from the administration of one that causes only a minor illness. D can legitimately claim

---

[106] *R v Mendez* [2010] EWCA Crim 516, [2011] QB 876 (CA (Crim Div)).
[107] Ibid, [47]; see M Dyson, 'More Appealing Joint Enterprise' (2010) 69 *CLJ* 425–28.
[108] See D Ormerod, 'Case Comment: R v Mendez (Reece)' [2010] *Crim LR* 874, 877.
[109] *Mendez*, above n 106, [20].
[110] Ormerod, above n 108, 877.
[111] JC Smith, 'Case and Comment: R v Powell and Daniels' [1998] *Crim LR* 48, 50; Ashworth, above n 1, 425; Ormerod, above n 2, 214; Clarkson et al, above n 4, 563.
[112] Smith, above n 111, 51.
[113] See Ashworth, above n 1, 425.

that he would not have been part of the joint venture had he known the true nature of the drug.[114] This statement of the test of fundamental difference must be qualified, however, to deal with the kinds of situations discussed below, where D will not be responsible for the offence committed by P but may nonetheless be liable for a lesser offence arising out of the same act done by P.[115]

C. Conviction for a Different Offence

A further refinement of the contemplation or foresight requirement is introduced in the case where D foresees only that P might resort to violence in the course of the joint enterprise; D does not foresee P's murderous state of mind. In this situation, can D be convicted of the lesser offence of manslaughter while P is held guilty of murder, or must D be acquitted completely? English courts have not been uniform in their decisions on this matter, and there are both authorities supporting D's conviction for the lesser offence[116] and authorities that would acquit him altogether.[117] The difference turns essentially on what the accessory's foresight determines – his level of culpability, or the scope of the joint venture. For instance, in *Smith*, Lord Parker CJ considered that the accessory's liability stems from the scope of the joint venture, and that his foresight determines only the level of his culpability.[118] A similar rationale was propounded in *Gilmour*[119] and *Day*,[120] which support accessorial liability for the lesser offence in cases where the principal may have 'larger intentions', on the basis of the accessory's personal state of mind.[121] The cases that reject secondary liability for manslaughter, on the other hand, rely on the fact that violence that is of a gravity which D did not foresee takes P's conduct outside the scope of the joint venture.[122]

The former approach would approximate more closely the general shift from assessing D's culpability on the basis of the derivative theory of responsibility to one that evaluates his conduct independently.[123] On this theory, D could indeed be convicted of manslaughter based on what he

---

[114] JC Smith, 'Commentary: R v Day (M) and Others' [2001] *Crim LR* 984, 985; Ormerod, above n 2, 354.

[115] Ormerod, above n 2, 352–54.

[116] *R v Betty* (1964) 48 Cr App R 72; *R v Reid* (1976) 62 Cr App R 109 (CA); *R v Stewart and Scholfield* [1995] 1 Cr App R 441 (CA).

[117] *R v Dunbar* [1998] Crim LR 693; *Uddin*, above n 104; *Powell and English*, above n 96.

[118] *R v Smith* [1963] 1 WLR 1200 (CCA). See Smith, *Criminal Complicity*, above n 9, 226–27.

[119] *R v Gilmour* [2002] 2 Cr App Rep 407 (NICA).

[120] *R v Day* [2001] Crim LR 984 (CA (Crim Div)).

[121] Clarkson et al, above n 4, 562, citing commentary to *Day*, above n 120, 985.

[122] GR Sullivan, 'Participating in Crime: Law Com No 305 – Joint Criminal Ventures' [2008] *Crim LR* 19, 24.

[123] See Ashworth, above n 1, 426.

foresaw, and P's deviation would not result in his acquittal. This conclusion is also supported in more recent jurisprudence.[124] In *Yemoh*,[125] during an attack on V by D and others, V was stabbed and died. D had foreseen that P might use a knife to inflict harm, but might not have foreseen P's intention to kill. The Court of Appeal, relying on the reasoning in *Rahman*, upheld D's conviction for manslaughter, as D had foreseen the essential elements of manslaughter and P's having acted with intent to kill was not fundamentally different from what D had contemplated.[126] In any event, under Part 2 of the Serious Crime Act 2007, D may be convicted of encouraging and assisting the crime he contemplated, regardless of P's subsequent conduct.[127]

D. Joint Enterprise as a Distinct Mode of Accomplice Liability

The status of joint enterprise liability as a form of secondary responsibility, as opposed to principal responsibility, is uncontroversial in English law.[128] It is less certain whether joint enterprise is simply a variant of other forms of secondary liability, or whether it forms a distinct category of accessorial responsibility. The Law Commission's Consultation Paper No 131[129] appears to support the latter position, as does the decision in *Stewart and Schofield*, where Hobhouse LJ distinguished joint enterprise from aiding, abetting, etc, stating that 'when the allegation is joint enterprise, the allegation is that one defendant participated in the criminal act of another'.[130]

Simester and Sullivan strongly favour the position that joint enterprise is distinct from liability as an aider and abettor, both normatively and structurally.[131] Structurally, liability for aiding and abetting involves only a single offence which is aided or encouraged by D and eventually committed by P. Joint enterprise doctrine has nothing special to say about this scenario; it comes into its own in the cases that Smith labels 'parasitic' secondary liability which consist of two offences: the joint venture to commit offence X by D and P, and the further offence Y which P commits alone. D does not contribute to offence Y; his connection to offence Y operates through the joint venture and his liability consists in having foreseen

---

[124] See Simester and Sullivan, above n 1, 241–42.
[125] *R v Yemoh* [2009] EWCA Crim 930, [2009] Crim LR 888.
[126] See Simester and Sullivan, above n 1, 241–42.
[127] See Ashworth, above n 1, 426.
[128] In contrast, parties to an unlawful joint enterprise are considered co-principals in South African law. See eg, J Burchell, 'Joint Enterprise and Common Purpose: Perspectives in English and South African Criminal Law' (1997) 10 *South African Journal of Criminal Justice* 125, 139.
[129] Law Commission, *Assisting and Encouraging Crime* (Consultation Paper No 131, 1993).
[130] *R v Stewart and Scholfield*, above n 116.
[131] Simester, above n 79, 593; Simester and Sullivan, above n 1, 243.

its commission as a possible consequence of the venture.[132] Simester argues that if joint enterprise were merely a sub-species of assistance and encouragement, one could dispense with the requirement of crime X altogether and then apply the same criteria for secondary liability for crime Y as would exist for the other forms of secondary liability. This is not the case, however: at the very least, the conduct element differs widely. In contrast with other forms of secondary liability, D need not directly assist or encourage crime Y. Instead, he must participate in the joint venture, and it is his commitment to the common purpose that makes him liable for crime Y. Such a showing of common purpose is not required for standard cases of accomplice liability.[133]

According to Simester and Sullivan, it is the element of an unlawful agreement or concert that distinguishes joint enterprise liability from standard cases of aiding and abetting.[134] In the latter case, it is D's intentional or knowing association with P's unlawful conduct that makes his conduct a wrong. In contrast, in joint enterprise liability, D's wrong consists in his deliberate participation in a common endeavour to commit a crime.[135] It is D's voluntary affiliation with a shared criminal purpose (to commit crime A) which justifies his assumption of responsibility for crime B which he only foresees, and which exempts him from the more demanding requirements of having actually encouraged or helped crime B, as would be the case in standard forms of complicity.[136]

The majority of the commentators, however, consider joint enterprise a species of liability for assistance and encouragement. This is partly based on the law's shift from the requirement of tacit agreement to one based on the accomplice's contemplation to ground liability for the collateral offence. This test of (subjective) foresight of the further offence is similar to the basis for holding D liable under other modes of secondary responsibility.[137] Smith also argues against the proposition that one can simply drop crime X (the basic offence) out of the picture and assess D's liability directly in relation to crime Y: since D's liability for crime Y is parasitic on the joint venture to commit crime X, logically, it cannot exist without the basic liability for crime X.[138] This also makes the the *actus reus* elements of joint enterprise cases relatively similar to those of standard forms of secondary liability. D can only participate in the acts of P through assistance or encouragement in either case; the only difference is that in joint enterprise cases, the aiding or abetting takes the form of a joint venture to

---

[132] Ibid, 593; ibid, 243–44.
[133] Ibid, 593, 595, 598.
[134] Ibid, 598; Simester and Sullivan, above n 1, 243.
[135] Ibid, 598–99; ibid, 243.
[136] Ibid, 598–99; ibid, 243.
[137] Dennis, above n 58, 43; G Virgo, 'Clarifying Accessorial Liability' (1998) 57 *CLJ* 13, 15.
[138] Smith, above n 90, 462.

commit crime X and there is no need to prove any further acts of facilitation in respect of crime Y.[139]

This crucial element of the joint venture which results in the commission of additional wrongs for which D can be held liable, however, deserves to be taken as seriously as urged by Simester and Sullivan. The common purpose results in a shared bond of affiliation between D and P and other members of the joint venture which the mere aider or abettor, who need not have a purposive attitude towards P and his acts, lacks. The normative position of the voluntarily committed gang member D1 is thus very different from that of the independent aider and abettor D2.[140] It is moreover this shared purpose that broadens the liability of D for the collateral offence Y, to which he does not contribute in any manner. Thus, while the conduct element for standard forms of accessorial responsibility must exist in relation to crime X which is ultimately committed, the conduct element for joint enterprise responsibility need only exist in relation to X, and not for crime Y which P eventually commits. Moreover, joint enterprise liability has a representational value that distinguishes it from liability for aiding and abetting: it is a more accurate account of the roles played by different members in a criminal enterprise committed to the commission of certain offences during the course of which one or more members go on to commit collateral offences.[141]

E. Justification for Joint Enterprise Responsibility

At first glance, liability arising out of participation in a joint criminal venture, particularly D's liability for the collateral offence committed by P, appears to extend unduly the scope of D's liability for offences to which he has made no direct contribution. Several arguments, both normative and pragmatic, have been adduced, however, to support this extension. One set of arguments focuses on the conduct of the secondary party and is grounded in his voluntary association with a criminal venture. The element of collusion not only constitutes a manifestation of D's criminal proclivities,[142] but also makes his conduct an independent wrong.[143] D's participation in the unlawful enterprise represents his affiliation with a segment of society that has set itself against the rule of law.[144] Even if D does not make any direct contribution to the collateral offence, he is indirectly causally connected to it, as he helps to create or contributes to the

---

[139] Ibid, 463; Ormerod, above n 2, 341.
[140] Simester, above n 79, 598–99; Simester and Sullivan, above n 1, 244.
[141] See Dennis, above n 58, 43.
[142] Smith, above n 9, 6.
[143] Simester, above n 79, 600–01; Simester and Sullivan, above n 1, 244, fn 260.
[144] Ibid, 600; ibid, 244.

situation in which it occurs.[145] In more close-knit ventures, D may also be in a position of authority to exercise supervision over the other members and restrain their conduct.[146] This reasoning appears to base D's conviction on his 'criminal proclivities', and is not particularly persuasive. Apart from being circular, the argument does not have anything to say about how the same logic should not then apply to D's liability for aiding and abetting. D's purported affiliation with anti-rule-of law sentiments as a basis for his extended liability is also unconvincing. Arguably, anyone who commits or facilitates the commission of an offence in any manner exhibits the same characteristics.

A second set of justifications for joint enterprise liability rests on a risk/endangerment rationale similar to that used for inchoate offences. Through his association in a criminal enterprise, D increases the likelihood that the collateral offence will occur.[147] Criminal enterprises also represent a greater threat to public safety than individuals acting alone, as the members of the enterprise tend to mutually reinforce individual criminal tendencies, discouraging withdrawal and often resulting in an escalation of crime.[148] Moreover, liability based on participation in the joint enterprise deters people from associating with criminal ventures, and thus makes the offences less likely to occur.[149] These are empirical claims that have some merit, but they need to be supported further by fairly comprehensive studies in other areas of the social sciences. The argument on deterrence especially does not seem very plausible. At least in cases of joint enterprise that involve spontaneous outbreaks of violence such as street fights, it is unlikely that the potential for punishment would feature very strongly in the decision-making calculus of a party to the enterprise. Neither is it entirely clear that even if one or more persons were to be deterred from participating in the joint venture, this would reduce the chances of the offence being committed. Offences that are committed pursuant to joint ventures which involve a relatively large number of persons, or in which individual actors are more or less dispensable, would be just as likely to occur.

V. CONCLUSION

As the analysis in this chapter reveals, the English law on secondary liability is not entirely straightforward or coherent. While causal, agency and endangerment explanations ground various aspects of accessorial

---

[145] See PH Robinson, 'Imputed Criminal Liability' (1984) 93 *Yale Law Journal* 609, 633.
[146] See Smith, above n 9, 233.
[147] Ibid, 6.
[148] Simester, above n 79, 600–01; Ashworth, above n 1, 403; Simester and Sullivan, above n 1, 244.
[149] Smith, above n 9, 233; see also Ashworth, above n 1, 404.

responsibility, no single policy rationale serves to tie together the different means by which D is held accountable as a secondary party to the crime. Nevertheless, the emphasis on the fault element of subjective foresight for all forms of accomplice liability, when taken together with the creation of auxiliary offences of complicity under the Serious Crime Act 2007, points towards a focus on the mental attitude and conduct of the accessory, assessed independently from the principal, for the assignment of responsibility. This is true not only for the standard forms of complicity, but also for joint enterprise responsibility.

Before we examine whether the doctrinal bases for secondary responsibility in English law can support JCE liability in international criminal law, we shall examine whether German law has any equivalent for this mode of participation.

10

The Accessory in German Criminal Law Theory

I. THE FRAMEWORK FOR SECONDARY RESPONSIBILITY

T HE GERMAN CRIMINAL Code (*Strafgesetzbuch*, StGB – see also chapter seven) recognises two categories of accomplice liability: aiding and instigation:

Section 26 Instigation

Any person who intentionally induces another to intentionally commit an unlawful act (abettor) shall be liable to be sentenced as if he were a principal.

Section 27 Aiding

(1) Any person who intentionally assists another in the intentional commission of an unlawful act shall be convicted and sentenced as an aider.
(2) The sentence for the aider shall be based on the penalty for a principal. It shall be mitigated pursuant to section 49(1).

German criminal law conceives of the accessory as the marginal figure, who merely facilitates the course of events, without controlling it.[1] His participation is of such secondary weight that it is evaluated as a contribution to the unlawful act of a third party.[2] His act represents a different degree of attack against the legal interest protected by the elements of the offence (as compared to the perpetrator),[3] and his criminal responsibility is contingent on the existence of an unlawful act intentionally committed by the perpetrator.[4] This difference is also reflected in the operative provisions of judgments, where the verdict specifically mentions either instigation or assistance to denote participation in the act of another.[5]

---

[1] U Sieber and M Engelhart, *Strafbare Mitwirkung von Führungspersonen in Straftätergruppen und Netzwerken in Deutschland* (Max-Planck-Institut für ausländisches und internationales Strafrecht, unpublished report, 2009) ('MPICC Report') 13.
[2] Ibid.
[3] Ibid.
[4] Ibid.
[5] Ibid, 14.

The distinction between principals and accessories also has significant practical consequences.[6] For instance, the rules for attempts under Sections 22 to 24 of the StGB regulate only the conduct of perpetrators, whereas accessorial attempts are regulated under Section 30. Attempted instigation is criminalised, and there is an obligatory mitigation of punishment under Section 49(1); attempted aid remains unpunished.[7] As Section 27(2) makes clear, there is also an obligatory mitigation of punishment for the aider as compared to the perpetrator. This is based on the reasoning that the aider merely renders help to an actor who is already determined to carry out an unlawful act.[8]

The rationale for accessorial responsibility in German criminal law mirrors the conventional account of accomplice liability in English criminal law – the accessory's liability derives from the main act of the perpetrator. However, unlike the traditional requirement in English law of an 'offence' by principal P which forms the basis of accessory D's criminal liability, German law recognises the concept of *limitierte Akzessorietät* which signals the limited dependence of accessorial liability on the main offence. Thus, D's liability derives from the unlawful act of P,[9] and his culpability is assessed separately from that of P under Section 29 of the StGB.[10] Consequently, if the main act by P is not intentional or is justified, or does not fulfil the elements of the offence, D will not be liable; conversely, if P only lacks culpability and is excused, D may still be subject to criminal responsibility.[11]

The principle of *limitierte Akzessorietät* does not explain fully the rationale behind the criminal responsibility of accessories. Five main theories have been put forward, three of which endorse an independent evaluation of accessorial conduct:

(a) the doctrine of participation in guilt;
(b) the doctrine of solidarity with wrongfulness; and
(c) the pure causation theory.

The fourth, accessory-orientated causation theory, considers the accessory to have caused the perpetrator's behaviour, which makes him criminally responsible. The fifth is the doctrine of accessorial attack on the legally protected interest, and it combines elements of both these approaches.

---

[6] Ibid, 15.

[7] Ibid.

[8] Ibid, 11, 14.

[9] M Bohlander, *Principles of German Criminal Law: Studies in International and Comparative Criminal Law* (Oxford, Hart Publishing, 2009) 168; H Laufhütte et al (eds), *Strafgesetzbuch Leipziger Kommentar (Großkommentar): Band 1* (Berlin, de Gruyter Recht, 2006) 1977.

[10] S 29, StGB. Every participant shall be punished according to his own guilt irrespective of the guilt of the other.

[11] J Wessels and W Beulke, *Strafrecht, allgemeiner Teil: Die Straftat und ihr Aufbau (Schwerpunkte)* (CF Müller Verlag, 2012) 209–10; MPICC Report, above n 1, 34–35; *Leipziger Kommentar*, above n 9, 1977.

Under the doctrine of participation in guilt or culpability, the accessory's criminal responsibility stems from the fact that he corrupts the perpetrator and entangles him in culpable conduct.[12] The pure version of this theory is clearly rejected by the positive law, which does not require the existence of a culpable main act for accessorial liability.[13] A modified guilt participation doctrine has been proposed by Trechsel, who views the accessory as liable for having involved the perpetrator in wrongful acts. The perpetrator himself may not necessarily be culpable, but the accessory's actions still lead to the perpetrator being subjected to a criminal investigation and, in some cases, to the imposition of sanctions.[14] However, this modified theory does not account for the standard case of aiding, where the perpetrator is already resolved to commit an unlawful act.[15] It also severely understates the role of the perpetrator in the commission of an offence – the perpetrator is not a victim but an independent person responsible for his own acts and decisions; he cannot make the accessory a scapegoat for his conduct.[16] As is the case with the agency rationale in English law, the guilt participation theory risks reversing the relationship between the perpetrator and the accomplice, such that the accomplice becomes the central figure in the commission of the crime.

Another theory that emphasises the independent wrongfulness of the accessorial act is the doctrine of solidarity with the wrongfulness of a third party. The accessory's culpability lies in his solidarity, as manifested by his intentional contribution to the unlawful act of a third party; the accessory thus makes common cause with the unlawful act of the perpetrator.[17] The solidarity theory is helpful in explaining why situations like neutral everyday actions (such as the sale of a screwdriver to a person who uses it to commit theft) would not be punishable as aid, for lack of solidarity with the perpetrator.[18] Nonetheless, it does not adequately explain the rationale for the accessory's punishment, as it fails to refer to the accessory's role in the fulfilment of the elements of an offence.[19] If D instigates P to commit a murder, his criminal responsibility stems from the death of the victim, and not merely from his solidarity with P.[20] It also does not describe accurately the relation between D and P in many cases. Even if D exclusively pursues his own interests in instigating P, he should still be liable as an instigator. Similarly, the fact that D aids P in exchange

---

[12] *Leipziger Kommentar*, above n 9, 1973; C Roxin, *Täterschaft und Tatherrschaft* (Berlin, de Gruyter Recht, 2006) 133.

[13] *Leipziger Kommentar*, above n 9, 1973; Roxin, above n 12, 133.

[14] Ibid, 1973; ibid, 133.

[15] Ibid, 1973; ibid, 133.

[16] Roxin, above n 12, 134.

[17] *Leipziger Kommentar*, above n 9, 1976; Roxin, above n 12, 134.

[18] Ibid, 1976; ibid, 135.

[19] Ibid, 1976; ibid, 135.

[20] Roxin, above n 12, 135.

for a small fee and is quite indifferent to, or even disapproving of, the main act carried out by P does not affect his liability as an aider.[21]

The pure causation theory makes the accessory responsible for the result of the elements of the offence intentionally caused by him, and independently from the perpetrator's act.[22] In its most radical form, accessorial responsibility is dependent on whether the legal interest protected by the elements of the offence is protected against injury by the accessory. If that is the case, the accessory will be liable despite the lack of a main act by the perpetrator.[23] Thus, for example, secondary participation in suicide will be punishable, since the life of the victim is protected against all third parties, even if the victim cannot realise the elements of the offence (of suicide, which is not criminalised) in his own person.[24] The pure causation theory is, however, incompatible with Sections 26 and 27 of the StGB which incorporate the principle of *limitierte Akzessorietät*.[25] It also leads to an unjustified expansion of liability by relinquishing the connection between the wrongfulness of the perpetrator's act and the conduct of the accessory.[26]

The theory endorsed by the majority of the commentators and the BGH is the doctrine of accessory-orientated causation, which bases D's punishability on his causation of P's intentional and unlawful conduct.[27] The wrongfulness of D's act consists in his participation in the injury to a norm brought about by P; it is thus dependent on the reason and measure of the wrongfulness of the main act.[28] The doctrine rejects alternative theories that are premised on the independence of the accessory's wrongful conduct.[29] Lackner/Kühl summarise the predominant view thus: the instigator and aider facilitate and/or co-cause the unlawful act committed by the perpetrator.[30] The accessory-orientated causation theory, which resembles the doctrine of causation and derivative liability in English law, accords with the principle of *limitierte Akzessorietät* in Sections 26 and 27.[31] It cannot, however, explain certain aspects of the positive law, such as the impunity of the agent provocateur[32] or the non-criminalisation of neutral actions (as aid), even though such cases represent the causing of a punishable main act in an accessorial manner.[33]

---

[21] Ibid.
[22] Ibid, 131.
[23] *Leipziger Kommentar*, above n 9, 1974; Roxin, above n 12, 131.
[24] *Leipziger Kommentar*, above n 9, 1974.
[25] Ibid, 1974–75; Roxin, above n 12, 131.
[26] Ibid, 1975; ibid, 131.
[27] Ibid, 1975; ibid, 136.
[28] Ibid, 1975; ibid, 136.
[29] Roxin, above n 12, 136.
[30] *Leipziger Kommentar*, above n 9, 1975; Roxin, above n 12, 136.
[31] Ibid, 1975; ibid, 136.
[32] Ibid, 1976; ibid, 137.
[33] Ibid, 1976; ibid, 136, 137.

These concerns are accounted for in Claus Roxin's doctrine of secondary responsibility as an accessorial attack on the legally protected interest, which is based partly on the independence of the accessorial wrong and partly on its connection to the wrongfulness of the perpetrator's act.[34] It is derivative in that the intentional wrong committed by the perpetrator is attributed to the accessory. It is also independent to the extent that this attribution is possible only when the accessory's conduct also represents an independent attack on the protected legal interest.[35] Thus D, who requests P to kill him but survives, cannot be punished as an instigator because his life is not protected against an attack by himself (suicide is not criminalised).[36] This also justifies the impunity of the agent provocateur recognised in the law, since his action is not aimed at the fulfilment of the elements of the offence and thus not directed towards the injury of a protected legal interest.[37] The doctrine limits the range of criminal responsibility based on causal contribution by requiring an independent attack on the legal interest protected by the elements of the offence.[38] At the same time, it emphasises the nature of accomplice liability as a secondary concept to perpetration, by deriving its unlawfulness from the wrong committed by the perpetrator.[39]

II. INSTIGATION

According to Section 26 of the StGB (see section I. above), the instigator is someone who intentionally induces another person to commit an intentional and unlawful act. In this respect, instigation resembles assistance, which also calls for an intentional and unlawful main act. However, in contrast with assistance, instigation is a more serious form of participation, as the instigator is responsible for provoking the unlawful resolution of the perpetrator to commit an offence, whereas the aider merely assists a person who has already decided to commit it.[40] The instigator is thus jointly responsible (along with the perpetrator) for the causing of the act resolution, which justifies a higher punishment than that of the aider.[41]

---

[34] Roxin, above n 12, 130–31; *Leipziger Kommentar*, above n 9, 1972.
[35] Ibid, 131; ibid, 1971–72.
[36] *Leipziger Kommentar*, above n 9, 1970.
[37] Ibid, 1971.
[38] Ibid.
[39] Ibid, 1971–72.
[40] MPICC Report, above n 1, 36–37.
[41] *Leipziger Kommentar*, above n 9, 1986–87; see A Schönke and H Schröder, *Strafgesetzbuch: Kommentar*, 27th edn (Munich, CH Beck, 2006) 543.

A. The Instigator Must 'Induce' the Perpetrator

The instigation by D must be causal, or at least co-causal, for the perpetrator P's decision to commit the unlawful act.[42] The question then is whether any inducement that is causal for P's act resolution would qualify as instigation, or must D influence P's will in some fashion?[43] This issue has proved most controversial in cases where D's conduct merely leads to a situation that might provoke an unlawful act by P. For instance, can a thief who leaves money or jewellery on his trail to slow down his pursuers be guilty of instigating theft? Similarly, can a man who tells a bad-tempered husband that his wife is having an affair, and who supplies him with the name and address of the paramour, be liable for instigating bodily injury?[44] The situation also came up in a case before the BGH[45] (which unfortunately did not address this particular issue) in which D raped V and then asked P, who had been standing nearby and had not decided on having sexual intercourse with V, 'Do you want, too?'. P also then raped V. The BGH held D guilty of instigating the rape on the basis that he had a conditional intent to instigate. As commentators have pointed out, the BGH should first have considered whether a mere question, in the absence of factors such as pressure on P to prove his manhood, could suffice for instigation.[46]

Some commentators would hold D liable as an instigator in such situations lest more refined and subtle ways of inducement that still have some influence on P go unpunished.[47] However, this interpretation stretches the range of conduct covered by instigation a little too far. Unlike a concrete act of inducement, the mere creation of an act-provoking situation is in some ways too close to circumstances in everyday life that might potentially tempt a person into committing an offence.[48] It also belies the rationale for secondary responsibility as an independent attack on the legally protected interest. This would more readily be present in more direct cases of inducement by the accessory, where there is a concrete communicative influence by D on P.[49] Moreover, it makes the link between the conduct of the accessory and the unlawful act too tenuous to justify the equal punishment meted out to the perpetrator and the instigator.

On the other end of the spectrum, some scholars demand that the communicative influence should reach the level of a collusive agreement

---

[42] *Leipziger Kommentar*, above n 9, 1991 and references therein.
[43] Schönke and Schröder, above n 41, 543–44.
[44] See *Leipziger Kommentar*, above n 9, 1987; Roxin, above n 12, 153.
[45] BGH GA 1980, 183.
[46] Bohlander, above n 9, 169; *Leipziger Kommentar*, above n 9, 2002–03; Roxin, above n 12, 155.
[47] *Leipziger Kommentar*, above n 9, 1987.
[48] Ibid, 1987–88; Roxin, above n 12, 153.
[49] *Leipziger Kommentar*, above n 9, 1988; Schönke and Schröder, above n 41, 544.

between the instigator and the perpetrator.[50] Puppe calls this a 'wrongfulness pact', whereby P enters into an agreement with D who extracts a promise or an obligation from P that he will commit the unlawful act. This agreement is not legally but factually binding.[51] This doctrine does not accord with the terminology in Section 26 StGB. 'Obligating' P is different from 'inducing him' to commit an act: causing someone to reach the decision to commit an unlawful act through skilful persuasion is inducement and hence instigation; it still does not reach the level of an obligation.[52] On the other hand, if D gives P some money to beat up V, whom P had already decided to injure for personal reasons, this may count as an obligation, though not, as we shall see in section II.B below, incitement (as P is already resolved to commit the act).[53]

A more promising course is charted by the dominant doctrine of intellectual or mental contact, which requires that the instigator must influence the will of the perpetrator through overt intellectual or mental contact.[54] This would involve inciting P to commit the act such that it opens the possibility that P makes the incitement (in addition to his other motives and reasons) a basis for his act resolution.[55] In addition, however, D's statement that mentally influences P must have an objectively inciting character.[56] For instance, if D simply reports similar unlawful acts committed by others to P, this would not qualify as instigation, even if he took into account the possibility that P might be incited by his description.[57] Appropriate means of influencing P's will might include express statements in the form of persuasion, promises of rewards or gifts, or more subtle ones such as suggestions or questions.[58]

B. The Perpetrator Must be Able to be Induced

Since the instigation must be causal for the perpetrator's act resolution, one cannot instigate a perpetrator who is already resolved on committing the unlawful act (the so-called *omnimodo facturus*). Such cases are instead classified as psychological aid or attempted instigation (Section 30, StGB).[59] The boundary between psychological aid and instigation requires

---

[50] *Leipziger Kommentar*, above n 9, 1989.
[51] Ibid.
[52] See ibid, 1990; Roxin, above n 12, 152.
[53] Roxin, above n 12, 152.
[54] Wessels and Beulke, above n 11, 216; *Leipziger Kommentar*, above n 9, 1987.
[55] Wessels and Beulke, above n 11, 216.
[56] *Leipziger Kommentar*, above n 9, 1988; Roxin, above n 12, 155.
[57] Ibid, 1988; ibid, 155.
[58] Wessels and Beulke, above n 11, 216; *Leipziger Kommentar*, above n 9, 2002; Schönke and Schröder, above n 41, 544.
[59] Wessels and Beulke, above n 11, 216; *Leipziger Kommentar*, above n 9, 1992.

further clarification, however, since one cannot insist on P's absolute certainty that he will commit the act – the provision for withdrawal (Section 24, StGB) clearly accounts for the perpetrator's changing his mind.[60] Commentators have therefore suggested that when the reasons and motives pushing towards the commission of a crime have gained clear ascendence in P's psyche, he cannot be further instigated.[61] Thus, if P is still in two minds about the commission of the act, or has serious misgivings about embarking on it, D, who persuades him to carry it out, can still be held liable as an instigator.[62] However, if P is more or less resolved to commit the act and only has last-minute doubts, D will in all likelihood be liable only as an aider.[63] Given the obligatory mitigation of punishment for aid as compared to instigation, this guideline, while helpful, is not as precise as one might wish.

Problems arise in situations where D instigates P to commit an act other than the one he is resolved to commit. Three categories of cases come up most frequently:

(a) the *Umstiftung*;
(b) the *Abstiftung*;
(c) the *Übersteigerung or Aufstiftung*.

i. The Umstiftung

This category refers to cases where D induces P to commit an act different from the one he planned. The question then arises whether this change represents the causing of a new act resolution (instigation), or whether the change constitutes only a modification of the existing act plan (aid).[64] The change may concern the perpetrator, the elements of the offence, the object of the act, the motive for the act or the means for carrying out the act.[65]

Commentators are unanimous that causing a change of the perpetrator qualifies as instigation rather than aid, on the basis that changing the concrete perpetrator always changes the act. Thus, if D persuades A instead of B to commit the same terrorist attack on an airplane, he would be responsible not as an aider but as an instigator.[66] For the same reason, a change in the elements of the offence also represents instigation rather than aid. If D persuades P, who wants to cause bodily injury to V, instead to destroy V's car, he is liable as an instigator for damage to the property.

---

[60] *Leipziger Kommentar*, above n 9, 1992; Roxin, above n 12, 150.
[61] Ibid, 1992; ibid, 150.
[62] Ibid, 1992; Schönke and Schröder, above n 41, 544–45.
[63] *Leipziger Kommentar*, above n 9, 1992; Roxin, above n 12, 150.
[64] *Leipziger Kommentar*, above n 9, 1993.
[65] Roxin, above n 12, 158.
[66] *Leipziger Kommentar*, above n 9, 1993; Roxin, above n 12, 159.

This applies even if the elements of the offence protect the same legal interest (for instance, in the case of extortion and fraud).[67]

In cases of causing a change in the object of the act, the criterion of 'plan domination' has been widely accepted. If D charts a new plan through changing the object targeted by P, he qualifies as an instigator; if his conduct merely inserts itself into, or improves, P's existing plan, he is an aider.[68] Thus, if P wants to steal whisky to entertain his guest, and D induces him to steal vodka instead, D is only an aider. On the other hand, if D induces P to steal the vodka and sell it for his own profit, and entertain the guest with beer, then he is liable as an instigator to the theft since he promotes an entirely new plan.[69] However, the evaluation of what counts as a new plan, and what is considered a mere insertion into an existing plan, can be fairly subjective.[70]

Causing a change in motive or mode of commission (for the same act) is classified as aiding rather than instigation. If D persuades P to steal the whisky in the above example for the purpose of selling it, rather than to entertain his guests, he will only be an aider, since the concrete act of theft as such remains the same.[71] Similarly, if D gives a master key to P, who intends to break into a house with a screwdriver, he will be liable for assistance.[72]

ii. *The* Abstiftung

If D induces P to commit a less grave crime than he intended (for instance, theft (Section 242, StBG) instead of theft with weapons (Section 244, StBG))[73] then he is not liable for instigating the less serious offence. This is because the act resolution for the basic offence is encompassed within P's resolution for the more serious offence.[74] This is also the case when D persuades P to inflict a smaller injury within the same elements of the offence – for instance, to steal €100 instead of the planned €1,000.[75] In such cases, D may not even be liable as an aider, since he actually causes a reduction of the risk in relation to the protected legal interest.[76]

---

[67] Ibid, 1993; ibid, 159.
[68] Ibid, 1993; ibid, 159.
[69] Ibid,1993–94; ibid, 160.
[70] Roxin, above n 12, 160.
[71] *Leipziger Kommentar*, above n 9, 1994; Roxin, above n 12, 161.
[72] Ibid, 1994; see ibid, 161.
[73] *Leipziger Kommentar*, above n 9, 1994.
[74] Ibid,1994; Roxin, above n 12, 151.
[75] Ibid, 1994; ibid, 151.
[76] Ibid, 1994–95; ibid, 151.

iii. The Übersteigerung *or* Aufstiftung

The most controversial cases concern situations where D persuades P to commit a more serious offence than the one he intends – for instance causing V grievous injury, instead of simply administering a slap.[77] The BGH addressed this issue in a case[78] where P, who had decided to commit a robbery, was induced by D to carry along a club with which he struck the victim unconscious, resulting in aggravated robbery (under Section 250, StGB) instead of simple robbery (Section 249, StGB). The BGH held P liable as an instigator on the basis that due to the use of a club, the measure of wrongfulness of the original act had been increased considerably.[79] Some of the jurisprudence rejects this reasoning and proposes the 'analytical separation principle', whereby instigation can exist only in relation to that part of the elements of the offence in relation to which P was not already resolved.[80] The analytic separation principle is difficult to accept, however, because it ignores the insight that the whole is more than simply the sum of its parts – robbery is more than simply theft plus use of force or theft plus injury. To hold the instigator responsible only for an independent part of this offence understates his role in the offence ultimately committed.[81]

C. The Intent of the Instigator

The instigator must have a double intent, that is, intent in relation to his act of instigation, as well as intent with respect to the commission of the main act by the perpetrator.[82] Intent to the extent of *dolus eventualis* is sufficient in both cases – D must consider as possible and accept the fact that his conduct will give rise to P's act resolution.[83] In addition, he must possess *dolus eventualis* with respect to all essential objective and subjective elements of the offence, and the circumstances that justify the punishment of the main act (the main act is unlawful and intentionally committed by P).[84] The instigator's intent must generally be directed to the actual completion of the main act by P.[85] Hence, D who instigates P to commit a theft and informs the police so that P is arrested in the attempt, is not liable as an instigator.[86]

---

[77] *Leipziger Kommentar*, above n 9, 1995.
[78] BGHSt 19, 339.
[79] *Leipziger Kommentar*, above n 9, 1995; Roxin, above n 12, 162.
[80] Ibid, 1995–96; ibid, 162.
[81] Ibid, 1996; ibid, 162–63.
[82] MPICC Report, above n 1, 39; Wessels and Beulke, above n 11, 217.
[83] MPICC Report, above n 1, 39; *Leipziger Kommentar*, above n 9, 2004.
[84] Ibid, 39; ibid, 2005.
[85] MPICC Report, above n 1, 41; Wessels and Beulke, above n 11, 218.
[86] Wessels and Beulke, above n 11, 218; *Leipziger Kommentar*, above n 9, 2012.

The instigator must intend to instigate a concrete perpetrator towards a concrete criminal act, though the extent of concreteness required is heavily disputed. For instance, a generic prompting to commit some general criminal act cannot be classified as instigation, because the connection between the prompter and the offence ultimately committed is too attenuated to justify punishment equal to that of the perpetrator.[87] The element of steering or inducement that proves causal for the perpetrator's act requires that the instigator must have a more exact conception of the offence in question.[88] An early decision of the *Reichsgericht* confirms this:[89] D had remarked to P, who was a domestic helper, that it was stupid not to use such an opportunity to make money. The *Reichsgericht* absolved D of liability for instigation for misappropriation, as it was unclear to which elements of the offence the instigation was directed. Thus, the instigation must be with reference to specific offence elements.[90]

On the other hand, the instigator need not know the precise circumstances of the act, such as the time, place or method of execution.[91] If D incites P to rob a supermarket, it is irrelevant whether P does so on Monday or Tuesday, and whether D knows the date and time. The BGH[92] had occasion to address this issue in a case where P needed money in order to flee abroad. Initially, D had advised P to make money by selling some things, and when this proved impractical, D remarked, 'then you would have to rob a bank or a gas station'. P made no reply to this, but he committed a bank robbery worth 40,000 DM two days later. The BGH rejected D's liability for instigation on the ground that the act being incited was too indefinite, because it lacked any particularising circumstances (object, place, time and other circumstances of the execution). This was despite the fact that the elements of the offence (robbery) and the objects of the act (bank or gas station) had been specified. The court held that while the instigator does not need to know every detail of the offence committed, he must be aware of the circumstances that make the act recognisable as a concrete, particularised happening. The exact nature of these circumstances depends on the individual case and cannot be outlined in the abstract.[93]

Commentators have proposed an alternative to the BGH's determinacy criterion, where the instigator is liable if his intent is directed towards certain elements of the offence and encompasses the 'essential dimensions' of the wrongfulness of the main act.[94] These essential dimensions include

---

[87] See Wessels and Beulke, above n 11, 217; Roxin, above n 12, 173.
[88] Schönke and Schröder, above n 41, 547.
[89] RGSt 1,110 f.
[90] Roxin, above n 12, 165, 173.
[91] Wessels and Beulke, above n 11, 217–18; Schönke and Schröder, above n 41, 547.
[92] BGHSt 34 63.
[93] See *Leipziger Kommentar*, above n 9, 1997–78; Roxin, above n 12, 173.
[94] Ibid, 1998; ibid, 174.

the approximate degree of the harm, and the type and manner of injury towards the planned object of the act. [95] Thus in the case above, D had intent with respect to all three – the elements of the offence (robbery), the extent of injury (he knew how much money the perpetrator needed), and the manner and type of attack (an attack on a savings bank or gas station).[96] The BGH rejects this approach on the ground that a focus on a generally abstract 'wrongfulness dimension' weakens the ties between the act of instigation and the main act. This makes it difficult to justify the culpability of the instigator and his identification with the act of the perpetrator.[97] However, this criticism ignores the fact that this wrongfulness dimension must exist in the context of concrete elements of the offence.[98]

In fact, it is not the criterion of essential dimensions of wrongfulness but the BGH's own approach that falls victim to the charge of abstraction. Leaving the decision of which elements suffice to demarcate the concrete act to the discretion of the judges is open to attack for lack of legal certainty.[99] Neither does the BGH's doctrine fit the reality of organised crime – the leader of a terrorist group who instructs its members to rob a bank to procure funds for the group, should not escape liability merely because he left it to his minions to decide which bank they would target and when.[100]

Commentators agree that prompting an indeterminate and undefined group of people to commit a crime will not suffice for instigation.[101] At the same time, it is not necessary to induce a determinate individual, as long as one person in a determinate group is incited. For instance, if D tells a group of five people, 'whoever amongst you beats X will receive €500 from me', he will be liable as an instigator if one of them commits the act.[102]

D. The Equivalence of the Instigator's Intent and the Perpetrator's Act

The instigator's (D's) intent determines the extent of his responsibility for the unlawful main act of the perpetrator. If P goes beyond the act intended by D, D cannot normally be attributed with this excess of P. Thus, if D instigates P to cause injury to V and P kills V instead, D will be liable only for the injury that is realised as part of the murder.[103] Disputes arise in

---

[95] Roxin, above n 12, 174.
[96] Ibid. The instigation would still fail on the ground that the statement did not have an objectively inciting character: *Leipziger Kommentar*, above n 9, 1999.
[97] *Leipziger Kommentar*, above n 9, 1998; Roxin, above n 12, 175.
[98] Ibid, 1998; ibid, 175.
[99] See ibid, 1999; ibid, 175–76.
[100] See ibid, 1998; ibid, 175.
[101] MPICC Report, above n 1, 39; *Leipziger Kommentar*, above n 9, 2000; Schönke and Schröder, above n 41, 547.
[102] Ibid, 39; ibid, 2000; ibid 547.
[103] Schönke and Schröder, above n 41, 549.

cases where P commits an act different from that intended by D. The majority opinion endorses a standard of foreseeability akin to that in English criminal law in these cases: if D had taken into account the possibility of the deviation, he would be responsible for it.[104] The jurisprudence goes further, however, and holds D responsible if he should have foreseen the deviation given the circumstances of case.[105] The scope of the liability is limited, though, by the fact that the instigator is not responsible for significant deviations, such as deviations in the elements of the offence.

There is little debate on what counts as a significant deviation. Roxin refers briefly to cases of deviation that are relevant to instigation liability. Deviations in the details of the act execution, such as a change in the modality of execution (a theft is committed by means of a truck instead of a van) or the motive for the act (robbing a bank for private gain, and not to support a terrorist organisation), have no bearing on the responsibility of the instigator. Such specific conditions are often not strictly planned, or are left open or make no significant difference to the ultimate outcome.[106] On the other hand, deviations in the object of the act (P beats X instead of Y as intended by D) or the elements of the offence (D instigates P to commit theft but P commits fraud) cannot be attributed to the instigator. In the first case, P realises a completely different plan from that instigated by D, while in the second, D's intent has reference to different elements of the offence.[107] Roxin uses the test of 'wrongfulness dimension' to distinguish cases of excess that concern a shift in the kind of wrongfulness within the same elements of the offence. If P's act causes the same type and measure of injury to the protected legal interest intended by D, D is liable as an instigator.[108] Thus, if D incites P to clear out the window display of a jewellery shop, and P plunders the entire shop instead, D is liable for instigation as P's act falls within the wrongfulness dimension of the act instigated by D. The 'lesser' intent of D is relation to P's excess is taken into account during the sentencing stage.[109]

III. AID

Aid is intentional assistance to the intentionally committed unlawful act of another. Aiding is distinguished from co-perpetration on the basis that the aider lacks hegemony over the act and is a marginal figure who merely advances the unlawful act of another.[110]

---

[104] MPICC Report, above n 1, 40.
[105] Ibid.
[106] *Leipziger Kommentar*, above n 9, 2015; Roxin, above n 12, 164–65.
[107] Roxin, above n 12, 165.
[108] *Leipziger Kommentar*, above n 9, 2015–16; Roxin, above n 12, 166.
[109] Roxin, above n 12, 166.
[110] MPICC Report, above n 1, 41; Wessels and Beulke, above n 11, 221.

A. Causality and Aid

In contrast with instigation, which undisputedly requires a causal connection between the act of the instigator and the result of the offence, the causation requirement in the case of aiding is highly disputed.[111] If, for instance, D gives P a knife to kill V but P poisons V instead, can D be punished as an aider? In the leading decision on this issue,[112] the *Reichsgericht* adopted the view that aiding does not require the causal promotion or facilitation of the *result of the elements of the offence*. Even if the aid has no influence on the result, D's conduct would still be considered aid if it actually promoted or facilitated the *act* of the perpetrator. The BGH has affirmed this holding.[113] This standard avoids difficulties in proof that arise with a causation requirement, especially in cases of psychological aid and aid through omissions.[114] However, it has been convincingly criticised by commentators. Since the act of the perpetrator is directed towards the realisation of the elements of the offence, it is difficult to see how D's assistance could promote P's act in the concrete circumstances of the case without having a causal effect on the result of the elements of the offence.[115]

Indeed, the BGH has mostly used the standard in cases where actual causality exists.[116] Thus the BGH[117] convicted the driver of a car as an aider because he continued to drive as instructed by two robbers in the car while they robbed a co-passenger such that the victim's screams could not be heard and there was no opportunity for a third party to intervene. The BGH held that, by driving, the accused had 'facilitated' the commission of the act. However, the decision could as easily have been rendered using a causation analysis, since the act of driving was clearly causal for the commission of the robbery.[118]

The reluctance of the BGH to adopt a causation standard may arise from its understanding of the causation requirement in terms of a *sine qua non* for the result of the elements of the offence.[119] This is not, however, the interpretation of causation favoured in scholarly opinion, which stipulates only that the aider's contribution must make possible, facilitate, intensify or secure the commission of the act.[120] Thus, causation includes situations of 'modification causality', where the assistance merely affects the commission of the offence in some manner, for instance handing a

---

[111] See, eg, Roxin, above n 12, 192–97.
[112] RGSt 58, 113ff (114 / 115).
[113] BGH MDR (D) 1972, 16.
[114] Schönke and Schröder, above n 41, 551 and references therein.
[115] *Leipziger Kommentar*, above n 9, 2044; Roxin, above n 12, 194.
[116] Ibid, 2045; ibid, 194.
[117] BGH DAR 1981, 226.
[118] *Leipziger Kommentar*, above n 9, 2045.
[119] See references ibid, 2030.
[120] MPICC Report, above n 1, 42; *Leipziger Kommentar*, above n 9, 2030.

burglar a pair of gloves so that he can prise open a window without leaving fingerprints. The deciding factor is whether the course of events was transformed through the act of assistance.[121] It is for this reason that the effect of the aid must be considered in the concrete circumstances of the case, and no hypothetical situations may be taken into account.[122] Thus, in the oft-quoted example of D who carries a ladder to the scene of the crime for the burglar P, liability on account on assistance cannot be ruled out simply because P might well have carried the ladder himself. Any contrary holding would also make essential help rendered by D, such as supplying a master key to P, non-punishable if P could have procured it through other means.[123]

For the same reason, contributions that later prove to be superfluous are still considered aid. Thus D who acts as a lookout during a robbery would be punished as an aider even if there was ultimately no occasion for him to sound an alarm, on the basis that his presence served *ex ante* to increase the chances of the commission of the offence and reduced the element of risk undertaken by the perpetrator.[124] However, the effect of the aiding contribution must, at the very least, extend till the stage of attempt by the perpetrator. If, while carrying the ladder to the house P plans to burgle, D sees a window in the house open from a distance and simply abandons the ladder, he will not be responsible for aiding P's burglary.[125]

A minority viewpoint in the literature rejects the causality requirement and interprets aid as an endangerment offence, where D is liable as an aider if his contribution poses an abstract or concrete danger to the legal interest protected by the elements of the offence.[126] This doctrine blurs the distinction between aid and non-punishable attempted aid.[127] The nature of the abstract danger that would suffice for aid is also unclear: for instance, if D hands P a drink, thus ensuring that P carries out a theft in a better frame of mind, would that constitute an abstract danger to the legal interest?[128] Moreover, treating aid as an independent endangerment offence uncouples the aider's conduct from the elements of the offence injured by the perpetrator. This is difficult to reconcile with the general structure and reasoning behind secondary responsibility in German criminal law as an accessorial attack on the legally protected interest.[129]

---

[121] *Leipziger Kommentar*, above n 9, 2030; Roxin, above n 12 (n 975) 193.
[122] Ibid, 2032; ibid, 193.
[123] *Leipziger Kommentar*, above n 9, 2032; Schönke and Schröder, above n 41, 552.
[124] Ibid, 2033; ibid, 552.
[125] Ibid, 2032–33; ibid, 552.
[126] See references at *Leipziger Kommentar*, above n 9, 2045–46.
[127] *Leipziger Kommentar*, above n 9, 2030; Schönke and Schröder, above n 41, 552.
[128] *Leipziger Kommentar*, above n 9, 2046; Roxin, above n 12, 196.
[129] See Schönke and Schröder, above n 41, 552.

B. The Requirements of a Causal Risk Increase and Psychological Connection

The bulk of the academic commentary holds co-causation of the realisation of the elements of the offence as a necessary, but not sufficient, condition for responsibility as an aider.[130] Even contributions that do not assist P may modify the manner and type of the act execution, and hence be deemed co-causal (for instance, if D gave the thief P a master key which P never intended to use because he knew that the door was unlocked). A causal act contribution will be punished as aid, however, only if it increases the risk for the victim and/or the probability that the result of the elements of the offence will occur.[131]

Thus, if D hands a beer to burglar P, who is fatigued by his efforts to drill a hole through a bank vault, so as to revive his strength, he increases the chances of the successful execution of the burglary and may be punished as an aider. On the other hand, if a sympathiser, D, passes a glass of champagne to an illegal squatter, P, to celebrate his occupation of the house, this cannot be considered assistance to the squatting as it does not facilitate P's continuing to do so.[132]

Apart from co-causation and risk increase, an additional precondition for assistance liability is either that P is aware of D's act of assistance, or that D's act is objectively recognisable as increasing the probability that P's act will succeed.[133] If he prevents a policeman from approaching a house which P is burgling, D would be an aider even if P does not notice his aid.[134] On the other hand, D's mere readiness to help P, should the occasion arise, would not be punished as aid, as this would amount to criminalising his attitude rather than his behaviour. Thus, if D, a colleague of pickpocket P, stands near the scene of the prospective theft without P's knowledge, and in order to create a diversion to assist P if needed, he will not be punished as an aider despite the fact that his conduct increases the probability that P's act will be successful.[135]

C. Means of Aid and Psychological Aid

Aid may be physical or intellectual in nature. Physical aid consists of act contributions such as the provision of a weapon used to commit the crime.[136]

---

[130] *Leipziger Kommentar*, above n 9, 2030; Roxin, above n 12, 203.
[131] Ibid, 2031; ibid, 203.
[132] Ibid, 2032; ibid, 203.
[133] Ibid, 2034; ibid, 205.
[134] Ibid, 2034; ibid, 205.
[135] Ibid, 2034; ibid, 205.
[136] MPICC Report (n 972) 43; Roxin, above n 12 (n 975) 198.

Intellectual aid comprises contributions that influence the psyche of the perpetrator, and the extent to which it is punishable is heavily disputed.[137] Relatively uncontroversial cases of intellectual aid are situations of technical advice, where D gives P advice that facilitates the act, for instance detailed descriptions of the place where the crime is to be committed.[138] Cases of previous assistance that are directed towards making the potential subsequent prosecution of the perpetrator more difficult are also widely accepted as aid. Thus D who hands P a mask so that he will be unrecognisable during a robbery, would be liable as an aider.[139]

Situations where D's assistance merely reinforces or confirms P's act resolution represent problematic cases of intellectual aid.[140] Some commentators argue that instances where the perpetrator's resolution is stabilised or strengthened through the provision of additional motivating factors are punishable as aid; mere expressions of solidarity with the perpetrator or approval of his actions remain unpunished. In the former case D's actions are in fact co-causal for P's final act resolution, and thus also for the result of the elements of the offence.[141] Thus, if P decides to carry out an abortion and D gives her money to secure its execution,[142] he supplies her with an additional motive for its commission and reinforces the chances of the result's occurring. The BGH has gone further, however, and held expressions of sympathy to constitute aid (for example, expressing solidarity with illegal squatters constitutes aiding their infliction of injuries on policemen).[143] It is difficult to see how these situations represent a causal indirect attack on the legally protected interest.[144]

The BGH's jurisprudence on aid through omissions has been inconsistent.[145] In one case,[146] in the course of a return trip from Holland to Germany, the accused realised that the co-defendants in the car wanted to import heroin into Germany. He protested, but when the co-defendants outlined a plan to fool the border police, he simply remained silent. The 2nd Senate of the BGH rejected the suggestion that the accused's failure to object constituted aid. The 3rd Senate, however, reached a different conclusion in a very similar scenario,[147] where the accused, who was a lawyer, was silent at a meal during which his two lawyer colleagues and three others planned an act of extortion. The BGH held him liable as an aider, as his

---

[137] *Leipziger Kommentar*, above n 9, 2034; Roxin, above n 12, 198.
[138] *Leipziger Kommentar*, above n 9, 2034; Schönke and Schröder, above n 41, 554.
[139] Ibid, 2035; ibid, 555.
[140] MPICC Report, above n 1, 43; Roxin, above n 12, 198.
[141] *Leipziger Kommentar*, above n 9, 2035; Schönke and Schröder, above n 41, 555; Roxin, above n 12, 198–89, 200.
[142] RG HRR 1939, Nr 1275.
[143] BGHZ 63,124, 130; Roxin, above n 12, 200.
[144] See *Leipziger Kommentar*, above n 9, 2052.
[145] See discussion ibid, 2036; Roxin, above n 12, 200–01.
[146] BGH StV 1982, 516.
[147] BGH StV 1982, 517.

silent presence constituted a promotion of the extortion, even though he could only have registered his disapproval by walking away, or by confronting his colleagues. The omission to do so should, however, have been punishable only if there was a positive duty on the part of the accused to leave or to protest.[148]

D. The Intent of the Aider and Excess

The *mens rea* requirements for liability as an aider resemble those for instigation responsibility (see section II.C. above), with some important variations. Similar to the intent of the instigator, the aider's intent has a twofold component: it must be directed towards his own act of assistance to an intentional unlawful act of the perpetrator, and to the injury (by the perpetrator) to the legal interest protected by the elements of the offence.[149] Since aid must be rendered intentionally, negligent aid does not suffice for liability. Conversely, *dolus directus* is not required and mere *dolus eventualis* fulfils the conditions for assistant liability.[150]

It is not necessary that D approves of or endorses P's act; if he is aware that his contribution will facilitate the main act, his personal misgivings or disapproval do not affect his liability.[151] If, on the other hand, the contribution is not suited to promoting P's act and D knows this, he will not incur responsibility.[152] Since the aider's intent must be directed towards an actual injury to the protected legal interest by the perpetrator, he will not be liable if he intends that the act only reaches the stage of attempt. Thus, if D knows that P will not succeed in his theft because he has already informed the police about it, he is not an aider.[153]

Some of the requirements for intent in aiding are less stringent than those for instigation. The bulk of the academic commentary holds that the aider must be aware of the wrongfulness dimension and the direction of attack on the legally protected interest intended by the perpetrator. He may not, however, have any knowledge of the extent of harm, or of the type and manner of the attack on the legal interest protected by the elements of the offence.[154] If D lends P a gun for 'a robbery' and has no further information on the details of the proposed robbery, he may still be punished on account of aiding.[155] The BGH has applied different standards with respect to the

---

[148] *Leipziger Kommentar*, above n 9, 2036; Roxin, above n 12, 201.
[149] *Leipziger Kommentar*, above n 9, 2054; Schönke and Schröder, above n 41, 556.
[150] Ibid, 2054; ibid, 556.
[151] Ibid, 2054; ibid, 556.
[152] Ibid, 2054; ibid, 556.
[153] Wessels and Beulke, above n 11, 224.
[154] *Leipziger Kommentar*, above n 9, 2055; Schönke and Schröder, above n 41, 556.
[155] Roxin, above n 12, 225.

requirement for determinateness.[156] In one case,[157] D had sold members of a revolutionary cell an alarm that was used by them to delay the detonation of a bomb attack in the Lufthansa premises in Cologne. He was punished as an aider to the offence of inducing an explosion, even though he had known only that the alarm would be used for a bomb attack on some political opponents of the cell. The BGH convicted D since his intent encompassed the essential wrongfulness dimension and the direction of the attack on the protected legal interest.[158]

A later decision[159] concerned D, a jewellery expert, who wrongly certified the value of some jewels as 300,000 DM, despite being aware his valuation might result in their being sold for a higher price or serving as security. The jewels were used by P to obtain a credit of 270,000 DM from the bank, which he could not later repay, and the bank was unable to sell the stones. The jewellery expert was convicted of aiding P's fraud on the ground that his abstract conception of the elements of the offence (of fraud) and his foreseeability of P's act were sufficient to establish intent.[160] However, the BGH contradicted its earlier position that the aider need not be aware of the time, place or manner of commission of the offence. It held that foresight of the commission of an offence must include knowledge of the essential details of the act plan, including the circumstances that make the commission of the act sufficiently probable. Nonetheless, it held D liable even though he was unaware of any details of the act plan.[161]

As in the case of the instigator, the aider is liable only within the framework of his intent; the rules for 'excess' in instigation are also applicable to assistance.[162] Thus, if D supplies P with tools for house-breaking, and P then kills X who surprises him in the act, D will not be liable for aiding the killing. He is responsible only if he had foreseen the deviation from the original plan, and according to the jurisprudence, if he should ordinarily have foreseen such a deviation.[163]

E. Neutral Actions

'Neutral actions' are everyday transactions that the potential aider would carry out irrespective of whether they ultimately were being used for criminal purposes, for example selling knives, which the members of a

---

[156] *Leipziger Kommentar*, above n 9, 2056–57; Roxin, above n 12, 226–29.
[157] BGHR, StGB § 27 Abs 1, Vorsatz 6.
[158] Roxin, above n 12, 226.
[159] BGHSt 42, 135.
[160] Roxin, above n 12, 227.
[161] Ibid, 228.
[162] MPICC Report, above n 1, 45; Schönke and Schröder, above n 41, 557.
[163] Ibid, 45; ibid, 557.

violent gang buy to commit crimes, in a household goods shop.[164] Some commentators argue that such conduct should not be subject to criminal sanctions, while others support criminalising neutral actions but based on criteria that differ from ordinary cases of aid.[165]

The jurisprudence, following commentators such as Roxin, uses a combination of objective and subjective criteria to criminalise neutral actions, with particular emphasis on the aider's state of mind. If D knew, rather than simply accepted as a possibility, that his actions would support the unlawful act of P, and that the act of P served an exclusively criminal purpose, he will be liable as an aider.[166] The first element of this test stipulates that aid in the case of neutral actions requires the higher level of *dolus directus* instead of *dolus eventualis*. The BGH applied the second element of the test[167] in a case where D was charged with aiding in the organisation of landmines along the former GDR's internal border, on the basis that he assisted in the drafting of standing orders for the general organisation of the border regime. The BGH acquitted D on the ground that this general organisation of the border regime was a useful and legal act for the perpetrators, even in the absence of the minefields.[168] The only exception to this two-pronged standard is in cases where D foresees that his actions may be used by P for committing an offence, and where the risk of the punishable behaviour is acknowledged by him to be so high that he supports an actor recognisably determined to carry out the act.[169]

Both the requirement for *dolus directus* and cases where it is dispensed with are explained by German commentators using the 'trust principle', that is, people must normally be able to act on the assumption that other people around them are not rushing to commit criminal acts. Without such trust, everyday commercial activities such the sale of lighters, knives, etc, which are indispensable for modern life, would become impossible.[170] Roxin illustrates this principle with the help of two cases. In the first, a salesman (D) thinks that customer (P) looks suspicious, but nevertheless sells him a screwdriver. The screwdriver is used by P for breaking into a house. The salesman will not be an aider because his subjective impression of P's suspicious appearance must be reinforced by a concrete criterion that establishes P's inclination to commit an unlawful act.[171] This will exist in the second case scenario, where P and other members of his gang are engaged in a gang fight on the street, and P goes to a shop from which

[164] Wessels and Beulke, above n 11, 222.
[165] See references at *Leipziger Kommentar*, above n 9, 2041–42.
[166] Bohlander, above n 9, 173; Wessels and Beulke, above n 11, 223; Roxin, above n 12, 207–08.
[167] BGH NJW 2001, 2410.
[168] See Bohlander, above n 9, 173.
[169] *Leipziger Kommentar*, above n 9, 2039.
[170] Ibid, 2039; Roxin, above n 12, 214–16.
[171] Roxin, above n 12, 214–15.

the fight is visible to procure additional knives. If salesperson D sells him the knives and foresees that these will be used to inflict injuries during the course of the fight, he will be liable as an aider.[172]

IV. CONCLUSION

As the discussion above demonstrates, German law on secondary responsibility grapples with issues similar to those encountered in English jurisprudence. The doctrinal basis of accessorial responsibility, causality requirements, the extent to which the intent of the accessory must be determinate, the treatment of neutral actions and cases of excess by the perpetrator, all feature prominently in both systems. One of the most striking differences between the two systems, however, lies in the very subject that is most of interest to this study – the absence of any special mode of participation such as joint enterprise in German criminal law. The reason for this may be that German criminal law treats cases of parasitic joint enterprise liability under excess configurations in aiding and abetting.

Chapter eleven will compare the treatment of accessories in German and English criminal law and theory to assess whether liability under JCE II and JCE III may be justified under the principles of secondary responsibility in both legal systems.

---

[172] *Leipziger Kommentar*, above n 9, 2039; Roxin, above n 12, 215.

11

Joint Criminal Enterprise Liability for International Crimes

I. LESSONS FROM DOMESTIC CRIMINAL LAW AND THEORY

ENGLISH AND GERMAN criminal law and theory distinguish between parties to a crime, both in terms of the rationale for attribution of criminal responsibility (as principals or accessories) and as a matter of certain practical consequences that follow from this classification.[1] This is despite the fact that under English law an accessory may be punished to the same extent as a perpetrator. There is some overlap in the different doctrinal justifications for holding the accessory criminally responsible in the two legal systems, though there is a marked divergence in the weight accorded to them. This is particularly true of the causal basis for accessorial responsibility. Following the orthodox formulation of causation put forward by Hart and Honoré, English criminal law in general rejects the requirement of a causal link for accomplice liability. However, causation features to some extent in the case of specific modes of secondary responsibility such as procuring and encouragement.[2] In addition, influential commentators on English criminal law argue that the attribution of secondary responsibility assumes that the accessory makes a causal contribution to the offence, albeit one that is mediated through the perpetrator.[3] This view is similar to the dominant justification for accomplice liability in the German criminal law system: the accessory-orientated causation doctrine articulated by the BGH, according to which the accomplice must facilitate and/or co-cause the principal's unlawful act.[4]

The risk or endangerment rationale that features prominently in recent developments in the English law of complicity[5] does not have a strict counterpart in German criminal law. The reason for this may be due to the centrality of the principle of *limitierte Akzessorietät* in Sections 26 and 27 of the StGB, whereby the accessory D's liability derives from the unlawful act

---

[1] See ch 9, text to nn 5–6; and ch 10, text to nn 1–11.
[2] See ch 9, text to nn 15–18.
[3] See ch 9, text to nn 11–14.
[4] See ch 10, text to nn 27–30.
[5] See ch 9, text to nn 15–18 and nn 145–47.

of the principal (P) and his punishment corresponds to the punishment framework of P's act.[6] D's conduct must also result in an injury to the legal interest protected by the elements of the offence.[7] This is indeed the reason why the causal account favoured by scholars such as Roxin is supplemented by a further requirement: the accessory's act must represent an independent attack on the legally protected interest.[8] This connection between the harm caused to the legal interest protected by the elements of the offence and the conduct of the accessory is modified in cases of inchoate offences of complicity under the Serious Crime Act 2007 based on an endangerment rationale. Here, D may be convicted simply for doing an act that is capable of encouraging or assisting the commission of an offence, in the belief that it will be committed. Thus, the offence that P ultimately commits may differ from the one D's act is aimed at encouraging.

Despite the dominance of the accessory-orientated causation theory in German criminal law, the differences in English and German law may appear less stark when one considers the application of the causal link requirement to concrete modes of liability – aiding and abetting – in both jurisdictions. For instance, there is consensus that liability for instigation in German criminal law requires that the instigation by D is causal or at least co-causal for P's decision to commit an unlawful act.[9] Causality, however, is also important if D is to be convicted as an abettor/instigator under English law – D must intend to encourage P, and in fact must encourage P in the commission of an offence.[10] Instigation in both systems requires a meeting of minds between P and D.[11] The difference in the causation requirements in English and German criminal law may then be one of degree – while English law requires only that D's encouragement is communicated to P, even if he is not ultimately influenced by it,[12] German criminal law poses a higher standard that D must influence P's will through overt intellectual contact.[13]

A similar picture emerges when one considers the necessity of a causal link for liability in case of aiding. Both systems reject a causation nexus, if causation is taken to mean that D's actions must constitute a *sine qua non* for the commission of the offence.[14] English law, however, recognises a diluted causation requirement, where D is liable as an aider if his conduct in fact helped, or could potentially have helped, P in the commission of an

---

[6] See ch 10, text to nn 9–11, 28–31.
[7] See ch 10, text to nn 34–37.
[8] See ibid.
[9] See ch 10, text to n 42.
[10] See ch 9, text to nn 34–36.
[11] See ch 9, text to nn 38 and 39; and ch 10, text to nn 54–55.
[12] See ch 9, text to n 36.
[13] See ch 10, text to nn 54–55.
[14] See ch 9, text to n 41; and ch 10, text to n 119.

offence.[15] D's assistance need not be substantial, however.[16] This is remarkably similar to the standard employed by the BGH and German criminal law commentators. According to the BGH, D is liable for aiding if his conduct promotes the act of P. As discussed, it is unlikely that D's conduct can facilitate P's act without also being causal for the commission of the offence.[17] Most commentators consider D's conduct causal if it makes possible, facilitates, intensifies or secures the commission of P's (unlawful) act. This facilitation need not be substantial, but it must increase the risk for the victim and/or the likelihood that the result of the elements of the offence will occur.[18]

Thus, notwithstanding the seeming divergence in English and German criminal law on the necessity of a causal link for accessorial responsibility, one might reasonably argue that a diluted form of causation (where causation is defined to exclude a *sine qua non* condition) underlies the primary modes of secondary responsibility in both legal systems. Exceptions to this general common standard may be found in each case – responsibility for instigation in German criminal law requires a greater causation nexus than that in English law, and inchoate offences of complicity in English criminal law abjure the requirement of a causal link.

The second major difference in the criteria for secondary responsibility in the two systems consists in the *mens rea* or subjective elements. The requirement of 'double intent' for accomplice liability is common to both systems: D's intent must exist in relation to his own conduct, as well as in relation to the commission of the main act by P.[19] However, the level of intent required is different in the two systems. In order to convict D as an accessory under German law, *dolus eventualis* with respect to both aspects is sufficient: D must consider as possible and accept that his conduct will result in P's act, and possess *dolus eventualis* with respect to all essential objective and subjective elements of the offence.[20] In English criminal law, on the other hand, the first prong of the *mens rea* element requires D to know that his conduct will facilitate the commission of the offence intended by P, whereas the second prong is satisfied as long as D foresees the essential matters relating to P's conduct which make it an offence.[21] The knowledge standard is higher than that required in German law, whereas recklessness/foresight is lower than the German law requirement of *dolus eventualis*.

German and English criminal law treat the question of specificity of knowledge/foresight required of D with respect to the elements of the

---

[15] See ch 9, text to n 29.
[16] See ch 9, text to n 28.
[17] See ch 10, text to nn 113–15.
[18] See ch 10, text to nn 120–21 and 131.
[19] See ch 9, text to n 45; and ch 10, text to nn 82 and 149.
[20] See ch 10, text to nn 83–84 and 150.
[21] See ch 9, text to n 46.

offence somewhat differently. According to English law, D must know the essential elements of the offence, which has been interpreted to mean that D must know either the type of offence intended (and ultimately committed) by P (*Bainbridge*), or that P would commit any one of a shopping list of offences (one of which P commits) (*Maxwell*).[22] This is different from the two dominant tests for instigation in German criminal law. The BGH's requirement that D is aware of the circumstances that make the (unlawful) act identifiable as a concrete, particularised occurrence[23] is stricter than either of the two tests in English law. The majority scholarly opinion, on the other hand, holds that D's intent must be directed towards certain elements of the offence and the essential dimensions of the wrongfulness of the main act. The latter comprise the degree of harm and the manner and type of attack on the legally protected interest.[24] While the second prong of this test may be likened to the *Maxwell* standard, it is more rigid in its reference to certain elements of the offence. The specificity requirements are lowered in the case of liability for aiding under German criminal law.

English law and German law have different responses to the challenge posed by neutral actions. English case law and commentary mostly acknowledge D's liability if he knows that his act will assist the offence intended by P, but a minority holds that D must act in order to assist its commission.[25] In contrast, German criminal law requires not only that D be aware that his actions will support P's unlawful act, but also that P's act must serve an exclusively criminal purpose. It dilutes the knowledge requirement in cases where D takes into account the possibility that his actions will facilitate P's commission of an offence, if there is such a high risk that P will commit an offence that D's actions are regarded as having supported a person who is clearly determined to carry out the crime.[26]

Joint enterprise as a distinct form of secondary liability in English criminal law has no obvious German counterpart; cases of 'parasitic accessory liability' would be dealt with under principles of 'excess' in German law. D is liable for the acts of P on the basis of joint enterprise liability if three conditions are met:

(a) D and P act in concert to commit crime X;
(b) D had foreseen that in the course of committing X, there was a real risk that P would also commit crime Y; and
(c) Y occurred as an incident of the joint venture and did not fundamentally differ from the crime foreseen by D.[27]

---

[22] See ch 9, text to nn 70–75.
[23] See ch 10, text to nn 92–93.
[24] See ch 10, text to nn 94–95.
[25] See ch 9, text to nn 47–62.
[26] See ch 10, text to nn 166–69.
[27] See ch 9, text to n 92.

German cases of 'excess' concern liability for aiding or instigation in cases where P commits an act that deviates from that intended by D.[28] There is thus no requirement of an agreement or a joint venture to commit a crime. German law applies a test of foreseeability to hold D liable: if D had, or should have, taken into account the possibility of the deviation in P's conduct, he will be liable for P's act.[29]

There are some overlaps between the English law requirement that Y should not be fundamentally different from the act foreseen by D, and the German law standard that P's conduct should not constitute a significant deviation from that intended by D. Deviations in the modality of the execution of the act or the motive for the act are irrelevant in both systems.[30] The test of foresight in English law seems most closely connected to the expected consequences of P's conduct.[31] This standard corresponds to some of the specific instances of deviation identified in German criminal law: changes in the object of the act, or in the elements of the offence, count as significant deviations. If the measure and type of injury to the protected legal interest are different from those foreseen by D, he would not be liable.[32]

II. SUPPORT FOR JCE II AND JCE III IN DOMESTIC CRIMINAL LAW

Now that we have studied the differences in the treatment of secondary responsibility in English law and German law, the next step is to assess whether the *actus reus* and *mens rea* elements of JCE II and JCE III find any support in these domestic systems.

The *actus reus* elements common to JCE II and JCE III are:

(a) a plurality of persons;
(b) the existence of a common plan or design;
(c) the participation of the accused in the common plan.[33]

In order to satisfy the first element, the accused must act along with a number of persons to commit the crime. There is no requirement for a maximum or minimum number, or for any kind of organisational structure, for the plurality.[34] This is true of joint enterprise liability in England, and also of liability for aiding and instigation in Germany.

The second element is the existence of a common plan which involves the commission of a crime. The plan may arise extemporaneously and need not

---

[28] See ch 10, text to nn 103–05 and 162–63.
[29] See ch 10, text to nn 104–09 and 163.
[30] See ch 9, text to nn 100–09; and ch 10, text to n 106.
[31] See ch 9, text to nn 111–13.
[32] See ch 10, text to nn 107–09.
[33] *Prosecutor v Tadić*, No IT-94-1-A, Appeals Chamber Judgment (15 July 1999) para 227.
[34] See ch 3, text to nn 3–4.

be explicit.[35] This position also accords with joint enterprise liability in the UK.[36] Liability for aiding or instigation in German criminal law does not require a common plan. However, it is possible to have instigation in the form of '*Mitanstiftung*', ie co-perpetrated instigation, where several persons act in concert to instigate the perpetrator to commit the act. In this situation, the elements for co-perpetration must be present, including the existence of a common plan.[37]

Tribunal jurisprudence has interpreted the common plan requirement differently in cases of JCE II which concern concentration camp scenarios. Here, no agreement is needed, and the entire system of repression in place in the concentration camp is treated as a common plan.[38] The ICTY has put forward two potentially inconsistent criteria in interpreting this condition: first, that if the accused is involved in the system of repression, it is less important to prove the fact of an agreement; and secondly, that the accused knew of the system and agreed to it, without it being necessary that he entered into an agreement with the principal perpetrators. The second test, as discussed, seems to interpret 'agree' to mean 'acquiesce'.[39] Mere acquiescence would not, however, be sufficient for establishing the elements of co-perpetration (for *Mitanstiftung*) in German criminal law, which presupposes a mutual understanding or consent between the co-perpetrators that forms the basis of the further joint action.[40] If one agrees with commentators such as Simester, one can make the same argument for common purpose in English criminal law: the distinction between the aider/abettor and the party to a joint enterprise lies in the fact that the latter and the perpetrator have a shared bond of affiliation resulting from the common purpose. The accessory's voluntary and purposive affiliation with the act of the perpetrator distinguishes his normative position from the aider/abettor.[41] If this reading of common purpose is correct, simple acquiescence will not satisfy the test of a common plan in English criminal law.

Joint enterprise cases in English law may be interpreted as confirming the *Brdanin* Trial Chamber's opinion that the common plan or agreement must exist between the accused and the physical perpetrators of the crime[42] – in almost every case the accused has some contact or understanding with the physical perpetrator. The ICTY has subsequently rejected this criterion, to hold that the physical perpetrator does not need

---

[35] See ch 3, text to nn 11–13.
[36] See ch 9, text following nn 96 and 97.
[37] H Laufhutte et al (eds), *Strafgesetzbuch Leipziger Kommentar (Großkommentar): Band 1* (Berlin, de Gruyter Recht, 2006) 2023.
[38] See ch 3, text to nn 21–23.
[39] See ch 3, text following n 23.
[40] See ch 7, text to nn 54–56.
[41] See ch 9, text to n 140.
[42] See ch 3, text to nn 26–29.

to be a member of the JCE. The most important factor is that the criminal plan is not only the same but also common to all persons acting within the enterprise; and that even if the accused's contribution to this common purpose is not substantial, it should be significant for the crimes for which he is found responsible.[43] This latter test tracks the debates on the requirement of a causal link for secondary responsibility in domestic law. Neither English law nor German law requires D's contribution to the unlawful act of P to have been substantial. However, both systems consider a minimal causal link between D's conduct and the crime committed by P to be necessary. The only exception is in cases of parasitic joint enterprise liability in English law and 'excess' cases in German law. The very purpose behind these forms of liability is that the accused should be able to be held liable for crimes towards which he did not make a significant contribution.

Thus, the three elements of the *actus reus* requirement in JCE II and JCE III do find some support in domestic criminal law principles, but the latter point the way towards some useful modifications. The criterion of an 'agreement' in the case of a common plan should mean exactly that: a mutual understanding or consent to commit the crimes in question. The accused and the physical perpetrators should be members of the common plan. This does not mean that they should have met each other; it merely implies that they should act with the awareness that there are other participants in the plan, all working towards the same common goal. For JCE II, the accused must causally contribute to the commission of the crimes that are a result of the common plan, although his contribution need not be a *sine qua non* for their commission.

The *mens rea* requirements for JCE II and JCE III differ. In order to be held liable under JCE II, the accused must have personal knowledge of the criminal nature of the system in place in a concentration camp as well as the intent to further the criminal purpose. The latter intent may be inferred from two factors: knowledge of the criminal plan, and participation in its advancement.[44] As was noted in Part One, this has the potential to lead to an unjustified expansion of liability in the case of neutral actions, such as the performance of duties as a cook in a concentration camp. In this case, the cook may well have some knowledge of the purpose for which the camp has been set up, and participate in the camp through his activities as a cook. It is, however, difficult to use this function to convict him to the same level as a perpetrator for all the crimes that are committed within the camp.[45] The problem posed by neutral actions to a *mens rea* requirement grounded in knowledge, rather than purpose, is also found in domestic law systems. English law has struggled to come up with a principled solution to this issue, with some commentators advocating

---

[43] See ch 3, text to nn 68–74.
[44] See ch 3, text to nn 83–88.
[45] See ch 3, text following n 89.

that an exception should be carved out for neutral actions which warrant a more rigid standard of purpose. The bulk of the law, though, supports a knowledge standard, with the defences of duress and necessity as potential safeguards to the expansion of liability.[46] However, the defences of duress and necessity are permitted in extremely limited circumstances in international criminal law. The German criminal law option of adding an additional element – the conduct of the perpetrator must serve an exclusively criminal purpose[47] – also does not seem particularly helpful in the concentration camp context; a concentration camp by its very nature serves an entirely criminal purpose.

There may still be some justification for permitting neutral actions to be subject to the knowledge standard. The objection that this equates the conduct of a cook with that of a physical perpetrator of a crime loses some of its bite once JCE II is acknowledged as a mode of accessorial rather than perpetrator responsibility. The treatment of the accessory's conduct as deserving of criminal sanctions is not as harsh as might initially appear. His liability is ultimately based on his knowing association with the camp's criminal purpose. The knowledge standard does not require him to take any extraordinary steps to fathom the camp's activities, or to prevent the perpetrators in a camp from performing criminal acts. The accessory need only desist from voluntarily facilitating the camp's endeavours when he knows that it is engaged in heinous acts. If the only reason for his participation in the camp is an imminent and real threat to his life, he may have some limited protection under the defences of duress and necessity.

The most controversial *mens rea* requirements are found in the case of JCE III. The participant in a JCE, D, may be held liable for the crimes committed by another JCE member, P, even if the crime goes beyond the common purpose, as long as it was a natural and foreseeable consequence of the common plan and D willingly took this risk.[48] D should have foreseen that P was likely to commit the additional crimes (subjective foreseeability), and it should have been objectively foreseeable that the additional crimes might be committed by P. The foreseeability standards have not been applied consistently by ICTY tribunals, however.[49] German criminal law has no strict equivalent to cases of JCE III, which would instead be governed by principles of 'excess' in liability for aiding and instigation. D would thus be liable under 'excess' principles as long as it was objectively foreseeable that P would commit the crimes he did. However, there is an additional qualifying condition – P's conduct should not significantly deviate from that contemplated by D.[50] This is an extremely significant

---

[46] See ch 9, text to nn 48–57.
[47] See ch 10, text to nn 166–68.
[48] See ch 3, text to nn 104–08.
[49] See ch 3, text to nn 109–16.
[50] See ch 10, text to nn 104–09.

factor for limiting D's liability as a secondary party. The English doctrine of joint enterprise similarly limits D's liability, but to a lesser extent, by stipulating that the additional crime committed by P must not differ fundamentally from the crime foreseen by D. Thus, under German criminal law, if D's intent had reference to different elements of the offence – torture instead of murder – this would count as a significant deviation.[51] In English criminal law, if D had contemplated that P would beat V, but P killed V instead, D will not be liable, or under some of the case law will be liable only for the lesser offence which he did contemplate.[52]

If one transposes the domestic criminal law requirements to international criminal law, JCE III can be compared to JCE under English law, but only in so far as it is regarded as accessorial in nature. Moreover, its operation will be somewhat limited. For instance, even for crimes that do not require special intent, D will be liable on account of JCE III only if he contemplated that one or more members of the JCE would act so as to fulfil the elements of the offence, which would include the intent requirement for the offence. It is much more difficult to justify JCE III as a form of secondary responsibility based on the rationale for accessory liability in German criminal law. Even in 'excess' cases, a change in the elements of the offence to which D's intent was directed will be considered a significant deviation which will make it difficult to sustain his liability for additional crimes committed by P.

III. JCE AS A DISTINCT MODE OF ACCESSORIAL RESPONSIBILITY

Since domestic criminal law comparisons will yield inconsistent results for the feasibility of JCE III, we must evaluate whether there are good independent reasons for its retention as a distinctive international mode of participation. In English law, the crux of joint enterprise liability lies in the existence of a common purpose between the members of the joint venture, where the accessory has a purposive attitude towards the commission of crimes by the perpetrator; the indifferent aider/abettor lacks any such community of purpose. It is this shared bond or affiliation between the accessory and the members of the enterprise that broadens his liability to cover cases that would traditionally not fall within the domain of liability for aiding and abetting.[53]

English law provides various justifications for this extension of responsibility, which need to be considered in light of the nature of international crimes. The first set of explanations is grounded in D's voluntary association with a criminal venture, which ostensibly demonstrates D's criminal

---

[51] See ch 10, text to nn 107–08.
[52] See ch 9, text to nn 116–26.
[53] See ch 9, text to nn 132–36.

proclivities and also helps contribute to the situation in which the additional crime occurs.[54] This argument is not particularly convincing. The fact that D has criminal proclivities cannot justify a broader imposition of liability on him in the absence of concrete conduct that offends against the law. If this conduct consists in his signing up to a criminal enterprise, the argument simply proves itself, and no more. Moreover, the mere fact that his conduct helps contribute to a situation where a crime occurs cannot, by itself, justify criminalising it. There are many situations in everyday life which do the same. Indeed, D's voluntary association with a criminal venture seems even more tenuous as a basis for his responsibility for international crimes. In a situation of mass atrocity, which involves individuals acting on different motives, and performing different actions across a dispersed geographical and temporal frame, D's participation in one aspect of the enterprise can easily be interpreted as having contributed to the general atmosphere of permissibility which results in the additional crimes. This would result in an unwarranted expansion of liability.

The risk/endangerment rationale provides two distinct explanations for D's liability: the first is a normative justification which holds D liable because he assumes the risks that flow from his subscription to the common criminal purpose; the second is an empirical claim that through D's association with the criminal enterprise, he increases the risk that the collateral crime will occur.[55] These arguments will have some currency in the context of international crimes. The assumption of risk rationale has been criticised for equating the cognitive element of foresight (of risk) with the volitional element of its conscious or deliberate acceptance. It is acknowledged, however, that some risks are so closely attendant to the fulfilment of the criminal purpose, that in foreseeing the possibility of their occurrence, D is additionally deemed to have accepted it.[56] These exceptional conditions arguably exist in cases of mass atrocity, where the criminal purposes of the enterprise are generally defined in fairly broad terms and often have multiple means of execution. If D becomes a member of a joint venture with the aim of ethnically cleansing a certain region in a country, the risk that torture and rape will be likely tools of accomplishing this objective is relatively high. Thus, D might be said to have assumed the risk that in additional to forcible transfer (the crux of ethnic cleansing), members of the JCE may also commit the additional offences of rape and torture.

The enhancement of risk approach is also pertinent in the context in which international crimes occur. Through his voluntary association with an unlawful venture, D increases the risk that the collateral crime will occur because group members reinforce each other's resolve to commit

---

[54] See ch 9, text to nn 142–46.
[55] B Krebs, 'Joint Criminal Enterprise' (2010) 73 *MLR* 578, 594–96.
[56] Ibid, 594–95.

crimes, discouraging withdrawal and often resulting in an escalation of atrocities.[57] This phenomenon is considered useful for explaining the behaviour of 'ordinary' perpetrators in mass atrocities, where the average individual becomes capable of committing heinous crimes in group settings.[58] However, the legal literature on international crimes rarely refers to concrete empirical research in support of this assertion, and more data would be needed to substantiate it.

Lastly, it is argued that joint enterprise liability presents a more accurate picture of the nature of mass atrocity and the role of various participants in its commission, than that offered by traditional forms of secondary responsibility. In chapter one, three distinctive aspects of international crimes were identified: their collective nature, conformity to the prevailing social norms, and widespread participation in their commission by different levels of participants acting on different motives.[59] The first and third of these features would support using JCE as a distinct mode of accessorial responsibility. While there is no theoretical limit to the number of parties that may be liable as aiders and abettors, typical cases of aiding and abetting do not involve large groups of people who are dispersed over time and place. In contrast, JCE manages to capture the peculiarly collective aspects of mass atrocity: the fact that the perpetrator usually commits an international crime in furtherance of a collective criminal project, and with the consciousness that he is part of a larger common project. Arguably, this consciousness is stronger in the leadership and administration level organs, rather than in the rank-and-file perpetrator. It nevertheless explains the attitudes and conduct displayed by different participants in mass atrocity cases far better than traditional modes of secondary responsibility.

IV. CONCLUSION

In this chapter, we set out to examine two main issues: whether JCE II and JCE III find any support in principles of criminal responsibility in domestic criminal law systems, and whether there is any merit to retaining them as distinct modes of liability for international crimes. The above analysis reveals a complicated response to these questions. Category JCE II is potentially justifiable, but only in the form of accessorial responsibility, if the *actus reus* elements are modified to some extent.

---

[57] See ch 9, text to nn 147–49.

[58] See, eg, the discussion and references in OS Liwerant, 'Mass Murder: Discussing Criminological Perspectives' (2007) 5 *Journal of International Criminal Justice* 917. See also A Cassese, 'The Proper Limits of Individual Responsibility under the Doctrine of Joint Criminal Enterprise' (2007) 5 *Journal of International Criminal Justice* 109, 117–18.

[59] See ch 1, text to nn 5–34.

The common plan or agreement must be defined as a mutual understanding or consent to commit the crimes in question; this does not include mere acquiescence. The accused and the physical perpetrators should be parties to the agreement. This means only that they should act in the knowledge that there are other participants in the plan, all working towards the common criminal goal. There must be a causal link, not necessarily amounting to a *sine qua non* condition, between the conduct of the accused and the commission of crimes that are a result of the common plan.

Domestic criminal law and theory yield inconsistent answers to the justification for JCE III liability. Its retention as a form of secondary (and not principal) responsibility may still be supported by transposing expressive and risk rationales derived from English law to the domain of international crimes. However, given that the wording of Article 25(3)(d) does not support JCE III, that systems such as German criminal law have no strict equivalent, that parasitic joint enterprise liability rests on shaky grounds even in English law and that more empirical research is needed to substantiate the risk rationale, international criminal law may be better served by abandoning the JCE III doctrine.

12

Conclusion

THIS STUDY REPRESENTS a new approach to the challenge presented by assigning individual responsibility for crimes that are collective by their very nature. The modified accounts of perpetration and accessorial responsibility proposed here engage with domestic criminal law principles, while simultaneously capturing the unique features of international crimes. The study assumes that principles of criminal responsibility developed in the domestic criminal law context are salient for international crimes. In this sense, there is no attempt to, as it were, reinvent the wheel; I take for granted the set of doctrinal justifications that have guided the ascription of responsibility in these systems, and make no claims to developing any alternative account of the theoretical foundations of criminal responsibility. At the same time, rather than making an indiscriminate commitment to any particular domestic conceptualisation of criminal responsibility, I use these divergent justifications in the form of guideposts to develop an account of modes of participation that are suited to the collective dimension of international crimes.

Using this methodology, I propose a modified version of *Organisation-sherrschaft* to attribute perpetrator responsibility to high-level leaders and policy makers in situations of mass atrocity. Though the specific elements of this new account of perpetration constitute a departure from settled principles of principal responsibility in both German and English criminal law (and by extension criminal law doctrine in other countries that borrow from these systems), they remain true to the fundamental concerns that guide the allocation of criminal responsibility in both jurisdictions. At the same time, I modify these principles to highlight the distinctive features of international crimes. When combined with co-perpetration as outlined above, this new version of *Organisationsherrschaft* takes us closer to an accurate picture of the role and function of high-level participants in international crimes, and situates them in the political context of mass atrocity perpetuated through the acts of several thousands of anonymous individuals. It is also capable of adoption as a theory of responsibility under Article 25(3)(a) of the Rome Statute, to hold an accused responsible for the commission of an international crime.

My analysis of JCE II and JCE III is developed with a view to assessing their feasibility as secondary forms of responsibility that are specifically tailored to represent the collective nature of international crimes. A true engagement with principles of responsibility in prominent domestic legal systems and with the nature of international crimes reveals that JCE II and JCE III are properly regarded as forms of secondary, and not principal, liability. The category JCE II can be retained in the form of secondary responsibility, provided its application is limited to situations where mutual consent in the form of a common plan exists, and there is a causal link between the conduct of the accused and the offence. Expressive and risk justifications may potentially support the acceptance of JCE III in international criminal law, but its insecure foundations in criminal law theory, and the lack of empirical research in favour of its retention, counsel in favour of its abandonment.

While this study is confined to evaluating forms of individual responsibility that cater to the collective aspect of international crimes, it reveals methodological and conceptual problems that persist in varied areas of international criminal law. The most glaring of these challenges is the failure to analyse in depth, compare and learn from domestic criminal law theory and conversations on various issues that are unsettled and controversial in international criminal law. This is not an easy problem to overcome, given the time and resource constraints under which international criminal tribunals operate, and the complications caused by the lack of accessibility of legal materials of different legal systems.[1]

The academic can play a vital role in overcoming these constraints faced by international criminal law which, despite rapid developments, remains chaotic, fragmented and under-theorised. This assessment is no less true of the Rome Statute of the ICC – while the Statute represents an admirable degree of progress in several areas of international criminal law, there are several places, such as the entire terrain of defences, which are defined in fairly basic terms.[2] These would need to be refined and developed through the evolution of a *Dogmatik* of international criminal law. The scholar, removed as she is from the pressures of producing quick judgments that must take into account vast amounts of legal and factual materials, may thus form a crucial part of the enterprise of international criminal justice, enabling the fashioning of doctrinally coherent explications of treaty provisions through careful consideration of criminal law principles in major legal systems.

---

[1] For instance, it is difficult to find a single textbook in English that explains, in detail, the main principles of German criminal law. Bohlander's work (M Bohlander, *Principles of German Criminal Law: Studies in International and Comparative Criminal Law* (Oxford, Hart Publishing, 2009)) is an excellent introduction to the basic principles of German criminal law, but is unfortunately not particularly helpful if one wants to understand in depth and critique these principles. Admittedly, this is also not the purpose of his project, which purports to give only an overview of the law and theory.

[2] C Kress, 'International Criminal Law' in *Max Planck Encyclopedia of Public International Law* (Oxford, Oxford University Press, 2009) para 40.

Bibliography

BOOKS

Amelung, K (ed), *Individuelle Verantwortung und Beteiligungsverhältnisse bei Straftaten in bürokratischen Organisationen des Staates, der Wirtschaft und der Gesellschaft* (Sinzheim, Pro Universitate Verlag, 2000).

Ashworth, A, *Principles of Criminal Law*, 6th edn (Oxford, Oxford University Press, 2009).

Bassiouni, MC (ed), *International Criminal Law Vol III: Enforcement*, 2nd edn (New York, Transnational Publishers, 1999).

Benton, WE and Grimm, G (eds), *Nuremberg: German Views of the War Trials* (Dallas, Southern Methodist University Press, 1955).

Bloxham, D, *Genocide on Trial* (Oxford, Oxford University Press, 2001).

Boas, G, Bischoff, JL and Reid NL, *International Criminal Law Practitioner Library Series Vol I: Forms of Responsibility in International Criminal Law* (Cambridge, Cambridge University Press, 2007).

Bohlander, M, *Principles of German Criminal Law: Studies in International and Comparative Criminal Law* (Oxford, Hart Publishing, 2009).

Burchard, C et al (eds), *The Review Conference and the Future of the International Criminal Court* (The Hague, Kluwer Law International, 2010).

Cassese, A et al (eds), *The Rome Statute of the International Criminal Court: A Commentary* Vol I (Oxford, Oxford University Press, 2002).

——, *International Criminal Law* (Oxford, Oxford University Press, 2003).

Chihiro, H et al (eds), *The Tokyo War Crimes Trial: An International Symposium* (Tokyo, Kodansha, 1986).

Clarkson, CMV, Keating, HM and Cunningham, SR, *Clarkson and Keating's Criminal Law: Text and Materials*, 7th edn (London, Sweet & Maxwell, 2010).

Cryer, R, *Prosecuting International Crimes: Selectivity and the International Criminal Law Regime* (Cambridge, Cambridge University Press, 2005).

Damgaard, C, *Individual Criminal Responsibility for Core International Crimes* (Berlin, Springer-Verlag, 2008).

Darcy, S and Powderly, J (eds), *Judicial Creativity at the International Criminal Tribunals* (New York, Oxford University Press, 2010).

Dower, JW, *Embracing Defeat: Japan In The Wake Of World War II* (New York, Norton, 1999).

Dressler, J, *Understanding Criminal Law* (LexisNexis, 2009).

Drumbl, MA, *Atrocity, Punishment, and International Law* (Cambridge, Cambridge University Press, 2007).

Fletcher, GP, *Rethinking Criminal Law* (Oxford, Oxford University Press, 2000).

Ginsburgs, G and Kudriavtsev, VN (eds), *The Nuremberg Trial and International Law* (London, Martinus Nijhoff, 1990).

Gourevitch, P, *We Wish to Inform You That Tomorrow We Will Be Killed with Our Families: Stories from Rwanda* (New York, Farrer Straus and Giroux, 1998).

Hart, HLA and Honoré, AM, *Causation in the Law* (Oxford, Clarendon Press, 1959).

Heller, KJ, *The Nuremberg Military Tribunals and the Origins of International Criminal Law* (Oxford, Oxford University Press, 2011).

Honoré, T, *Responsibility and Fault* (Oxford, Hart Publishing, 1999).

Hoyer, A et al (eds), *Festschrift für Friedrich-Christian Schroeder zum 70. Geburtstag* (Munich, CF Müller, 2006).

Jescheck, H-H, *Die Verantwortlichkeit der Staatsorgane nach Völkerstrafrecht* (Bonn, Röhrscheid, 1952).

Kadish, SH, *Blame and Punishment: Essays in the Criminal Law* (New York, Macmillan, 1987).

LaFave, WR, *Criminal Law* (St Paul, MN, West Academic Publishing, 2010).

Laufhütte, H et al (eds), *Strafgesetzbuch Leipziger Kommentar (Großkommentar): Band 1* (Berlin, de Gruyter Recht, 2006).

Lee, RS (ed), *The International Criminal Court: The Making of the Rome Statute: Issues, Negotiations, Results* (The Hague, Kluwer Law International, 1999).

MacCormack, TLH and Simpson, GJ (eds), *The Law of War Crimes: National and International Approaches* (The Hague, Kluwer Law International, 1997).

Macdonald, R St-J, Matscher, R and Petzold, H (eds), *The European System for the Protection of Human Rights* (London, Martinus Nijhoff, 1993).

Malanczuk, P, *Akehurst's Modern Introduction to International Law*, 6th rev edn (London, Routledge, 1997).

Mann, M, *The Dark Side of Democracy: Explaining Ethnic Cleansing* (Cambridge, Cambridge University Press, 2005).

McAdams, AJ (ed), *Transitional Justice and the Rule of Law in New Democracies* (Notre Dame, University of Notre Dame Press, 1997).

Minear, RH, *Victors' Justice: The Tokyo War Crimes Trial* (Princeton, Princeton University Press, 1971).

Moore, MS, *Causation and Responsibility* (Oxford, Oxford University Press, 2009).

Nersessian, DL, *Genocide and Political Groups* (Oxford, Oxford University Press, 2010).

Nino, CS, *Radical Evil on Trial* (New Haven, Yale University Press, 1996).

Nollkaemper, A and van der Wilt, H (eds), *System Criminality in International Law* (Cambridge, Cambridge University Press, 2009).

Nussbaum, A, *A Concise History of the Law of Nations* (New York, The Macmillan Company, 1947).

Olásolo, H, *The Criminal Responsibility of Senior Political and Military Leaders as Principals to International Crimes* (London, Hart Publishing, 2009).

Ormerod, D, *Smith and Hogan's Criminal Law: Cases and Materials*, 10th edn (Oxford, Oxford University Press, 2009).

Osiel, MJ, *Making Sense of Mass Atrocity* (Cambridge, Cambridge University Press, 2009).

——, *Mass Atrocity, Ordinary Evil, and Hannah Arendt: Criminal Consciousness in Argentina's Dirty War* (New Haven, CT, Yale University Press, 2001).

Reisman, WM, and Weston, BH (eds), *Toward World Order and Human Dignity: Essays in Honour of Myres S McDougal* (New York, The Free Press, 1976).

Roxin, C, *Täterschaft und Tatherrschaft*, 8th edn (Berlin, de Gruyter Recht, 2006).

Sadat, LN, *The International Criminal Court and the Transformation of International Law* (Ardsley, NY, Transnational, 2002).

Schönke, A and Schröder, H, *Strafgesetzbuch: Kommentar*, 27th edn (Munich, CH Beck, 2006).

Schroeder, F-C, *Der Täter hinter dem Täter: Ein Beitrag zur Lehre von der mittelbaren Täterschaft* (Berlin, Duncker & Humblot, 1965).

Schwarzenberger, G, *International Law as Applied by Interational Courts and Tribunals, International Law vol I*, 3rd edn (London, Stevens & Sons Limited, 1957).

——, *International Law as Applied by International Courts and Tribunals vol II* (London, Stevens & Sons, 1968).

Shklar, JN, *Legalism: Law, Morals, and Political Trials* (Cambridge, Harvard University Press, 1964).

Simester, AP and Sullivan, GR, *Criminal Law: Theory and Doctrine*, 4th edn (London, Hart Publishing, 2010).

Smith, B (ed), *The American Road to Nuremberg: The Documentary Record 1944-45* (Stanford, CA, Hoover Institute Press, 1982).

Smith, KJM, *A Modern Treatise on the Law of Criminal Complicity* (Oxford, Clarendon Press, 1991).

Smith, P (ed), *Criminal Law: Essays in Honour of J C Smith* (London, Butterworths, 1987).

Stahn, C and Sluiter, G (eds), *The Emerging Practice of the International Criminal Court* (Leiden, Martinus Nijhoff Publishers, 2009).

Tadros, V, *Criminal Responsibility* (Oxford, Oxford University Press, 2005).

Teitel, RG, *Transitional Justice* (Oxford, Oxford University Press, 2000).

Triffterer, O, (ed), *Commentary on the Rome Statute of the International Criminal Court*, 2nd edn (Baden-Baden, Nomos, 1999).

Tusa, A and Tusa, J, *The Nuremberg Trial* (London, BBC Books, 1995).

van Sliedregt, E, *Individual Criminal Responsibility in International Law* (Oxford, Oxford University Press, 2012).

——, *The Criminal Responsibility of Individuals for Violations of International Humanitarian Law* (The Hague, TMC Asser Press, 2003).

Vetlesen, AJ, *Evil and Human Agency: Understanding Collective Evildoing* (Cambridge, Cambridge University Press, 2005).

Wessels, J and Beulke, W, *Strafrecht, allgemeiner Teil: Die Straftat und ihr Aufbau* (Schwerpunkte) (Heidelberg, CF Müller Verlag, 2012).

Williams, G, *Criminal Law: The General Part*, 2nd edn (London, Stevens & Sons, 1961).

——, *Textbook of Criminal Law*, 2nd edn (London, Stevens & Sons, 1983).

Woetzel, R, *The Nuremberg Trials in International Law* (London, Stevens & Sons, 1962)

ARTICLES

'Developments in International Law – International Criminal Law' (2001) 114 *Harvard Law Review* 1943.

Akhavan, P, 'Justice in the Hague, Peace in the Former Yugoslavia? A Commentary on the United Nations War Crimes Tribunal' (1998) 20 *Human Rights Quarterly* 737.

Alldridge, P, 'The Doctrine of Innocent Agency' (1990) 2 *Criminal Law Forum* 45.

Alvarez, JE, 'Crimes of State/Crimes of Hate: Lessons from Rwanda' (1999) 24 *Yale Journal of International Law* 365.

——, 'Rush to Closure: Lessons of the Tadić Judgment' (1998) 96 *Michigan Law Review* 2031.

Ambos, K, 'Joint Criminal Enterprise and Command Responsibility' (2007) 5 *Journal of International Criminal Justice* 159.

——, 'Tatherrschaft durch Willensherrschaft kraft organisatorischer Machtapparate' (1998) *Goltdammer's Archiv für Strafrecht* 226.

——, 'The First Judgment of the International Criminal Court (*Prosecutor v. Lubanga*): A Comprehensive Analysis of the Legal Issues' (2012) 12 *International Criminal Law Review* 115.

——, 'The *Fujimori* Judgment: A President's Responsibility for Crimes Against Humanity as Indirect Perpetrator by Virtue of an Organized Power Apparatus' (2011) 9 *Journal of International Criminal Justice* 137.

Ashworth, A, 'Interpreting Criminal Statutes: A Crisis of Legality?' (1991) 107 *LQR* 419.

Badar, ME and Karsten, N, 'Current Developments at the International Criminal Tribunals (2008)' (2009) 9 *International Criminal Law Review* 227.

Badar, ME, '"Just Convict Everyone!" – Joint Perpetration: From *Tadić* to *Stakić* and Back Again' (2006) 6 *International Criminal Law Review* 293.

Bassiouni, M, 'The Time Has Come for an International Criminal Court' (1991) 1 *Indiana International & Comparative Law Review* 1.

Bloy, R, 'Grenzen der Täterschaft bei fremdhändiger Tatausführung' (1996) *Goltdammer's Archiv für Strafrecht* 424.

Bogdan, A, 'Individual Criminal Responsibility in the Execution of a "Joint Criminal Enterprise" in the Jurisprudence of the *ad hoc* International Tribunal for the Former Yugoslavia' (2006) 6 *International Criminal Law Review* 63.

Boister, N, 'The Application of Collective and Comprehensive Criminal Responsibility for Aggression at the Tokyo International Military Tribunal' (2010) 8 *Journal of International Criminal Justice* 425.

Burchell, J, 'Joint Enterprise and Common Purpose: Perspectives in English and South African Criminal Law' (1997) 10 *South African Journal of Criminal Justice* 125.

Carr, ASC, 'The Judgment of the International Military Tribunal for the Far East' (1948) 34 *Transactions of the Grotius Society* 141.

Cassese, A, 'Reflections on International Criminal Justice' (1998) 61 *MLR* 1.

——, 'The Proper Limits of Individual Responsibility under the Doctrine of Joint Criminal Enterprise' (2007) 5 *Journal of International Criminal Justice* 109.

Clapham, A, 'Extending International Criminal Law beyond the Individual to Corporations and Armed Opposition Groups' (2008) 6 *Journal of International Criminal Justice* 899.

Clark, RS, 'Drafting a General Part to a Penal Code: Some Thoughts Inspired by the Negotiations on the Rome Statute of the International Criminal Court and by the Court's First Substantive Law Discussion in the *Lubanga Dyilo* Confirmation Proceedings' (2008) 19 *Criminal Law Forum* 519.

Clark, RC, 'Return to *Borkum Island*: Extended Joint Criminal Enterprise Responsibility in the Wake of World War II' (2011) 9 *Journal of International Criminal Justice* 839.

Damaska, M, 'The Shadow Side of Command Responsibility' (2001) 49 *American Journal of Comparative Law* 455.

——, 'What is the Point of International Criminal Justice?' (2008) 83 *Chicago-Kent Law Review* 329.

Danner, AM and Martinez, JS, 'Guilty Associations: Joint Criminal Enterprise, Command Responsibility, and the Development of International Criminal Law' (2005) 93 *California Law Review* 75.

Danner, AM, 'Beyond the Geneva Conventions: Lessons from the Tokyo Tribunal in Prosecuting War and Terrorism' (2005) 46 *Virginia Journal of International Law* 30.

Darcy, S, 'Imputed Criminal Liability and the Goals of International Justice' (2007) 20 *Leiden Journal of International Law* 377.

Decker, JF, 'The Mental State Requirement for Accomplice Liability in American Criminal Law' (2008) 60 *South Carolina Law Review* 237.

Dennis, I, 'Intention and Complicity: A Reply' [1988] *Crim LR* 649.

Dressler, J, 'Reassessing the Theoretical Underpinnings of Accomplice Liability: New Solutions to an Old Problem' (1985–86) 37 *Hastings Law Journal* 91.

——, 'Reforming Complicity Law: Trivial Assistance as a Lesser Offense?' (2008) 5 *Ohio State Journal of Criminal Law* 427.

Drumbl, MA, 'Punishment, Postgenocide: From Guilt to Shame to *Civis* in Rwanda' (2000) 75 *New York University Law Review* 1221.

——, 'Collective Violence and Individual Punishment: The Criminality of Mass Atrocity' (2005) 99 *Northwestern University Law Review* 539.

——, 'Pluralizing International Criminal Justice' (2005) 103 *Michigan Law Review* 1315.

Duff, RA, '"Can I Help You?" Accessorial Liability and the Intention to Assist' (1990) 10 *Legal Studies* 165.

Dyson, M, 'More Appealing Joint Enterprise' (2010) 69 *CLJ* 425.

Ehard, H, 'The Nuremberg Trial Against the Major War Criminals and International Law' (1949) 43 *American Journal of International Law* 223.

Engvall, L, 'The Future of Extended Joint Criminal Enterprise – Will the ICTY's Innovation Meet the Standards of the ICC?' (2007) 76 *Nordic Journal of International Law* 241.

Farhang, C, 'Point of No Return: Joint Criminal Enterprise in *Brdanin*' (2010) 23 *Leiden Journal of International Law* 137.

Fletcher, GP and Ohlin, JD, 'Reclaiming Fundamental Principles of Criminal Law in the Darfur Case' (2005) 3 *Journal of International Criminal Justice* 539.

Fletcher, GP, 'The Storrs Lectures: Liberals and Romantics at War: The Problem of Collective Guilt' (2002) 111 *Yale Law Journal* 1499.

——, 'Collective Guilt and Collective Punishment' (2004) 5 *Theoretical Inquiries in Law* 163.

——, 'New Court, Old Dogmatik' (2011) 9 *Journal of International Criminal Justice* 179.

Fletcher, LE and Weinstein, HM, 'Violence and Social Repair: Rethinking the Contribution of Justice to Reconciliation' (2002) 24 *Human Rights Quarterly* 573.

Fletcher, LE, 'From Indifference to Engagement: Bystanders and International Criminal Justice' (2005) 26 *Michigan Journal of International Law* 1013.

Frankowska, M, 'The Vienna Convention on the Law of Treaties before United States Courts' (1988) 28 *Virginia Journal of International Law* 281.

Gardner, J, 'Criminal Law and the Uses of Theory: A Reply to Laing' (1994) 14 *OJLS* 217.

——, 'Complicity and Causality' (2007) 1 *Criminal Law & Philosophy* 127.

Garner, JW, 'Punishment of Offenders against the Laws and Customs of War' (1920) 14 *American Journal of International Law* 70.

Gillett, M and Schuster, M, 'Fast-Track Justice: The Special Tribunal for Lebanon Defines Terrorism' (2011) 9 *Journal of International Criminal Justice* 989.

Giustiniani, FZ, 'Stretching the Bounds of Commission Liability: The ICTR Appeal Judgment in *Seromba*' (2008) 6 *Journal of International Criminal Justice* 783.

——, 'The Responsibility of Accomplices in the Case Law of the *Ad Hoc* Tribunals' (2009) 20 *Criminal Law Forum* 417.

Goldstone, RJ, 'Justice as a Tool for Peace-making: Truth Commissions and International Criminal Tribunals' (1996) 28 *NYU Journal of International Law & Politics* 485.

Goy, B, 'Individual Criminal Responsibility before the International Criminal Court: A Comparison with the *Ad Hoc* Tribunals (2012) 12 *International Criminal Law Review* 1.

Greenawalt, AKA, 'Justice without Politics?: Prosecutorial Discretion and the International Criminal Court' (2007) 39 *NYU Journal of International Law & Politics* 583.

Grover, L, 'A Call to Arms: Fundamental Dilemmas Confronting the Interpretation of Crimes in the Rome Statute of the International Criminal Court' (2010) 21 *European Journal of International Law* 543.

Guifoyle, D, 'Responsibility for Collective Atrocities: Fair Labelling and Approaches to Commission in International Criminal Law' (2011) 64 *Current Legal Problems* 255.

Gustafson, K, 'The Requirement of an "Express Agreement" for Joint Criminal Enterprise Liability' (2007) 5 *Journal of International Criminal Justice* 134.

Haan, V, 'The Development of the Concept of Joint Criminal Enterprise at the International Criminal Tribunal for the Former Yugoslavia' (2005) 5 *International Criminal Law Review* 167.

Hola, B et al, 'International Sentencing Facts and Figures: Sentencing Practices at the ICTY and ICTR' (2011) 9 *Journal of International Criminal Justice* 411.

Horwitz, S, 'The Tokyo Trial' (1950) 466 *International Conciliation* 473.

Jakobs, G, 'Mittelbare Täterschaft der Mitglieder des Nationalen Verteidigungsrats' (1995) *Neue Zeitschrift für Strafrecht* 26.

Jeffries, JC, 'Legality, Vagueness and the Construction of Penal Statutes' (1985) 71 *Virginia Law Review* 189.

Jessberger, F and Geneuss, J, 'On the Application of a Theory of Indirect Perpetration in *Al Bashir*: German Doctrine at the Hague?' (2008) 6 *Journal of International Criminal Justice* 853.

Jorda, C, 'The International Criminal Tribunal for the Former Yugoslavia: Its Functioning and Future Prospects' (1999) 3 *Hofstra Law & Policy Symposium* 167.

Jordash, W and Martin, S, 'Due Process ad Fair Trial Rights at the Special Court: How the Desire for Accountability Outweighed the Demands of Justice at the Special Court for Sierra Leone' (2010) 23 *Leiden Journal of International Law* 585.

Jordash, W and van Tuyl, P, 'Failure to Carry the Burden of Proof: How Joint Criminal Enterprise Lost its Way at the Special Court for Sierra Leone' (2010) 8 *Journal of International Criminal Justice* 591.

Kadish, SH, 'Complicity, Cause and Blame: A Study in the Interpretation of Doctrine' (1985) 73 *California Law Review* 323.

Kelsen, H, 'Will the Judgment in the Nuremberg Trial Constitute a Precedent in International Law?' (1947) 1 *International Law Quarterly* 153.

Koessler, M, 'Borkum Island Tragedy and Trial' (1956) 47 *Journal of Criminal Law, Criminology and Police Science* 183.

Komarow, G, 'Individual Responsibility under International Law: The Nuremberg Principles in Domestic Legal Systems' (1980) 29 *ICLQ* 21.

Kopelman, ES, 'Ideology and International Law: The Dissent of the Indian Justice at the Tokyo War Crimes Trial' (1990–91) 23 *NYU Journal of International Law & Politics* 373.

Krebs, B, 'Joint Criminal Enterprise' (2010) 73 *Modern Law Review* 578.

Kremnitzer, M, 'A Possible Case for Imposing Criminal Liability on Corporations in International Criminal Law' (2010) 8 *Journal of International Criminal Justice* 909.

Kress, C, 'The Darfur Report and Genocidal Intent' (2005) 3 *Journal of International Criminal Justice* 562.

——, 'Claus Roxins Lehre von der Organisationsherrschaft und das Völkerstrafrecht' (2006) *Goltdammer's Archiv für Strafrecht* 304.

Küpper, G, 'Zur Abgrenzung der Täterschaftsformen' (1998) *Goltdammer's Archiv für Strafrecht* 519.

Lacey, N, 'In Search of the Responsible Subject: History, Philosophy and Social Sciences in Criminal Law Theory' (2001) 64 *Modern Law Review* 350.

Leonhardt, H, 'The Nuremberg Trial: A Legal Analysis' (1949) 11 *Review of Politics* 449.

Leventhal, H et al., 'The Nuernberg Verdict' (1947) 60 *Harvard Law Review* 857.

Levy, AG, 'Criminal Responsibility of Individuals and International Law' (1945) 12 *University of Chicago Law Review* 313.

Linton, S, 'Rediscovering the War Crimes Trials in Hong Kong, 1946-48' (2012) 13 *Melbourne Journal of International Law* 1.

Liwerant, OS, 'Mass Murder: Discussing Criminological Perspectives' (2007) 5 *Journal of International Criminal Justice* 917.

MacCormack, TLH, 'Selective Reaction to Atrocity: War Crimes and the Development of International Criminal Law' (1996–97) 60 *Albany Law Review* 681.

Manacorda, S & Meloni, C, 'Indirect Perpetration versus Joint Criminal Enterprise: Concurring Approaches in the Practice of International Criminal Law?' (2011) 9 *Journal of International Criminal Justice* 159.

Mansfield, JH, 'Hart and Honoré, Causation in the Law – A Comment' (1963) 17 *Vanderbilt Law Review* 487.

McNair, AD, 'The Functions and Differing Legal Character of Treaties' (1930) 11 *British Year Book of International Law* 100.

Milanovic, M, 'An Odd Couple: Domestic Crimes and International Responsibility in the Special Tribunal for Lebanon' (2007) 5 *Journal of International Criminal Justice* 1139.

Militello, V, 'The Personal Nature of Individual Criminal Responsibility and the ICC Statute' (2007) 5 *Journal of International Criminal Justice* 941.

Moore, MS, 'Causing, Aiding, and the Superfluity of Accomplice Liability' (2007–08) 156 *University of Pennsylvania Law Review* 395.

Muñoz-Conde, F and Olásolo, H, 'The Application of the Notion of Indirect Perpetration through Organized Structures of Power in Latin America and Spain' (2011) 9 *Journal of International Criminal Justice* 113.

Murmann, U, 'Tatherrschaft durch Weisungsmacht' (1996) *Goltdammer's Archiv für Strafrecht* 269.

O'Rourke, A, 'Joint Criminal Enterprise and Brdanin: Misguided Over-correction' (2006) 47 *Harvard International Law Journal* 307.

Ohlin, JD, van Sliedregt, E, and Weigend, T, 'Assessing the Control-Theory' (2013) 26 *Leiden Journal of International Law* 725.

Ohlin, JD, 'Second-Order Linking Principles: Combining Vertical and Horizontal Modes of Liability' (2012) 25 *Leiden Journal of International Law* 771.

——, 'Joint Intentions to Commit International Crimes' (2011) 12 *Chicago Journal of International Law* 693.

——, 'Three Conceptual Problems with the Doctrine of Joint Criminal Enterprise' (2007) 5 *Journal of International Criminal Justice* 69.

Olasolo, H, 'Joint Criminal Enterprise and its Extended Form: A Theory of Co-Perpetration Giving Rise to Principal Liability, a Notion of Accesorial Liability, Or a Form of Partnership in Crime?' (2009) 20 *Criminal Law Forum* 263.

——, 'Reflections on the Treatment of the Notions of Control of the Crime and Joint Criminal Enterprise in the Stakić Appeal Judgment' (2007) 7 *International Criminal Law Review* 143.

Ormerod, D, 'Case Comment: R v Mendez (Reece)' [2010] *Crim LR* 874.

——, 'Case Comment: R v A' [2011] *Crim LR* 61.

Osiel, MJ, 'Constructing Subversion in Argentina's Dirty War' (2001) 75 *Representations* 119.

——, 'Modes of Participation in Mass Atrocity' (2005) 38 *Cornell International Law Journal* (2005) 793.

——, 'The Banality of Good: Aligning Incentives Against Mass Atrocity' (2005) 105 *Columbia Law Review* 1751.

Otto, H, 'Täterschaft kraft organisatorischen Machtapparates' (2001) *Jura* 753.

Piacente, N, 'Importance of the Joint Criminal Enterprise Doctrine for the ICTY Prosecutorial Policy' (2004) 2 *Journal of International Criminal Justice* 446.

Powles, S, 'Joint Criminal Enterprise: Criminal Liability by Prosecutorial Ingenuity and Judicial Creativity?' (2004) 2 *Journal of International Criminal Justice* 606.

Radtke, H, 'Mittelbare Täterschaft kraft Organisationsherrschaft im nationalen und internationalen Strafrecht' (2006) *Goltdammer's Archiv für Strafrecht* 350.

Roberts, AE, 'Traditional and Modern Approaches to Customary International Law: A Reconciliation' (2001) 95 *American Journal of International Law* 757.

Robinson, D, 'The Identity Crisis of International Criminal Law' (2008) 21 *Leiden Journal of International Law* 925.

Robinson, PH, 'Imputed Criminal Liability' (1984) 93 *Yale Law Journal* 609.

Rose, C, 'Troubled Indictments at the Special Court for Sierra Leone: The Pleading of Joint Criminal Enterprise and Sex-Based Crimes' (2009) 7 *Journal of International Criminal Justice* 353.

Rotsch, T, 'Tatherrschaft kraft Organisationsherrschaft?' (2001) 112 *Zeitschrift für die gesamte Strafrechtswissenschaft* 518.

——, 'Neues zur Organisationsherrschaft' (2005) *Neue Zeitschrift für Strafrecht* 13.

Roxin, C, 'Straftaten im Rahmen organisatorischer Machtapparate' (1963) *Goltdammer's Archiv für Strafrecht* 193.

——, 'Anmerkung' (1995) *Juristen-Zeitung* 49.

——, 'Organisationsherrschaft und Tatentschlossenheit' (2006) 7 *Zeitschrift für Internationale Strafrechtsdogmatik* 293.

——, 'Bemerkungen zum Fujimori-Urteil des Obersten Gerichtshofs in Peru' (2009) 4 *Zeitschrift für Internationale Strafrechtsdogmatik* 565.

Sassòli, M and Olson, LM, 'The Judgment of the ICTY Appeals Chamber on the Merits in the *Tadić* Case' (2000) 839 *International Review of the Red Cross* 733.

Schabas, WA, 'The ICTY at Ten: A Critical Assessment of the Major Rulings of the International Criminal Tribunal Over the Past Decade: *Mens Rea* and the International Criminal Tribunal for the Former Yugoslavia' (2003) 37 *New England Law Review* 1015.

Schick, FB, 'The Nuremberg Trial and the International Law of the Future' (1947) 41 *American Journal of International Law* 770.

Schrag, M, 'Lessons Learned from ICTY Experience' (2004) 2 *Journal of International Criminal Justice* 427.

Schroeder, F-C, 'Der Sprung des Täters hinter dem Täter aus der Theorie in die Praxis' (1995) *Juristische Rundschau* 177.

Simester, AP, 'The Mental Element in Complicity' (2006) 122 *LQR* 578.

Sinclair, IM, 'The Principles of Treaty Interpretation and their Application by the English Courts' (1963) 12 *ICLQ* 508.

Sloane, RD, 'The Expressive Capacity of International Punishment: The Limits of the National Law Analogy and the Potential of International Criminal Law' (2007) 43 *Stanford Journal of International Law* 39.

Smith, JC 'Criminal Liability of Accessories: Law and Law Reform' (1997) 113 *LQR* 453.

——, 'Case and Comment: R v Powell and Daniels' [1998] *Crim LR* 48.

——, 'Commentary: R v Day (M) and Others' [2001] *Crim LR* 984.

——, 'Case and Comment: R v Yemoh' [2009] *Crim LR* 888.

Stewart, JG, 'The End of 'Modes of Liability' for International Crimes' (2012) 25 *Leiden Journal of International Law* 165.

Strippoli, A, 'National Courts and Genocide: The *Kravica* Case at the Court of Bosnia and Herzegovina' (2009) 7 *Journal of International Criminal Justice* 577.

Sullivan, G 'Intent, Purpose and Complicity' [1988] *Crim LR* 641.

——, 'Participating in Crime: Law Com No. 305 – Joint Criminal Ventures' [2008] *Crim LR* 19.

Sullivan, R, 'First Degree Murder and Complicity – Conditions for Parity of Culpability between Principal and Accomplice' (2007) 1 *Criminal Law & Philosophy* 271.

Tallgren, I, 'The Sensibility and Sense of International Criminal Law' (2002) 13 *EJIL* 561.

van der Wilt, H 'Joint Criminal Enterprise: Possibilities and Limitations' (2007) 5 *Journal of International Criminal Justice* 91.

van Sliedregt, E, 'Joint Criminal Enterprise as a Pathway to Convicting Individuals for Genocide' (2007) 5 *Journal of International Criminal Justice* 184.
——, 'The Curious Case of International Criminal Liability' (2012) 10 *Journal of International Criminal Justice* 1171.
Virgo, G, 'Clarifying Accessorial Liability' (1998) 57 *CLJ* 13.
Wassertrom, R, 'The Relevance of Nuremberg' (1971) 1 *Philosophy & Public Affairs* 22.
Watkins, JL and DeFalco, RC, 'Joint Criminal Enterprise and the Jurisdiction of the Extraordinary Chambers in the Courts of Cambodia' (2010) 63 *Rutgers Law Review* 193.
Weigend, T, 'Intent, Mistake of Law, and Co-perpetration in the *Lubanga* Decision on Confirmation of Charges' (2008) 6 *Journal of International Criminal Justice* 471.
——, 'Perpetration through an Organization: The Unexpected Career of a German Legal Concept' (2011) 9 *Journal of International Criminal Justice* 91.
Weisberg, R, 'Reappraising Complicity' (2000) 4 *Buffalo Criminal Law Review* 217.
Werle, G and Burghardt, B, 'Indirect Perpetration: A Perfect Fit for International Prosecution of Armchair Killers?' (2011) 9 *Journal of International Criminal Justice* 85.
Werle, G, 'Individual Criminal Responsibility in Article 25 ICC Statute' (2007) 5 *Journal of International Criminal Justice* 953.
Wessel, J, 'Relational Contract Theory and Treaty Interpretation: End-Game Treaties v. Dynamic Obligations' (2004) 60 *NYU Annual Survey of American Law* 149.
——, 'Judicial Policy-Making at the International Criminal Court: An Institutional Guide to Analyzing International Adjudication' (2006) 44 *Columbia Journal of Transnational Law* 377.
Williams, G, 'Complicity, Purpose and the Draft Code – I' [1990] *Crim LR* 4.
——, 'Innocent Agency and Causation' (1992) 3 *Criminal Law Forum* 289.
Wippman, D, 'Atrocities, Deterrence and the Limits of International Justice' (1999) 23 *Fordham International Law Journal* 473.
Wirth, S, 'Co-Perpetration in the Lubanga Trial Judgment' (2012) 10 *Journal of International Criminal Justice* 971.
Wright, Q, 'International Law and Guilt by Association' (1949) 43 *American Journal of International Law* 746.
Wright, Q, 'The Legal Liability of the Kaiser' (1919) 13 *American Political Science Review* 120.

MISCELLANEOUS

Report of Robert H. Jackson to the International Conference on Military Trials (Washington, US Government Printing Office, 1949).
'Statement of the Co-Prosecutors on the First Introductory Submission in the Extraordinary Chambers in the Courts of Cambodia' (18 July 2007) www.una-krt-online.org/Docs/Court%20Statements/2007-07-18%20Statement%20of%20Co-Prosecutors-First%20Submission.pdf.
Amicus Curiae Brief of Kai Ambos concerning Criminal Case File No. 001/18-07-2007-ECCC/OCIJ (PTC 02) (27 October 2008).

Amicus Curiae Brief of Professor Antonio Cassese and members of the Journal of International Criminal Justice on Joint Criminal Enterprise Doctrine, Case File No. 001/18-07-2007-ECCC/OCIJ (PTC 02) (27 October 2008).

Des Forges, A, *'Leave None to Tell the Story': Genocide in Rwanda* (New York, Human Rights Watch, 1999).

Easterday, J, 'Initial Reflections on JCE and Terrorism in the *Taylor* Judgment' (*IntLawGrrls*, 30 April 2012) http://www.intlawgrrls.com/2012/04/initial-reflections-on-jce-and.html#more

——, 'Joint Criminal Enterprise in the *Taylor* Judgment' (*IntLawGrrls*, 09 August 2012) http://www.intlawgrrls.com/2012/08/joint-criminal-enterprise-in-charles.html

History of the United Nations War Crimes Commission and the Development of the Laws of War (His Majesty's Stationery Office, 1948).

Humphrey W, 'Third Report on the Law of Treaties' in *Yearbook of the International Law Commission 1964*, vol II, 57 (New York, United Nations, 1965) UN Doc A/CN.4/SER.A/1964/Add.1.

Law Commission, *Assisting and Encouraging Crime* (Consultation Paper No. 131, 1993).

——, *Participating in Crime* (Law Com No 305, 2007).

Max Planck Encyclopedia of Public International Law (Oxford, Oxford University Press, 2009).

Memorandum to President Roosevelt from the Secretaries of State and War and the Attorney General, January 22, 1945 in *Report of Robert H Jackson, United States Representative to the International Conference on Military Trials* (Washington, 1949).

Pritchard, RJ (ed), *The Records of the International Military Tribunal for the Far East* (Queenston, The Edwin Mellen Press, 1998).

Schabas, W, 'Special Court for Sierra Leone Rejects Joint Criminal Enterprise' (*The Trial of Charles Taylor*, 25 June 2007) charlestaylortrial.org/expert-commentary/professor-william-schabas-on-afrc-decision.

Sieber, U and Engelhart, M, *Strafbare Mitwirkung von Führungspersonen in Straftätergruppen und Netzwerken in Deutschland* (Max-Planck-Institut für ausländisches und internationales Strafrecht unpublished report, 2009).

Sullivan, R, 'Principals and Accomplices – a Necessary and Useful Division' in Antony Duff and Christoffer Wong (eds), *Foundational Issues in the Philosophy of Criminal Law*, Special Workshop at the 23rd IVR Congress, 1-6 August 2007, Kraków, Poland 151.

The Secretary-General, Report of the Secretary-General Pursuant to Paragraph 2 of Security Council Resolution 808, delivered to the Security Council, U.N. Doc S/25704 (3 May 1993).

Toufayan, M, 'Human Rights Treaty Interpretation: A Postmodern Account of its Claim to "Speciality"' (2005) *NYU Center for Human Rights & Global Justice* Working Paper No 2.

Trial of the Major War Criminals Before the International Military Tribunal, vol I (Nuremberg, 1947).

Trial of the Major War Criminals Before the International Military Tribunal, vol II (Nuremberg, 1947).

Trial of the Major War Criminals Before the International Military Tribunal, vol VIII (Nuremberg, 1947).

Index

171 Joint enterprise lby clearly a form
of lndary lby in English law

171 Joint enterprise liab clearly a cgs of 2ndary
liab in English law - but is it distinct cgy?

173 It is diff representationally. Talks about
'affiliation w/ a segment f say' [I tho't
she was agst guilt by association?]
Yes - 174 - says cgy is unconvincing

177 German law - 5 theories to explain norm.
basis for unminimal liab.

202 JCE II allows acquiescence to count -
Eng + Ger law on 2ndary liab do nr.

203 3 element f a.r. in JCE II & III do
find some support in domestic crim law prs.

204   neutral actions & the "if" stp.

205   Extension f liab mediated by shared purpose.

206   Ex. of unwarranted extension f liab
         Risk/ endangerment rationale supported.

208   Conclusion to this section.

129 Qn Roxin structure — seems to have
size limitation. 130 Does not reflect
typical Intnl crime context.

130 Fungibility — why doesn't → no apply?

131 Principles of attribution may be diff. for
indiv. + collective criminality.
Intnl offcs have an inbuilt collectivity — this
defn.

132 So decoupling Hintermann from each idv microcrime
wld not → decoupling from macrocrime.

133 Praise for Roxin's 'law-detachedness' criterion.

135 bt - y Osschft can also save complexity.

136 Coperpetrator story can't. be substtd f Oschat
because there no common plan.

137 Theory does present foundational models.

138 No directness, no deep chain of causation.
No concept of mass criminality in Eng. crim. law.

139 German crim law emphasises control over causation.
Still an oversimplified picture.

140 Deliberately inflaming passions? — that's a diff
way they isn't it?

141 Spontaneity + initiative of lower works agst
overall control idea.
"control over the unleashing of a destructive
potential that can lead to mass atrocity
& is intended to do so — how does this
relate to fiery orator?
The clock/bomb maker.

149 Contrast w/ JCE — Key

150 Claims theory "engages with" domestic crim law
principles

154 Influence of risk/endangerment rationale.

25 co-perpetration ≠ JCE

75 ll attempts to under idea of "commission"

94 Terms spread to carry ord. meaning ⇒
so problematic to use national legal concepts
as guide to interpretation

95 Seems to raise esp. problem where it comes to
convicting ladders.

97 Dogmatik issue. Does nascent case of ICL
require Dogmatik approach?

98-9 Key intermediate conclusion.

103 The principal in English law - ref. to H + H
on causation

107 Prosecution for intnl crimes rarely concerned
w/ the Othellos s perpetrators.
ways of expanding "2nd-ary" lbly, lbly of 3rd-ary
party

Focus on wrong done, not on crime.

108 Problem in holding D guilty of more severe
crime than P - genocide / murder . Idv.
footsoldier commits murder, not genocide

110 Semi - innocent agency. im qus abt this

111 Non prosecutable wrong.

113 Claim that for typical intnl crime D is
logical principal

114 Criticism of Sullivan - outcome resp.

119 ff. German control theory.

124 Merit in any that on cooperation in execution
of plan w/ jnty rspy or co-perpetrator.

1 ider resp vs collective guilt
2 agent vs aider / instigator
   Intal crimes inherently collective

6 Dist. features of Intal crimes
7 why are of diff modes of ptcp— needed
   For of Intal con tral

8 2 competing dtes of modes I rspy

15 JCE defend

21 IMT wisnt collapsing idv & coll rspy.

28 Influence of IMT(FE) on subsequent dt.

30 tension between ICL & DCL — treaty, code,
   common law struct   NJ: ICL shld follow DCL model.

33 Model of small group I people all know each
   other & all interact.

36 Dachau — emphasis on continuing system

37 Objn to reliance on mere fact of being in a
   position of authority   [?? "must have known" ?]

41 Ref to driving spirit of N/berg trials.

42 Quble customary basis for JCE.

43 Principle vs 2nd'rs rspy

45 Tadic facts — small tight grp, but JCE dt much wider

47 "Must have occurred" inference — pretty tight one!

48 Concerns abt. breadth of JCE III

50 Empirical lbty to form I omission lbty

52 JCE — all actors are principals

54 "Fluid" common plan

61 JCE III — low m. r & ptcp— reqmts, makes lby of
   principal too like lby of necessary

65 Immaturity of ICL & dangers thereof.

71 CIL source for JCE III rejected.

PERPETRATORS AND ACCESSORIES IN INTERNATIONAL CRIMINAL LAW

International criminal law lacks a coherent account of individual responsibility. This failure is due to the inability of international tribunals to capture the distinctive nature of individual responsibility for crimes that are collective by their very nature. Specifically, they have misunderstood the nature of the collective action or framework that makes these crimes possible, and for which liability may be attributed to intellectual authors, policy makers and leaders. In this book, the author draws on insights from comparative law and methodology to propose doctrines of perpetration and secondary responsibility that reflect the role and function of high-level participants in mass atrocity, while simultaneously situating them within the political and social climate which renders these crimes possible. This new doctrine is developed through a novel approach which combines and restructures divergent theoretical perspectives on attribution of responsibility in English and German domestic criminal law, as major representatives of the common law and civil law systems. At the same time, it analyses existing theories of responsibility in international criminal law and assesses whether there is any justification for their retention by international criminal tribunals.